WORD 2010
Simplified®

Visual

by Elaine Marmel

WILEY

Wiley Publishing, Inc.

WORD 2010 SIMPLIFIED®

Published by
Wiley Publishing, Inc.
10475 Crosspoint Boulevard
Indianapolis, IN 46256

www.wiley.com

Published simultaneously in Canada

Library of Congress Control Number: 2010922572

ISBN: 978-0-470-57762-2

Manufactured in the United States of America

10 9 8 7 6 5 4 3 2 1

Trademark Acknowledgments

Wiley, the Wiley Publishing logo, Visual, the Visual logo, Simplified, Read Less - Learn More and related trade dress are trademarks or registered trademarks of John Wiley & Sons, Inc. and/or its affiliates. Microsoft is a registered trademark of Microsoft Corporation in the United States and/or other countries. All other trademarks are the property of their respective owners. Wiley Publishing, Inc. is not associated with any product or vendor mentioned in this book.

Disclaimer

In order to get this information to you in a timely manner, this book was based on a pre-release version of Microsoft Office 2010. There may be some minor changes between the screenshots in this book and what you see on your desktop. As always, Microsoft has the final word on how programs look and function; if you have any questions or see any discrepancies, consult the online help for further information about the software.

Contact Us

For general information on our other products and services please contact our Customer Care Department within the U.S. at 877-762-2974, outside the U.S. at 317-572-3993 or fax 317-572-4002.

For technical support please visit www.wiley.com/techsupport.

Wiley Publishing, Inc.

Sales

Contact Wiley at (877) 762-2974 or fax (317) 572-4002.

Credits

Executive Editor
Jody Lefevere

Project Editor
Jade L. Williams

Technical Editor
Vincent Averello III

Copy Editor
Lauren Kennedy

Editorial Director
Robyn Siesky

Editorial Manager
Cricket Krengel

Business Manager
Amy Knies

Senior Marketing Manager
Sandy Smith

Vice President and
Executive Group Publisher
Richard Swadley

Vice President and
Executive Publisher
Barry Pruett

Project Coordinator
Kristie Rees

Graphics and Production
Specialists
Joyce Haughey
Andrea Hornberger

Quality Control Technician
Lindsay Littrell

Proofreading
Melissa D. Buddendeck

Indexing
Johnna VanHoose Dinse

Screen Artist
Jill A. Proll
Ronald Terry

About the Author

Elaine Marmel is President of Marmel Enterprises, LLC, an organization which specializes in technical writing and software training. Elaine spends most of her time writing; she has authored and co-authored over 50 books about *Microsoft Project, Microsoft Excel, QuickBooks, Peachtree, Quicken for Windows, Quicken for DOS, Microsoft Word for Windows, Microsoft Word for the Mac, Windows 98, 1-2-3 for Windows,* and *Lotus Notes.* From 1994 to 2006, she also was the contributing editor to monthly publications *Peachtree Extra* and *QuickBooks Extra.*

Elaine left her native Chicago for the warmer climes of Arizona (by way of Cincinnati, OH; Jerusalem, Israel; Ithaca, NY; Washington, D.C. and Tampa, FL) where she basks in the sun with her dog Josh, and her cats, Watson and Buddy.

Dedication

To Cato, a sweet and loyal friend for 17 years. You are sorely missed by all of us, little girl.

Author's Acknowledgments

A book is far more than the work of the author; many other people contribute. I'd like to thank Jody Lefevere for once again giving me this opportunity. Sarah Cisco, it is a pleasure to work with you and I hope you'll get in touch with me the next time you visit your sister. My thanks to Lauren Kennedy for making me look good and to Vince Averello for helping to ensure that this book is technically accurate. Finally, my thanks to the graphics and production teams who labor tirelessly behind the scenes to create the elegant appearance of this book.

How to Use This Book

Who This Book Is For

This book is for the reader who has never used this particular technology or software application. It is also for readers who want to expand their knowledge.

The Conventions in This Book

❶ Steps

This book uses a step-by-step format to guide you easily through each task. Numbered steps are actions you must do; bulleted steps clarify a point, step, or optional feature; and indented steps give you the result.

❷ Notes

Notes give additional information — special conditions that may occur during an operation, a situation that you want to avoid, or a cross reference to a related area of the book.

❸ Icons and Buttons

Icons and buttons show you exactly what you need to click to perform a step.

❹ Simplify It

Simplify It sections offer additional information, including warnings and shortcuts.

❺ Bold

Bold type shows command names, options, and text or numbers you must type.

❻ Italics

Italic type introduces and defines a new term.

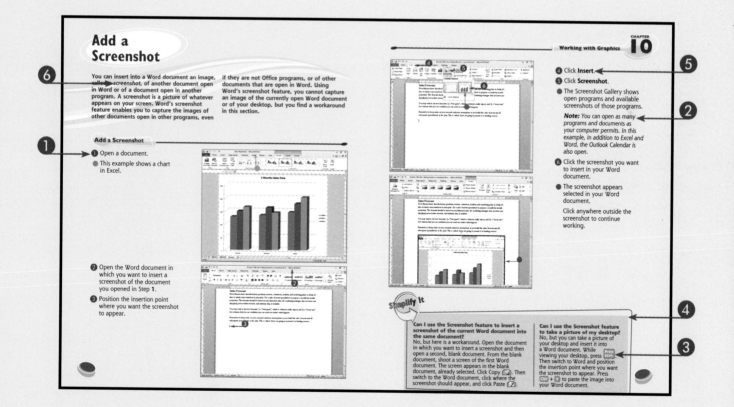

Table of Contents

Editing Text

Proofreading in Word

Table of Contents

Formatting Pages

Printing Documents

Table of Contents

9

Creating Tables and Charts

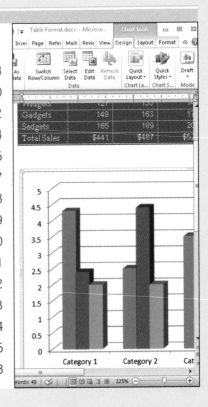

10

Working with Graphics

11

Customizing Word

12

Mailing Documents

Chapter 1

Getting Familiar with Word

Are you ready to get started in Word? In this first chapter, you become familiar with the Word working environment and you learn basic ways to navigate and to enter text. You explore the main Word window as well as read about the new Backstage view.

Using either your keyboard or your mouse, you find out how to navigate the Word window, launch dialog boxes, use the Mini toolbar that appears when you select text, and take advantage of context menus.

This chapter also shows you how to enter text into a document and how to move around the document.

Open Word

You can open Microsoft Word several ways. This section demonstrates the popular method of opening Word from the All Programs menu. After Word opens, a blank document, ready for you to type text, appears. The Ribbon, which contains commands that help you do things like apply boldface to type or create a numbered list, dominates the top of the Word window. In addition to opening Word from the All Programs menu, many of you might like to open Word and a specific document simultaneously, which you can accomplish by double-clicking any Word document.

Open Word

1 Click **Start**.

2 Click **All Programs**.

● All Programs changes to Back once you click it.

3 Click **Microsoft Office**.

4 Click **Microsoft Word 2010**.

● A blank document appears in the Word window.

Explore the Word Window

In addition to the document portion of the Word window, where you type and edit text, the Word window contains tools you can use to work quickly and efficiently while you create documents. Before you dive in and start using Word, take a few minutes to familiarize yourself with the basic screen elements that appear when you open Word. You will have occasion to use all of these screen elements at one time or another, so identifying them early on in your Word 2010 career will make you more proficient in the long run.

Quick Access Toolbar

Contains buttons that perform common actions, such as saving a document, undoing your last action, or repeating your last action. To customize, see Chapter 11.

Title Bar

Shows the program and document titles.

Ribbon

Contains commands organized in three components: tabs, groups, and commands. **Tabs** appear across the top of the Ribbon and contain groups of related commands. **Groups** organize related commands; each group name appears below the group on the Ribbon. **Commands** appear within each group. To customize the Ribbon, see Chapter 11.

Dialog Box Launcher

Appears in the lower-right corner of many groups on the Ribbon. Clicking this button opens a dialog box or task pane that provides more options.

Status Bar

Displays document information as well as the insertion point location. From left to right, this bar contains the number of the page on which the insertion point currently appears, the total number of pages and words in the document, the proofing errors button (⬚), the macro recording status button, the View buttons, and the Zoom Slider. To customize the Status Bar, see Chapter 11.

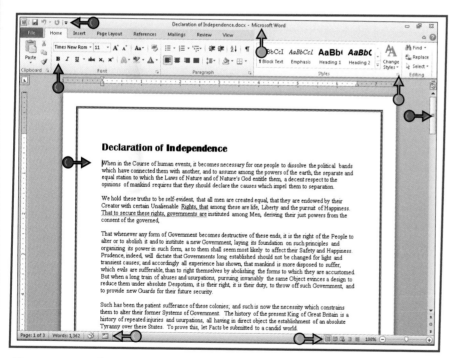

Document Area

The area where you type. The flashing vertical bar — called the *insertion point* — represents the location where text will appear when you type.

Scroll Bar

Enables you to reposition the document window vertically. Drag the scroll box within the scroll bar or click the scroll bar arrows (⬚ and ⬚).

Work with Backstage View

Clicking the File tab opens the Backstage view, which resembles a menu. The Backstage view in Word 2010 replaces the Office button in Word 2007 and, for the most part, the File menu in many earlier versions of Word.

In the Backstage view, you find a list of actions — commands — you can use to manage files and program options. For example, from the Backstage view you can open, save, print, and remove sensitive information from documents. You also can distribute documents via e-mail or post them to a blog, and set Word program behavior options.

Work with Backstage View

① Click the **File** tab.

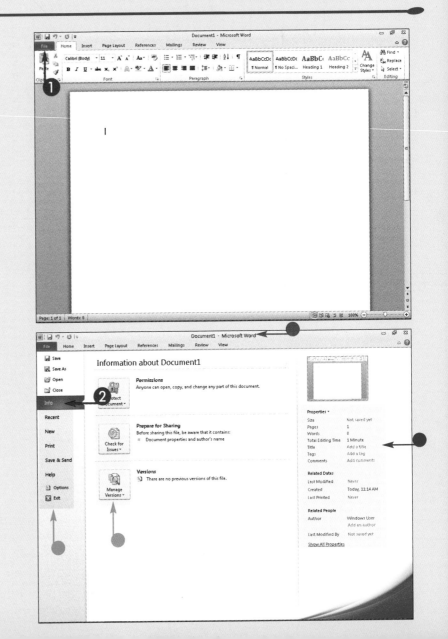

- In the Backstage view, commonly used file and program-management commands appear here.

- The title of the open document appears here.

- Information about the currently open document appears here.

- Buttons appear that you can click.

② Click Info.

③ Click an option in the left column; this example shows the results of clicking **Save & Send,** which contains commands that help you share Word documents.

● As you click a button in the Send column, the information shown to the right changes.

④ Repeat Step **3** until you find the command you want to use; this example shows the results of clicking **Recent**, which displays up to the last 25 documents opened. To select a document in this list to open it, see Chapter 2.

Is there a way to return to working in Word without making any selections in Backstage view?

Yes. You can click the **File** tab or press Esc on the keyboard. Although you might be tempted to click Exit, resist the temptation, because clicking Exit closes Word completely.

Select Commands with the Keyboard

In the world of Windows, a mouse is essential, and many of us would be lost without it. However, many good typists find that keeping their hands on the keyboard enables them to work efficiently and having to remove their hands to use the mouse to take an action slows them down. Although the Ribbon and the Quick Access Toolbar are exceedingly mouse-friendly, you can use your keyboard to select commands from the Ribbon or the Quick Access Toolbar. Try out this feature: You might find that you work faster and more efficiently than you do using both your keyboard and your mouse.

Select Commands with the Keyboard

① If appropriate for the command you intend to use, place the insertion point in the proper word or paragraph.

② Press **Alt** on the keyboard.

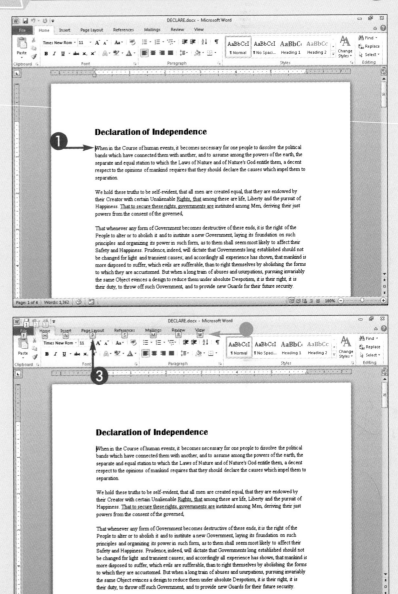

● Shortcut letters and numbers appear on the Ribbon.

Note: *The numbers control commands on the Quick Access Toolbar.*

③ Press a letter to select a tab on the Ribbon.

This example uses **P**.

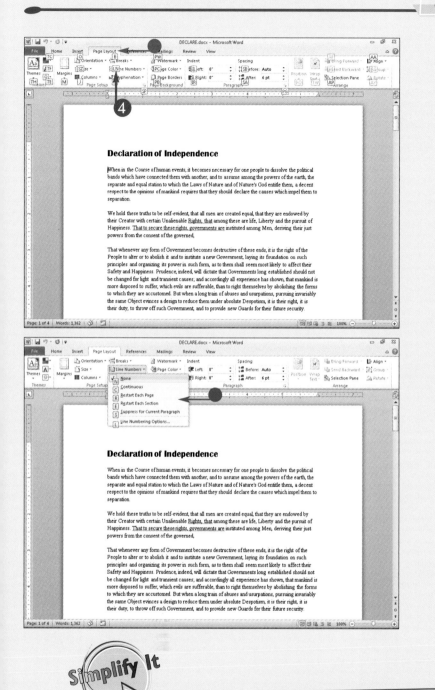

● Word displays the appropriate tab and letters for each command on that tab.

④ Press a letter or letters to select a command.

● Word displays options for the command you selected.

⑤ Press a letter or use the arrow keys on the keyboard to select an option.

Word performs the command you selected, applying the option you chose.

Simplify It

Is there a way to toggle between the document and the Ribbon using the keyboard?
Yes. Each time you press **F6**, Word changes the focus of the program, switching between the document, the Status bar, and the Ribbon.

What should I do if I accidentally press the wrong key?
You can press **Esc** to back up to your preceding action. For example, if you complete Steps **1** to **3** and, in Step **3**, you press **S** when you meant to press **W**, press **Esc** to redisplay the letters associated with tabs and then press **W**.

Select Commands with the Mouse

Using a mouse is second nature to most Windows users, and you can use the mouse to navigate the Ribbon or select a command from the Quick Access Toolbar (QAT) at the top of the window. The Ribbon organizes tasks using tabs. On any particular tab, you find groups of commands related to that task.

The QAT appears on the left side of the title bar, immediately above the File and Home tabs and contains three commonly used commands: Save, Undo, and Redo. Click a button to perform that command. To customize the QAT, see Chapter 11.

Select Commands with the Mouse

1 Click the tab containing the command you want to use.

2 Click in the text or paragraph you want to modify.

3 Point to the command you want to use.

● Word displays a ScreenTip describing the function of the button at which the mouse points.

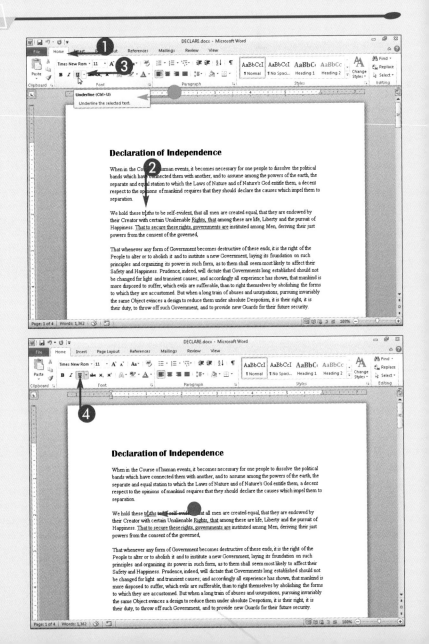

4 Click the command.

● Word performs the command you selected.

Work with the Mini Toolbar

The Mini toolbar contains a combination of commands available primarily in the Font group and the Paragraph group on the Home tab, and you can take advantage of the Mini toolbar to format text without switching to the Home tab.

When Word initially displays the Mini toolbar, it is transparent in the background of your document. But the closer you move the mouse pointer to the Mini toolbar, the darker the Mini toolbar becomes. This behavior keeps the Mini toolbar out of your way, but makes it available if you want to use it.

Work with the Mini Toolbar

① Select text.

● The Mini toolbar appears transparently in the background.

② Position the mouse pointer close to or over the Mini toolbar.

● The Mini toolbar appears solidly.

③ Click any command or button.

Word performs the actions associated with the command or button.

Work with Context Menus

You can use context menus to format text without switching to the Home tab. The context menu appears along with the Mini toolbar and contains a combination of commands available primarily in the Font group and the Paragraph group on the Home tab.

Like the Mini toolbar, the context menu is transparent in the background of your document. But the closer you move the mouse pointer to the context menu, the darker it becomes, which keeps the context menu out of your way until you want to use it. You can read more about the Mini toolbar in the section, "Work with the Mini Toolbar."

Work with Context Menus

① Select text.

● The Mini toolbar appears in the background.

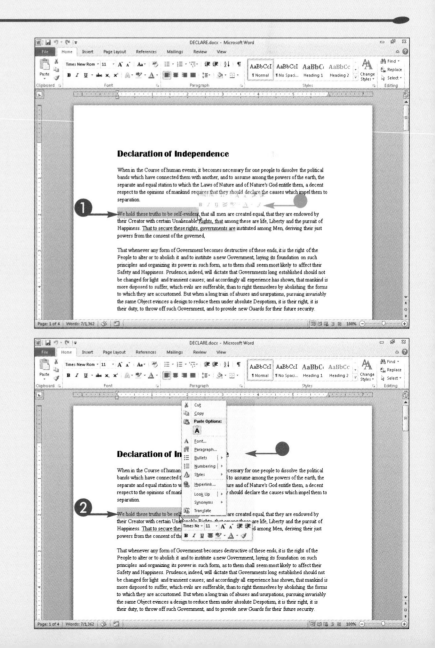

② Right-click the selected text.

● The context menu appears along with the Mini toolbar.

Note: *You can right-click anywhere, not just on selected text, to display the Mini toolbar and the context menu.*

③ Click any command or button.

Word performs the actions associated with the command or button.

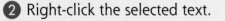

Launch a Dialog Box

Dialog boxes have been a part of Word from the very beginning of Word's life as a word-processing software package. Dialog boxes contain a series of related options that help you accomplish a task. In a dialog box, you select the options that apply to your situation. For example, you can use the Paragraph dialog box to describe the type of indentation you want to use for a particular paragraph.

Although the Ribbon contains most of the commands you use on a regular basis, you still need dialog boxes occasionally to select a command or refine a choice.

Launch a Dialog Box

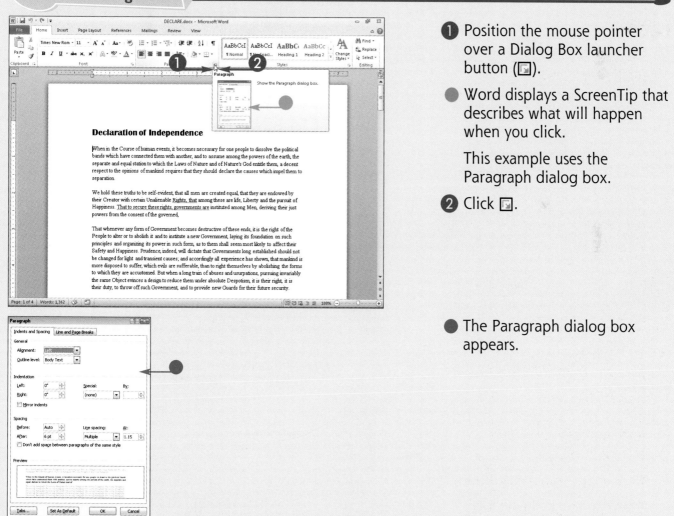

① Position the mouse pointer over a Dialog Box launcher button (⬜).

● Word displays a ScreenTip that describes what will happen when you click.

This example uses the Paragraph dialog box.

② Click ⬜.

● The Paragraph dialog box appears.

Work with Commands

When you select certain commands on the Ribbon, Word displays a gallery of choices. For example, in the Styles gallery, you find a variety of styles; each style contains a different set of font, font size, and paragraph formatting. You can use galleries to view the choices for a particular command.

In many cases, Word 2010 previews a command choice before you select it, giving you an opportunity "to try before you buy." For example, if you point the mouse at the Subtitle style in the Styles gallery, Word displays the text of the paragraph containing the insertion point in the Subtitle style.

Work with Commands

Work with Galleries

1 In galleries containing the More button (⬚), click ▲ and ▼ to scroll through command choices.

2 Click ⬚ to open the gallery and view additional choices.

● Word hides ⬚ to display the gallery.

3 Scroll over choices to see a live preview.

4 Click a choice from the gallery to apply it.

To close the gallery without choosing a command, click anywhere outside the gallery.

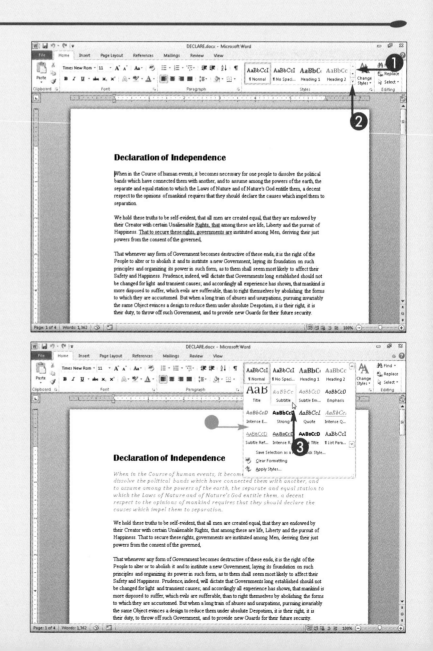

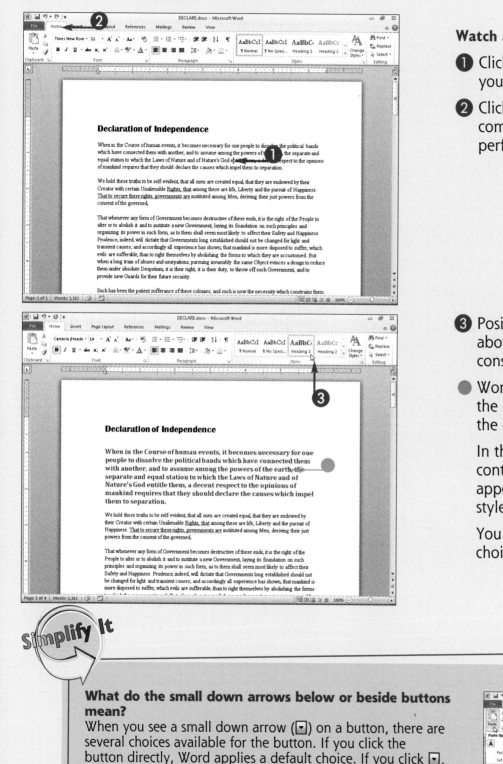

Watch a Live Preview

1 Click in the word or paragraph you want to modify.

2 Click the tab containing the command you are considering performing.

3 Position the mouse pointer above the choice you are considering applying.

● Word displays the effects of the choice without performing the command.

In this example, the paragraph containing the insertion point appears in the Heading 1 style.

You can click to select your choice.

Simplify It

What do the small down arrows below or beside buttons mean?
When you see a small down arrow (▾) on a button, there are several choices available for the button. If you click the button directly, Word applies a default choice. If you click ▾, Word displays additional options as either lists or galleries.

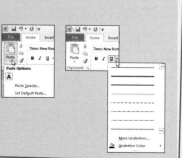

Enter Text

Word makes typing easy. For example, you do not need to press Enter to start a new line. Word calculates when a new line should begin and automatically starts it for you based on the font you select and its size. You need to press Enter only when you want to force Word to begin a new line or a blank line. See Chapter 3 for more information.

When you want to add more than one space between words, use the Tab key instead of the spacebar. This way you can properly align text when you use proportional fonts. See Chapter 6 for details on setting tabs.

Enter Text

Type Text

1 Type the text that you want to appear in your document.

● The text appears to the left of the insertion point as you type.

● As the insertion point reaches the end of the line, Word automatically starts a new one.

Press **Enter** only to start a new paragraph.

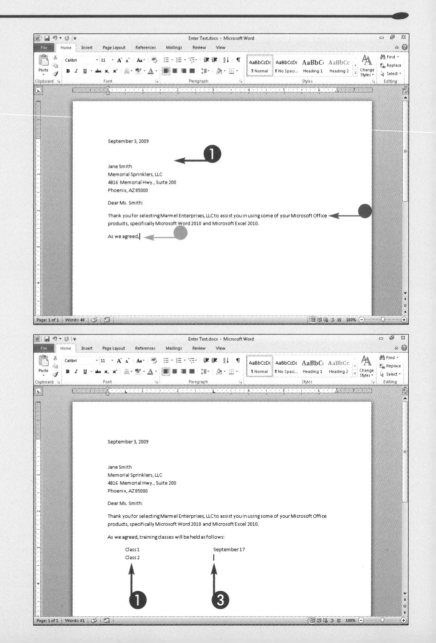

Separate Information

1 Type a word or phrase.

2 Press **Tab**.

To align text properly, you press **Tab** to include more than one space between words.

Several spaces appear between the last letter you typed and the insertion point.

3 Type another word or phrase.

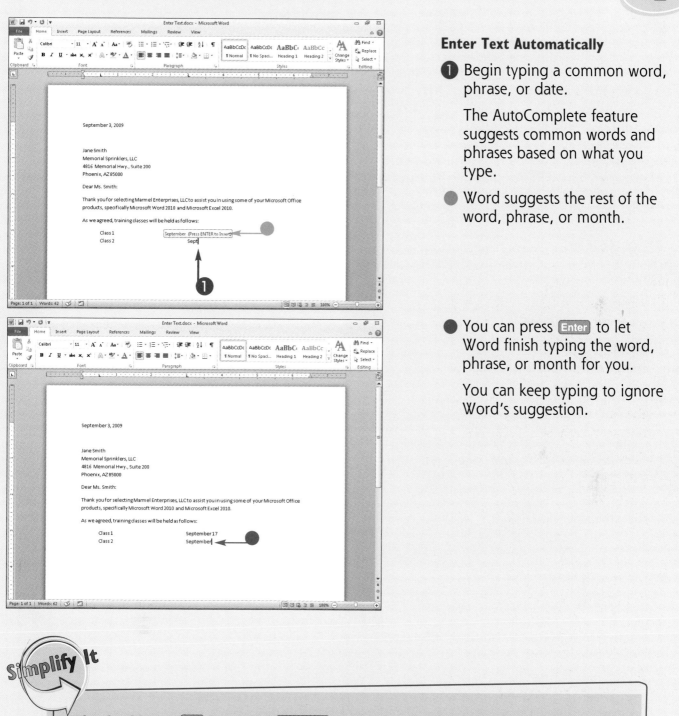

Enter Text Automatically

① Begin typing a common word, phrase, or date.

The AutoComplete feature suggests common words and phrases based on what you type.

● Word suggests the rest of the word, phrase, or month.

● You can press Enter to let Word finish typing the word, phrase, or month for you.

You can keep typing to ignore Word's suggestion.

Simplify It

Why should I use Tab instead of Spacebar to include more than one space between words?
Typically, when you include more than one space between words or phrases, you do so to align text in a columnar fashion. Most fonts are proportional, meaning each character of a font takes up a different amount of space on a line. Therefore, you cannot calculate the number of spaces needed to align words beneath each other. Tabs, however, are set at specific locations on a line, such as 3 inches. When you press Tab, you know exactly where words or phrases appear on a line. Word sets default tabs every .5 inches. To avoid pressing Tab multiple times to separate text, change the tab settings. See Chapter 6 for details.

Move Around in a Document

People rarely work in a strictly linear sense while creating a Word document. After you have typed three paragraphs, you might think of a sentence you should have included in the second paragraph. Or after typing five pages, you might decide that you need to delete something you wrote on page 4. You need to be able to efficiently move around your Word documents.

You can use many techniques to move to a different location in a document; the technique you select depends on the location to which you want to move.

Move Around in a Document

Move One Character

1 Note the location of the insertion point.

2 Press ➡.

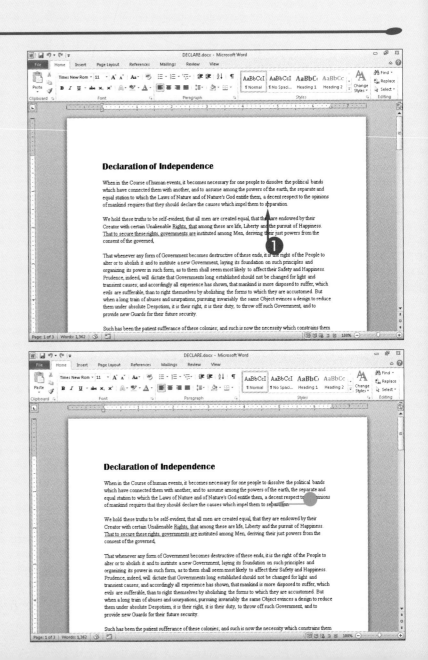

● Word moves the insertion point one character to the right.

You can press ⬅, ⬆, or ⬇ to move the insertion point one character left, up, or down.

Holding any arrow key moves the insertion point repeatedly in the direction of the arrow key.

You can press Ctrl + ➡ or Ctrl + ⬅ to move the insertion point one word at a time to the right or left.

Move One Screen

1 Note the last visible line on-screen.

2 Press **Page down**.

● Word moves the insertion point down one screen.

You can press **Page up** to move the insertion point up one screen.

● You can click **▲** to scroll up or **▼** to scroll down one line at a time in a document.

How do I quickly move the insertion point to the beginning or the end of a document?

Press **Ctrl** + **Home** to move the insertion point to the beginning of a document or **Ctrl** + **End** to move the insertion point to the bottom of a document. You can press **Shift** + **F5** to move the insertion point to the last place you changed in your document.

Is there a way to move the insertion point to a specific location?

Yes. You can use bookmarks to mark a particular place and then return to it. See Chapter 3 for details on creating a bookmark and returning to the bookmark's location. See Chapter 4 for details on searching for a specific word and, if necessary, replacing that word with a different one.

Get Help

You can search for help with the Word tasks you perform. The Word Help system is organized by various categories, such as ones for creating documents, setting up tables, or working with page breaks. When you select a category, the Word Help system displays topics available in that category. Locating help by selecting a category is similar to using the table of contents of a book.

If you prefer, you can search for help topics by providing keywords; this approach is similar to using the index of a book.

In either case, Word searches both the Internet and the Help file on your computer.

Get Help

1 Click the **Help** button (❓).

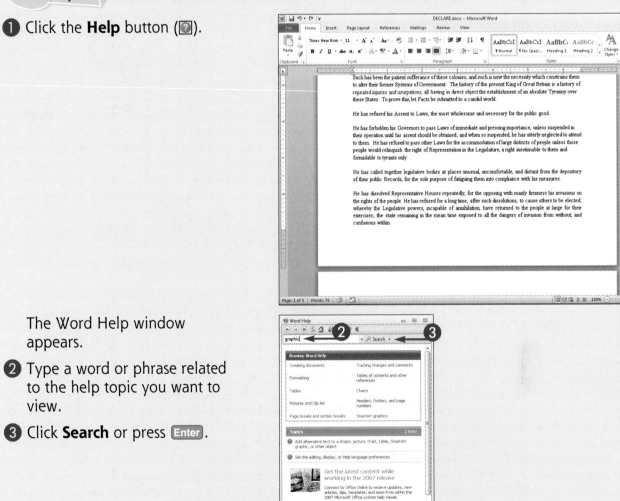

The Word Help window appears.

2 Type a word or phrase related to the help topic you want to view.

3 Click **Search** or press Enter.

Word Help

graphic   Search

Word

Searched for: "graphic"

Results 1-15 of 15   Page: [1]

Add alternative text to a shape, picture, chart, ta, SmartArt graphic, or other object
Help

Identify which program to use to create an organization chart
Help > SmartArt graphics

Insert a picture or clip art
Help > Pictures and Clip Art

Keyboard shortcuts for Microsoft Office Word

Adjust the spaces between lines or paragraphs
Help > Formatting

Compatibility changes between versions

Format Object (Alt text)

Add or delete a table
Help > Tables

Change the color, transparency, or recolor a picture
Help > Pictures and Clip Art

Word Help   Offline

Word Help

graphic   Search

Word

Add alternative text to a shape, picture, chart, table, SmartArt graphic, or other object

Show All

You can create alternative text (alt text) for shapes, pictures, charts, tables, SmartArt graphics, or other objects in your Office document. Alternative text helps people with screen readers understand the content of pictures. When you use a screen reader to view your document, or save it to a file format such as HTML or DAISY (Digital Accessible Information System), alternative text appears when you move the pointer over a picture in most browsers

This article discusses adding alternative text to a shape, picture, chart, table, SmartArt graphic, or other object and shows you how you can make the **Alt Text** command always available.

What do you want to do?

Word Help   Offline

● Help topics related to the word or phrase you typed appear in the task pane.

④ Click the topic most closely related to the subject on which you want help.

● The help topic information appears in the Word Help window.

⑤ To close the Help window, click ⊠.

The Word window reappears.

Simplify It

Can I leave the Word Help window open while I work in Word?
Yes. Simply do not perform Step **5**. By default, the Word Help window remains on top of the Word window. You can move the Word Help window by dragging its title bar. You can resize the window by positioning the mouse pointer over any edge of the window; when the mouse pointer changes to a two-headed arrow, drag in to make the window smaller and out to make the window larger.

I want to keep the Help window open, but not in front of the Word window. Is there a way to make it drop down to the Windows task bar?
Yes. Click the **pushpin** button (). When you subsequently click in the Word window, Word Help drops down to the Windows task bar. You can redisplay Word Help by clicking its task bar button.

Chapter 2

Managing Documents

Now that you know the basics, it is time to discover how to navigate among Word documents efficiently. In this chapter, you learn how to manage the Word documents you create.

You learn to save documents both as Word 2010 documents and as Word 97–2003 documents, and you can set a default folder location for documents you save.

You can open an existing Word document or start a new document, and, because you can have multiple documents open simultaneously, you learn to switch between open documents. You also find information in this chapter on closing documents and converting documents created with earlier versions of Word.

Save a Document

To avoid losing work you have done on a Word document, you can save a document. Saving a document also enables you to use it at another time in Microsoft Word. Word 2010 uses the same XML-based file format that Word 2007 uses. This XML-based file format is different than the file format used in prior versions of

Word, and it reduces the size of a Word document, improving the likelihood of recovering information from a corrupt file.

After you save a document for the first time, you can click the Save icon on the Quick Access Toolbar (QAT) to save it again.

Save a Document

- Before you save a document, Word displays a generic name in the title bar.

① Click the **File** tab.

The Backstage view appears.

② Click **Save As**.

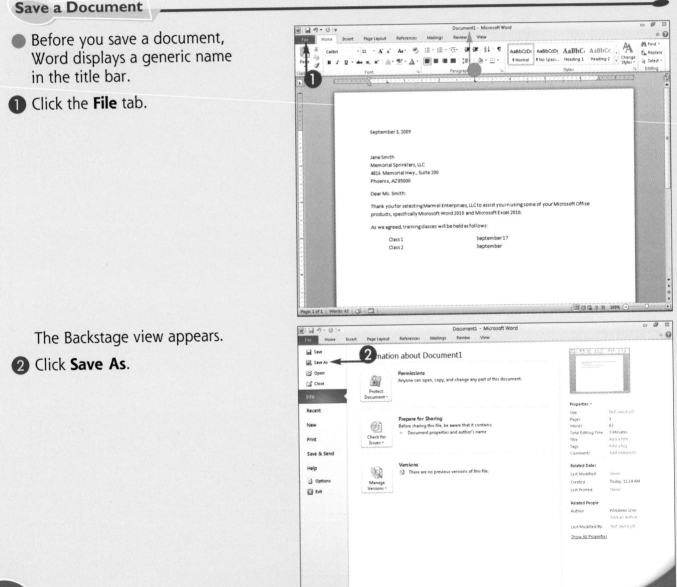

The Save As dialog box appears.

③ Type a name for the document here.

● You can click here to select a location on your computer in which to save the document.

● You can click the **New Folder** button to create a new folder in which to store the document.

④ Click **Save**.

● Word saves the document and displays the name you supplied in the title bar.

Simplify It

Will my associate, who uses Word 2003, be able to open a document I save in Word 2010?
Microsoft supplied a converter that enables Word 2003 users to open Word 2007 documents. You can create the document in Word 2010 and save it in Word 2003 format. See the section "Save a Document to Word 97–2003 Format" for more information.

How can I tell if I am working on a document saved in Word 2010 as opposed to one saved in Word 2003?
Word 2010 uses the file name extension .docx to designate its file format, while the file name extension for a Word 2003 document is .doc. If you set your computer's folder options to display extensions of known file types, the full file name of the document appears in the title bar of the program.

Class Schedule Letter.doc [Compatibility Mode] - Microsoft Word

Reopen an Unsaved Document

You can open documents you created within the last seven days but did not save because, as you work, Word automatically saves your document even if you take no action to save it.

For many years, Word saved your document in the background as you worked, but finding and using those files was unintuitive at best. But

now you can easily recover from the simple mistake of forgetting to save your work.

Recovering draft versions is optional and can create a lot of documents you do not necessarily want; use the Save tab of the Word Options dialog box to control this feature.

Reopen an Unsaved Document

① Click the **File** tab.

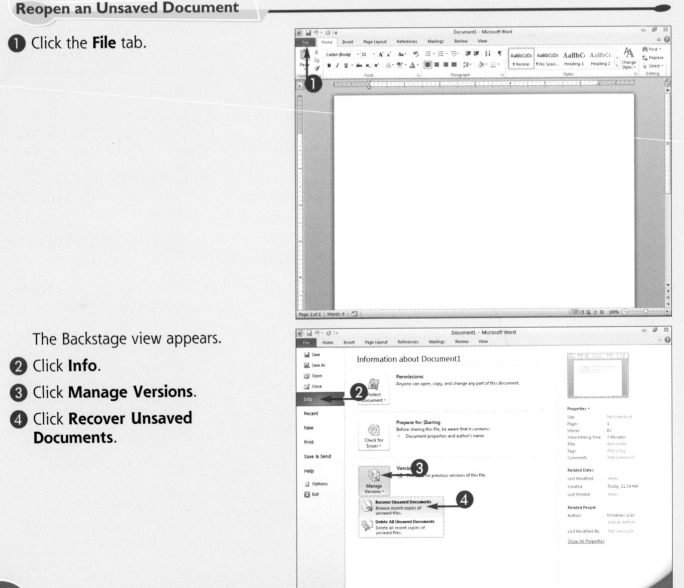

The Backstage view appears.

② Click **Info**.

③ Click **Manage Versions**.

④ Click **Recover Unsaved Documents**.

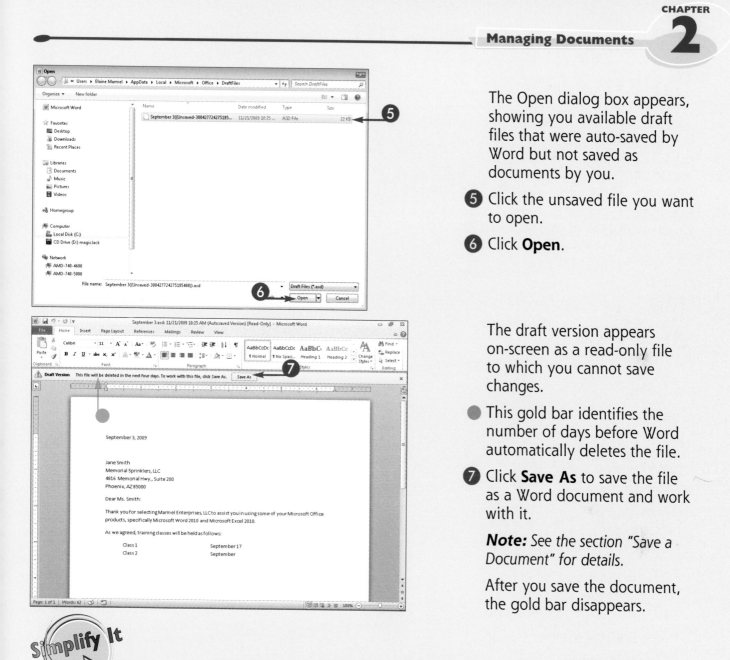

The Open dialog box appears, showing you available draft files that were auto-saved by Word but not saved as documents by you.

5 Click the unsaved file you want to open.

6 Click **Open**.

The draft version appears on-screen as a read-only file to which you cannot save changes.

● This gold bar identifies the number of days before Word automatically deletes the file.

7 Click **Save As** to save the file as a Word document and work with it.

Note: *See the section "Save a Document" for details.*

After you save the document, the gold bar disappears.

Simplify It

Is it possible to open documents that I closed without saving?
Yes, if you open them fairly soon after closing without saving. These documents appear in the Recent Documents list and remain there until you open 20 other documents. You can compare the unsaved version with the saved version or replace the saved version with the unsaved version. See the section "Open a Word Document" for details on using the Recent Documents list. See Chapter 4 for details on combining versions of a document.

Can I control any of the options associated with Word automatically saving my documents?
Yes. You can specify how often Word automatically saves your document and where Word stores the files it uses to help you recover lost work. You also can control whether Word keeps files if you close them without first saving them.

Save a Document to Word 97–2003 Format

You can save documents you create in Microsoft Word in a variety of other formats. For example, you might want to save a document as a Word template so that you can use it as a model for other documents. Or you might want to save a Word document as a Microsoft Works file, a text file, or in Word 97-2003 format to share the document with people who do not use Microsoft Word 2010 or Microsoft Word 2007.

Although the steps in this section focus on saving a document to Word 97–2003 format, you can use these steps to save a document to any file format Word supports.

Save a Document to Word 97–2003 Format

1 Click the **File** tab.

The Backstage view appears.

2 Click **Save As**.

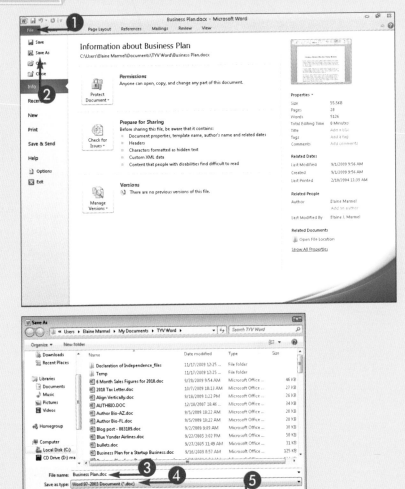

The Save As dialog box appears.

3 Type a name for the document.

4 Click here to display the formats available for the document and click **Word 97-2003 Document (*.doc)**.

5 Click **Save**.

Word saves the document in the format that you select.

Set the Folder Location for Saving Documents

You can set a variety of options for saving documents. For example, you can decide whether you want Word to save backup copies of your document as you work that you can open if you accidentally forget to save the document when closing.

You also can control the location Word suggests when you save your documents. Setting a default folder location helps you stay organized because you can easily save your Word documents in a single location on your hard drive. Setting a default location does not force you to save your documents to that location; you can always change the location when you save.

Set the Folder Location for Saving Documents

1 Click the **File** tab.

The Backstage view appears.

2 Click **Options**.

The Word Options dialog box appears.

3 Click **Save**.

4 Click **Browse** next to Default file location.

The Modify Location dialog box appears.

5 Click here to navigate to the folder where you want to save Word documents.

6 Click **OK** to redisplay the Word Options dialog box.

You can repeat Steps **4** to **6** to set the AutoRecover File and the Server drafts locations.

7 Click **OK** in the Word Options dialog box to save your changes.

Word saves your changes.

Open a Word Document

When you finish working on a document and save it, you typically close it as described in the section, "Close a Document," or you close Word, closing the document as well. If you need make changes to the document — add information to it, delete information from it, or change information in it — you open it to display it on-screen.

You can simultaneously open Word and a particular document by double-clicking that document. But if Word is already open, you do not need to find the document to double-click it. This section shows you how to open a document when Word is already open.

Open a Word Document

1 Click the **File** tab.

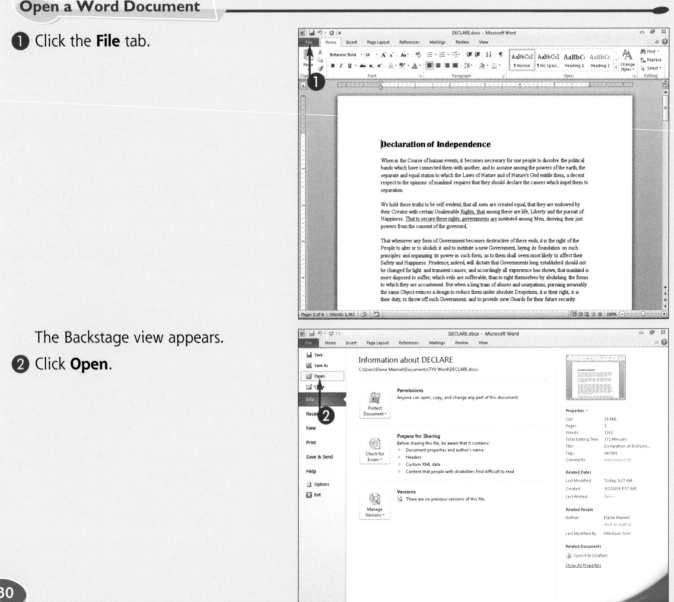

The Backstage view appears.

2 Click **Open**.

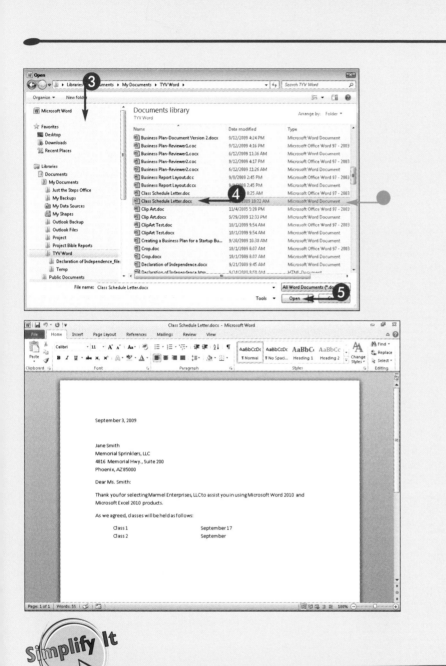

The Open dialog box appears.

③ Click here to navigate to the folder containing the document you want to open.

● Documents in a folder appear here.

④ Click the document you want to open.

⑤ Click **Open**.

The document appears on-screen.

Are there other ways to open a document?

Yes. The 25 most recently opened documents appear in Backstage view. You can click any of these documents to open them.

① Click the **File** tab to display Backstage view.

② Click **Recent**.

③ Click a document to open it.

Start a New Document

A new, blank document always appears when you start Microsoft Word. But suppose that you type in that document and save your work and then start another new document. You do not need to close and reopen Word to start a new, blank document.

In addition to starting a new, blank document, you can use a variety of templates — documents containing predefined settings that save you the effort of creating the settings yourself — as the foundation for a document. Many templates contain information; for example, your company might have created a template you can use to submit an expense report.

Start a New Document

① Click the **File** tab.

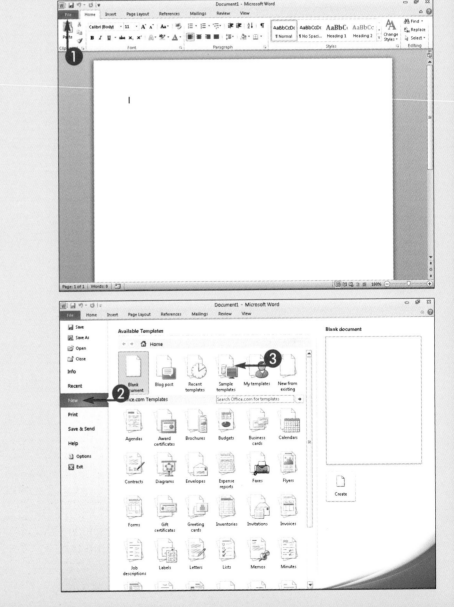

The Backstage view appears.

② Click **New**.

● Templates available on your computer appear here.

● Templates available online appear here.

③ Click an available type of template.

This example uses Sample templates.

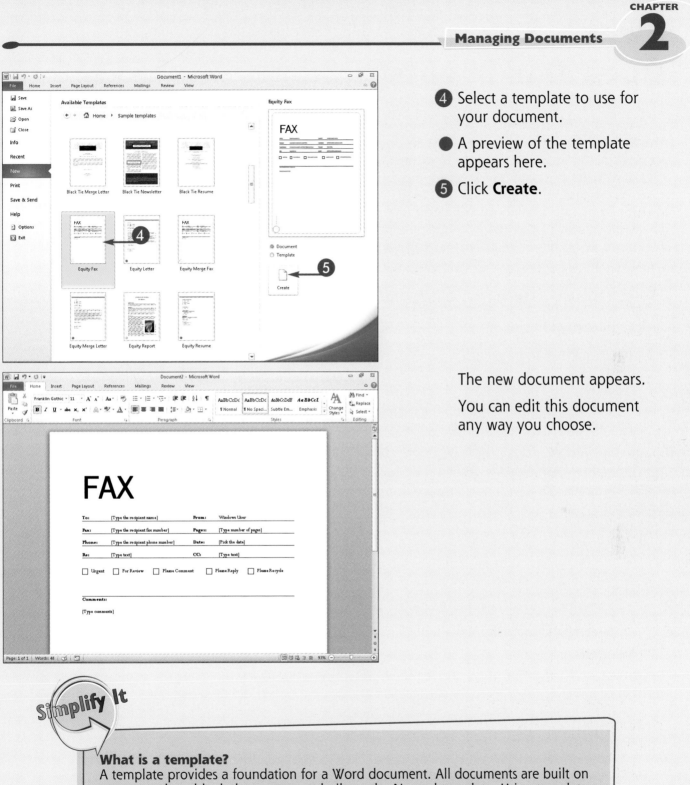

④ Select a template to use for your document.

● A preview of the template appears here.

⑤ Click **Create**.

The new document appears.

You can edit this document any way you choose.

Simplify It

What is a template?
A template provides a foundation for a Word document. All documents are built on some template; blank documents are built on the Normal template. Using templates, your company can create documents with consistent appearances because templates contain a specific set of fonts and styles and use the same formatting. Some Word templates, like the FAX cover sheets or the forms, also contain text that helps you quickly and easily create a document. Many of the available templates come from the Office Online Web site; when you select one, you download it.

Switch Between Open Documents

You can work in more than one document at the same time. Word does not limit the number of documents you open. And it is often convenient to open multiple documents because one might contain information you want to include in another, and you can copy and paste the information so that you do not need to retype it. For more information on copying and pasting, see Chapter 3.

If you have two or more documents open, you can switch between them from within Word or by using the Windows taskbar. If buttons representing each open document do not appear on the Windows taskbar, you can set options to display them.

Switch Between Open Documents

Switch Documents Using Word

① Click the **View** tab.

② Click **Switch Windows**.

● A list of all open documents appears at the bottom of the menu.

③ Click the document you want to view.

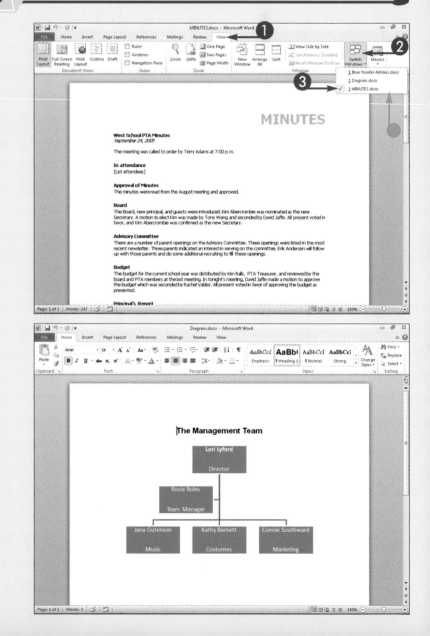

The selected document appears.

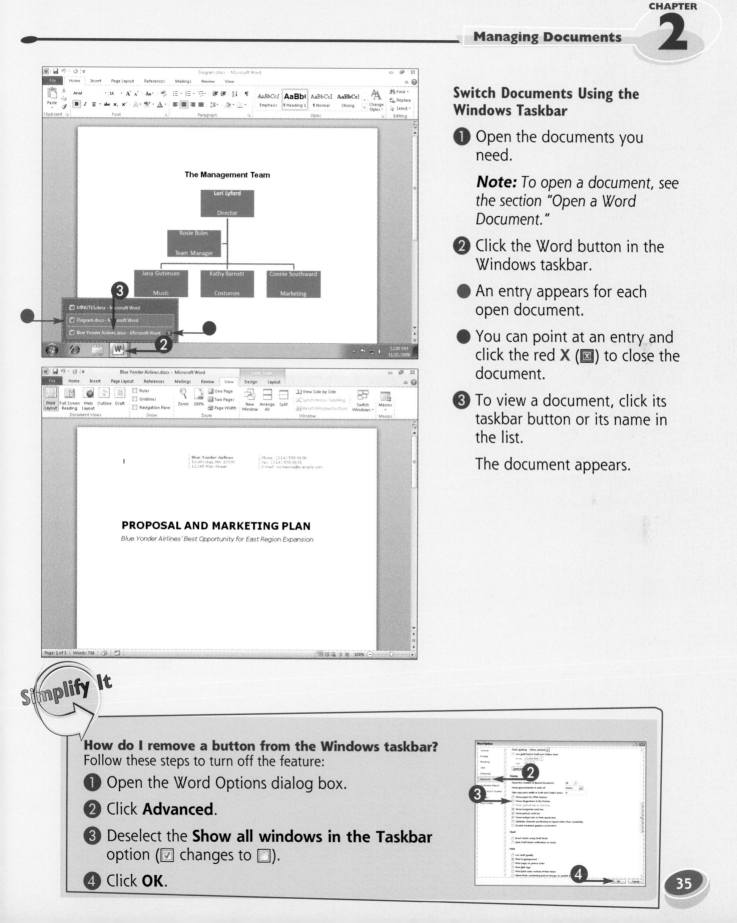

Switch Documents Using the Windows Taskbar

1 Open the documents you need.

Note: To open a document, see the section "Open a Word Document."

2 Click the Word button in the Windows taskbar.

● An entry appears for each open document.

● You can point at an entry and click the red **X** (⊠) to close the document.

3 To view a document, click its taskbar button or its name in the list.

The document appears.

Simplify It

How do I remove a button from the Windows taskbar?
Follow these steps to turn off the feature:

1 Open the Word Options dialog box.

2 Click **Advanced**.

3 Deselect the **Show all windows in the Taskbar** option (☑ changes to ☐).

4 Click **OK**.

Work with Document Properties

You can supply information about a document that you can then use when you search for documents. Word refers to this type of information as *document properties*. For example, you can supply a title that is not the same as the file name. You also can supply tags — *keywords* — that describe the document and you can add comments as document properties.

Windows Vista and Windows 7 users can use each operating system's built-in search engine. Windows XP users can search for files using document properties by downloading Windows Desktop Search from the Microsoft Web site.

Work with Document Properties

1 Click the **File** tab.

The Backstage view appears.

2 Click **Info**.

The Information panel appears.

3 Click **Properties**.

4 Click **Show Document Panel** to display the properties you can fill in above the document.

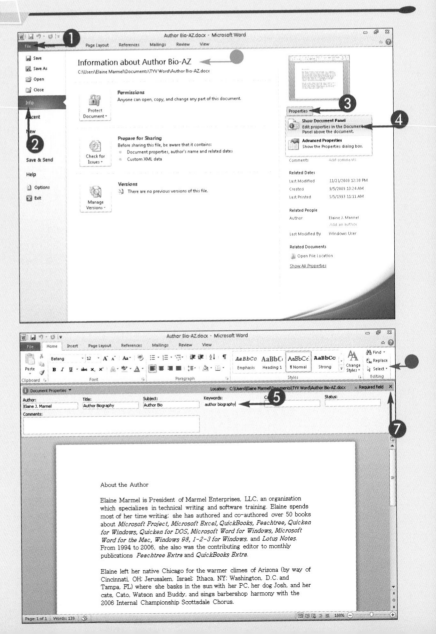

● The Document Properties panel appears above the document.

5 Click in a box and type information.

6 Repeat Step 5 as needed.

7 Click the **X** in the Document Properties panel to save your changes and return to editing the document.

Close a Document

When you finish working with a document, you close it. Closing a document removes it from your computer screen. Although Word does not limit the number of documents you can have open simultaneously, having too many documents open at the same time can lead to confusion. So, when you find you do not need a particular document open any longer, close it.

If you made any changes that you did not save, Word prompts you to save them before closing the document. You do not need to save changes; save them only if you want to keep the changes you made.

Close a Document

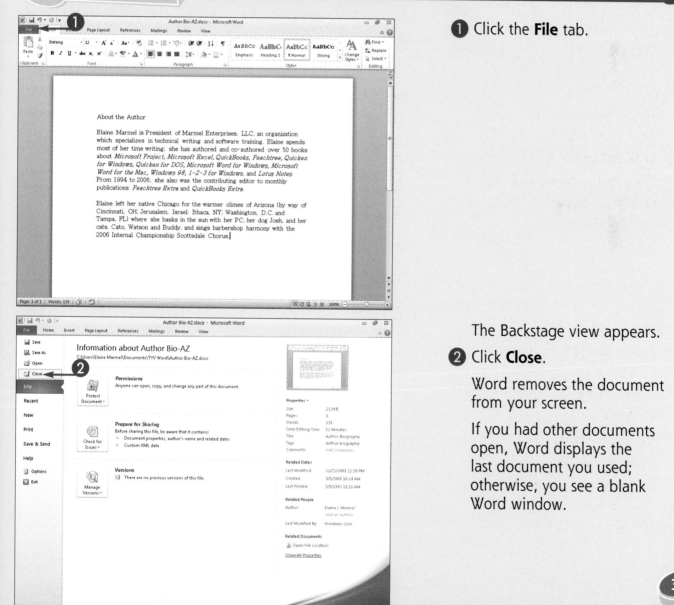

1 Click the **File** tab.

The Backstage view appears.

2 Click **Close**.

Word removes the document from your screen.

If you had other documents open, Word displays the last document you used; otherwise, you see a blank Word window.

Convert Word Documents from Prior Versions to Word 2010

Word 2010 uses a new XML-based file format that Microsoft introduced in Word 2007. However, you can still use Word 2010 to open Word documents created in earlier versions of Word. Once open, you can convert existing Word 97–Word 2003 documents to the new format. You also can convert Word 2007 documents to Word 2010 using the same approach.

While not a requirement to working on documents in Word 2010, converting documents created in older versions of Word enables you to incorporate new features in Word 2010 into those documents.

Convert Word Documents from Prior Versions to Word 2010

① Open any prior version Word document; this example uses a Word 2003 document.

Note: See the section "Open a Word Document" earlier in this chapter for details.

● In the title bar, Word indicates that the document is open in Compatibility Mode.

② Click the **File** tab.

The Backstage view appears.

③ Click **Info**.

④ Click **Convert**.

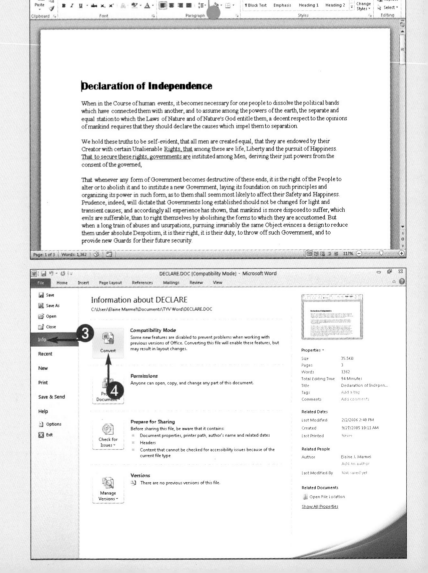

Word closes Backstage view and displays a message indicating it will convert the document to the newest file format.

● If you do not want to view this message in the future when you convert documents, select this option (☐ changes to ☑).

⑤ Click **OK**.

● Word converts the document and removes the Compatibility Mode indicator from the title bar.

⑥ Click ▤.

The Save As dialog box appears.

● Word suggests the same file name but the new file format extension .docx

⑦ Click **Save**.

Word saves the document in Word 2010 format.

Simplify It

Do I need to convert my documents from earlier versions of Word before I work on them in Word 2010?
No. You can work on a document created in an older version of Word and even incorporate Word 2010 features not available in earlier versions of Word. You only need to convert documents in which you expect to include features available only in Word 2010.

Is there any difference between using the method described in this section and opening a Word 97–Word 2003 document and then using the Save As command?
Not really; if you use the Save As method and choose Word Document (*.docx), Word prompts you to convert the older version document to the Word 2010 format using the Convert command, as described in this section.

Chapter 3

Editing Text

Once you know how to navigate around Word, it is time to work with the text that you type on a page. In this chapter, you learn some basic editing techniques that you can use to change text in documents you create. You learn methods to insert and delete text and blank lines and to undo actions you mistakenly take.

A basic staple of editing is the process of selecting the text on which you want to work, and this chapter describes several methods for selecting text. You also learn about the various ways to view your document and how to insert symbols.

Insert Text

Few of us ever write what we mean precisely on the first try, and inserting text is one way to change the meaning.

Word offers two ways to insert text. You can add to existing text or replace existing text. You use Insert mode, Word's default behavior, to add to existing text. And you can use Overtype mode to change existing text by simultaneously deleting text and replacing it with different text. In Overtype mode, Word replaces existing text to the right of the insertion point, character for character.

You cannot, by default, control switching between Insert and Overtype modes using your keyboard.

Insert Text

Insert and Add Text

1 Click the location where you want to insert text.

The insertion point flashes where you clicked.

You can press ➡, ⬅, ⬆, or ⬇ to move the insertion point one character or line.

You can press **Ctrl** + ➡ or **Ctrl** + ⬅ to move the insertion point one word at a time to the right or left.

2 Type the text you want to insert.

Word inserts the text to the left of the insertion point, moving existing text to the right.

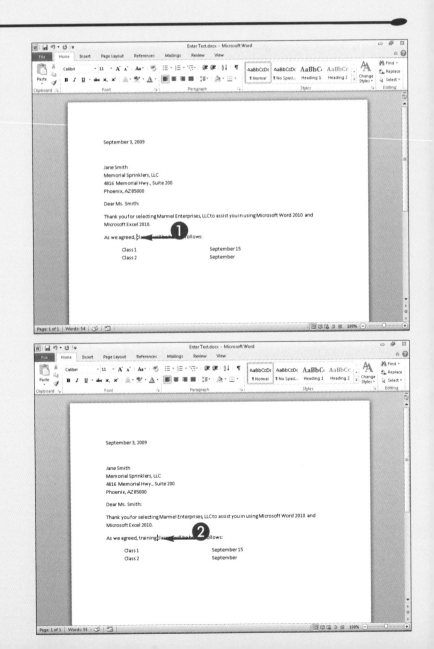

Insert and Replace Text

1 Right-click the status bar.

2 Click **Overtype**.

An indicator appears in the status bar.

3 Click the indicator to switch to Overtype mode.

Each time you click the indicator, you switch between Overtype and Insert mode.

4 Position the insertion point where you want to replace existing text and type the new text.

Simplify It

Can I control switching between Insert mode and Overtype mode using the keyboard?
Yes. Follow these steps:

1 Click the **File** tab and then click **Options** to display the Word Options dialog box.

2 Click **Advanced**.

3 Select the **Use the Insert key to control overtype mode** option (☐ changes to ☑).

4 Click **OK** and then press **Insert** on your keyboard.

Word switches between Insert mode and Overtype mode.

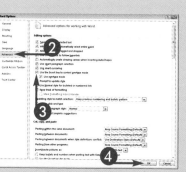

Delete Text

It is not uncommon to need to delete text. You might type something you did not mean to type, or you might think of a better way to write something, and it bears no resemblance to the way you previously wrote it. Or the facts of a situation might change, and you need to update the information.

Regardless of the reason, Word offers you two ways to eliminate text. You can easily remove text from a document using either the Delete or Backspace keys on your keyboard, and the method you choose depends on the placement of the insertion point.

Delete Text

Using the Delete Key

① Click to the left of the location where you want to delete text.

The insertion point flashes where you clicked.

You can press →, ←, ↑, or ↓ to move the insertion point one character or line.

You can press Ctrl + → or Ctrl + ← to move the insertion point one word at a time to the right or left.

② Press Delete on your keyboard.

● Word deletes the character immediately to the right of the insertion point.

You can hold Delete to repeatedly delete characters to the right of the insertion point.

You can press Ctrl + Delete to delete the word to the right of the insertion point.

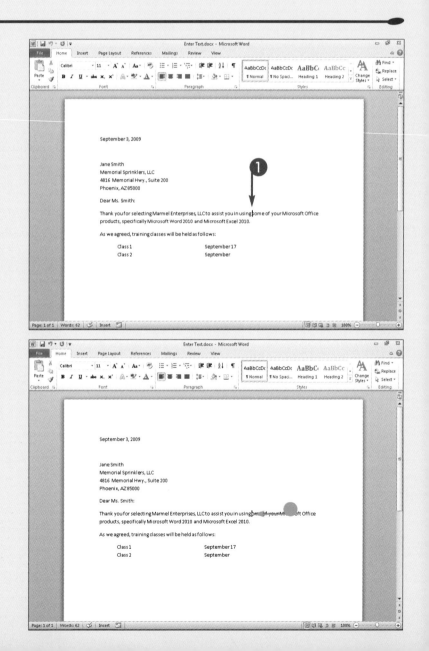

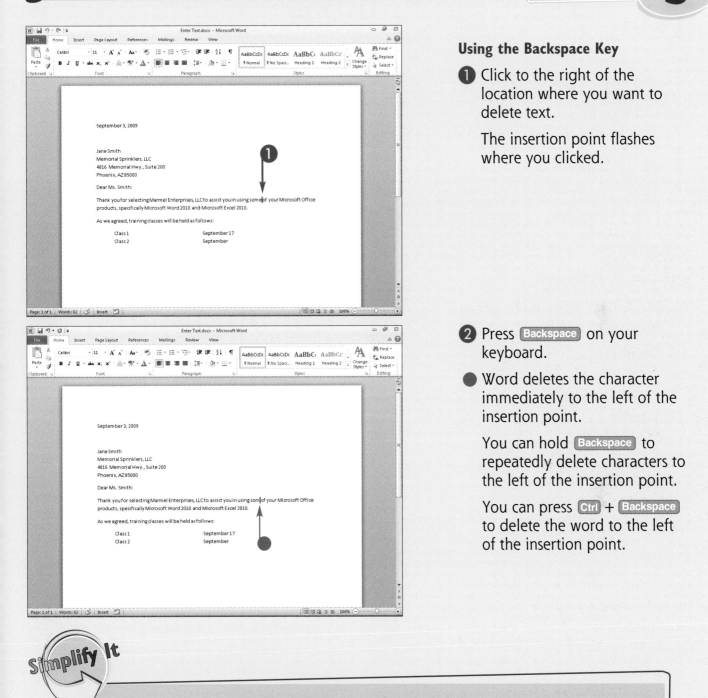

Using the Backspace Key

1 Click to the right of the location where you want to delete text.

The insertion point flashes where you clicked.

2 Press Backspace on your keyboard.

● Word deletes the character immediately to the left of the insertion point.

You can hold Backspace to repeatedly delete characters to the left of the insertion point.

You can press Ctrl + Backspace to delete the word to the left of the insertion point.

Simplify It

Do I have to delete a large block of text one character or one word at a time?
No. You can select the block of text and then press either Delete or Backspace; either key deletes selected text. For details on selecting text, see the section "Select Text" later in this chapter.

What should I do if I mistakenly delete text?
You should use the Undo feature in Word to restore the text you deleted. For details on how this feature works, see the section "Undo Changes" later in this chapter.

Insert Blank Lines

You can insert blank lines in your text to signify new paragraphs. Or you can start a new line without starting a new paragraph using a *line break*. For example, you might use line breaks when typing the lines of an address, particularly if pressing Enter starts a new paragraph, automatically inserting a blank line that you do not need between the lines of an address.

Word stores paragraph formatting in the paragraph mark shown in this section. You can change the formatting of one paragraph without affecting the formatting of the preceding paragraph. For more information on formatting paragraphs, see Chapter 6.

Insert Blank Lines

Start a New Paragraph

1 Click where you want to start a new paragraph.

2 Press **Enter**.

● Word inserts a paragraph mark and moves any text to the right of the insertion point into the new paragraph.

3 Repeat Steps **1** and **2** for each blank line you want to insert.

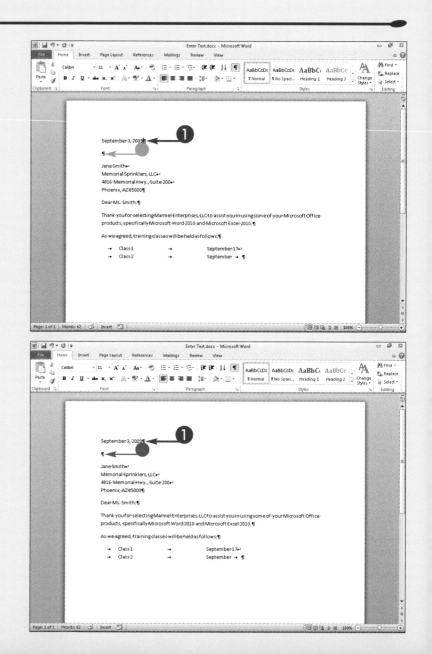

Insert a Line break

1 Click where you want to start a new paragraph.

2 Press **Shift** + **Enter**.

● Word inserts a line break and moves any text to the right of the insertion point onto the new line.

Undo
Changes

You can use the Undo feature to reverse actions you take while working in a document. For example, you might accidentally delete text that you need or apply formatting that you did not intend. In these cases, the Undo feature is particularly useful. Each time you use the Undo feature, Word reverses your last action. If you mistakenly delete text, you can use the Undo feature to recover it. If you deleted one character at a time, Word recovers one character at a time. If you deleted one word at a time, Word recovers one word at a time.

Undo Changes

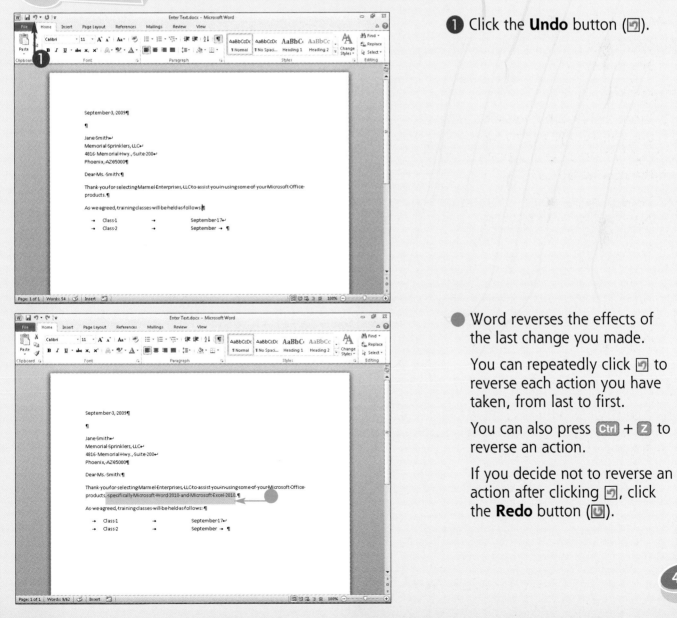

1 Click the **Undo** button (⬑).

● Word reverses the effects of the last change you made.

You can repeatedly click ⬑ to reverse each action you have taken, from last to first.

You can also press **Ctrl** + **Z** to reverse an action.

If you decide not to reverse an action after clicking ⬑, click the **Redo** button (⬐).

Select Text

Before performing many tasks in Word, you identify the existing text on which you want to work by selecting it. For example, you select existing text to underline it, align it, change its font size, apply color to it, or copy or move it.

Word offers you many ways to select text. And although you can always select text by dragging, you can become more efficient in Word if you use other methods, such as selecting words, a sentence, or your entire document.

You can use either the keyboard or your mouse to select text.

Select Text

Select a Block of Text

1 Position the mouse pointer to the left of the first character you want to select.

2 Click and drag to the right and down over the text you want to select and release the mouse button.

● The selection appears highlighted and the Mini toolbar appears faded in the background.

To cancel a selection, you can press ➡, ⬅, ⬆, or ⬇, or click anywhere on-screen.

Select a Word

1 Double-click the word you want to select.

● Word selects the word and the Mini toolbar appears faded in the background.

You can slide the mouse pointer closer to the Mini toolbar to make its options available.

Note: *See Chapter 1 for details on using the Mini toolbar.*

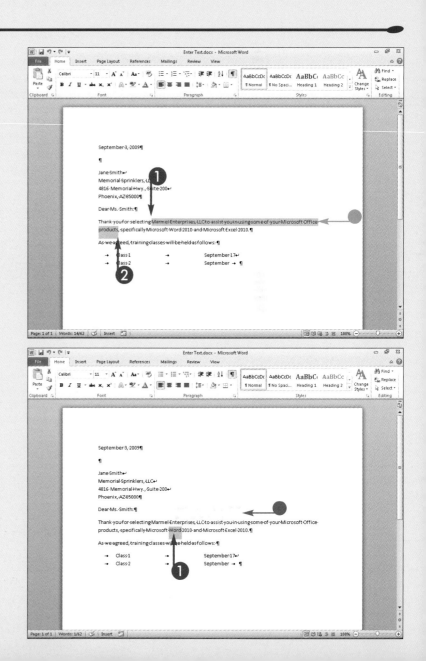

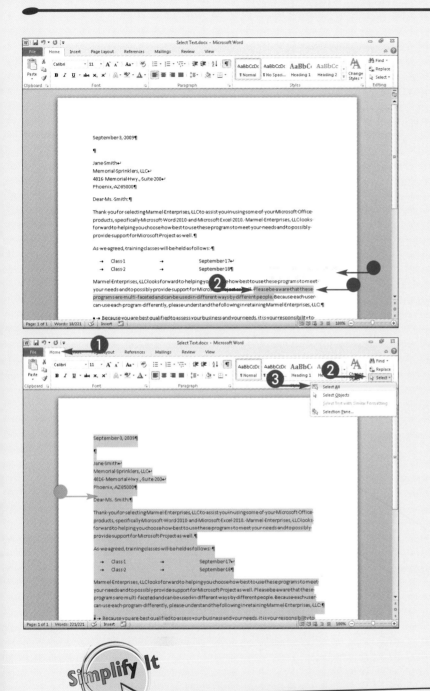

Select a Sentence

1 Press and hold **Ctrl**.

2 Click anywhere in the sentence you want to select.

● Word selects the entire sentence and the Mini toolbar appears faded in the background.

You can slide the mouse pointer closer to the Mini toolbar to make its options available.

Note: *See Chapter 1 for details on using the Mini toolbar.*

Select the Entire Document

1 Click the **Home** tab.

2 Click **Select**.

3 Click **Select All**.

● Word selects the entire document.

You also can press and hold **Ctrl** and press **A** to select the entire document.

To cancel the selection, click anywhere.

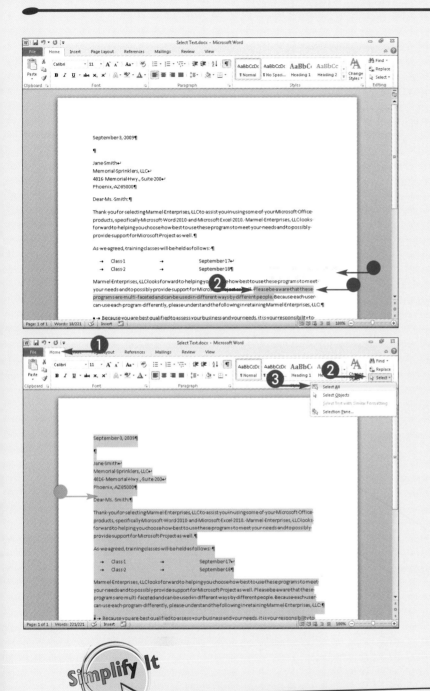
Simplify It

Can I select text using the keyboard?
Yes. Press and hold **Shift** while pressing
←, →, ↑, or ↓. You also can press
Shift + **Ctrl** to select, for example,
several words in a row. If you press and
hold **Shift** + **Ctrl** while pressing → five
times, you select five consecutive words
to the right of the insertion point.

Can I select noncontiguous text?
Yes. You select the first area using
any of the techniques described in
this section. Then press and hold
Ctrl as you select the additional
areas. Word selects all areas, even if
text appears between them.

Mark and Find
Your Place

Editing involves moving around a document to make changes, and most users find that they invariably need to return to a particular location. You can use the Bookmark feature to mark a location in a document so that you can easily return to it later.

Bookmarks do not print, nor are they visible in the document by default. Additionally, bookmarks serve other purposes besides marking a place in a document. You can also use bookmarks to store text, and Word uses bookmarks behind the scenes to operate some of its features.

Mark and Find Your Place

Mark Your Place

1 Click the location you want to mark.

Note: *If you select text instead of clicking at the location you want to mark, Word creates a bookmark containing text.*

2 Click the **Insert** tab.

3 Click **Bookmark**.

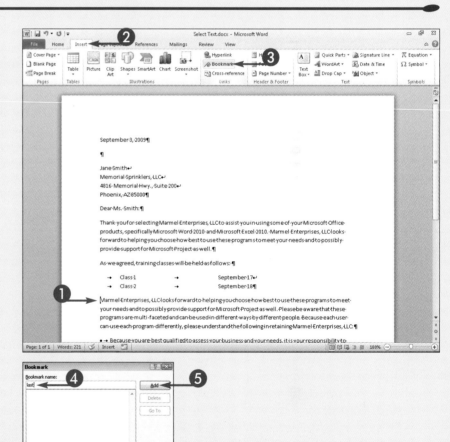

The Bookmark dialog box appears.

4 Type a name for the bookmark.

5 Click **Add**.

Word saves the bookmark and closes the Bookmark dialog box.

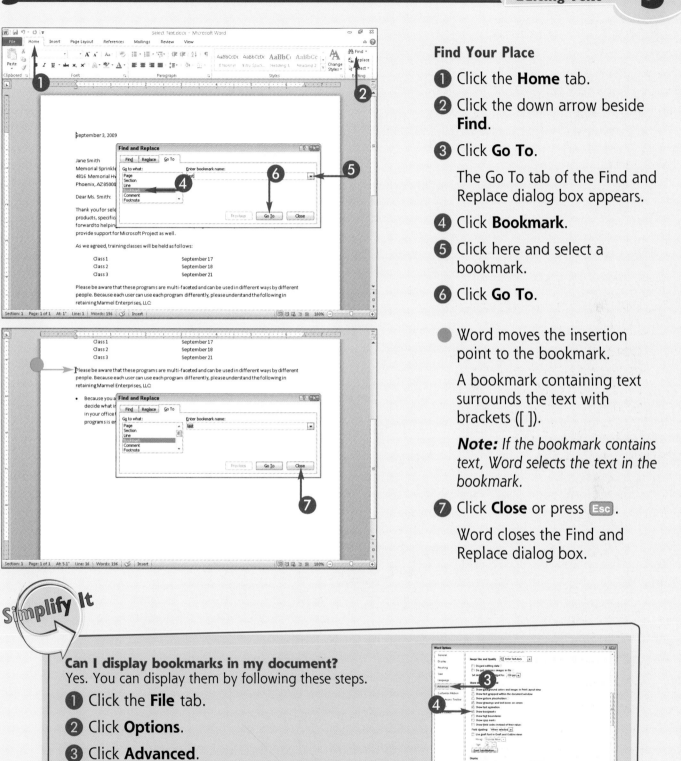

Find Your Place

1 Click the **Home** tab.

2 Click the down arrow beside **Find**.

3 Click **Go To**.

The Go To tab of the Find and Replace dialog box appears.

4 Click **Bookmark**.

5 Click here and select a bookmark.

6 Click **Go To**.

● Word moves the insertion point to the bookmark.

A bookmark containing text surrounds the text with brackets ([ ]).

Note: If the bookmark contains text, Word selects the text in the bookmark.

7 Click **Close** or press Esc.

Word closes the Find and Replace dialog box.

Simplify It

Can I display bookmarks in my document?
Yes. You can display them by following these steps.

1 Click the **File** tab.

2 Click **Options**.

3 Click **Advanced**.

4 Select the **Show bookmarks** option (☐ changes to ☑).

5 Click **OK** and Word displays open and close bookmark brackets.

Move or Copy Text

You can reposition text in your document by cutting and then pasting it. You also can repeat text by copying and then pasting it. Cutting and pasting or copying and pasting can save you a great deal of time and effort because you do not need to retype text simply because it appears in the wrong place in your document.

When you move text by cutting and pasting it, the text disappears from the original location and appears in a new one. When you copy and paste text, it remains in the original location and also appears in a new one.

Move or Copy Text

Using Ribbon Buttons

1. Select the text you want to move or copy.

   Note: To select text, see the section "Select Text."

2. Click the **Home** tab.

3. To move text, click the **Cut** button (); to copy text, click the **Copy** button ().

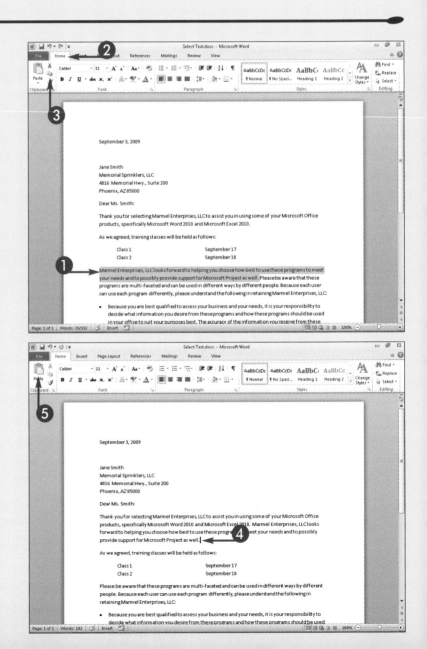

4. Click to place the insertion point at the location where you want the text to appear.

5. Click the **Paste** button ().

   The text appears at the new location.

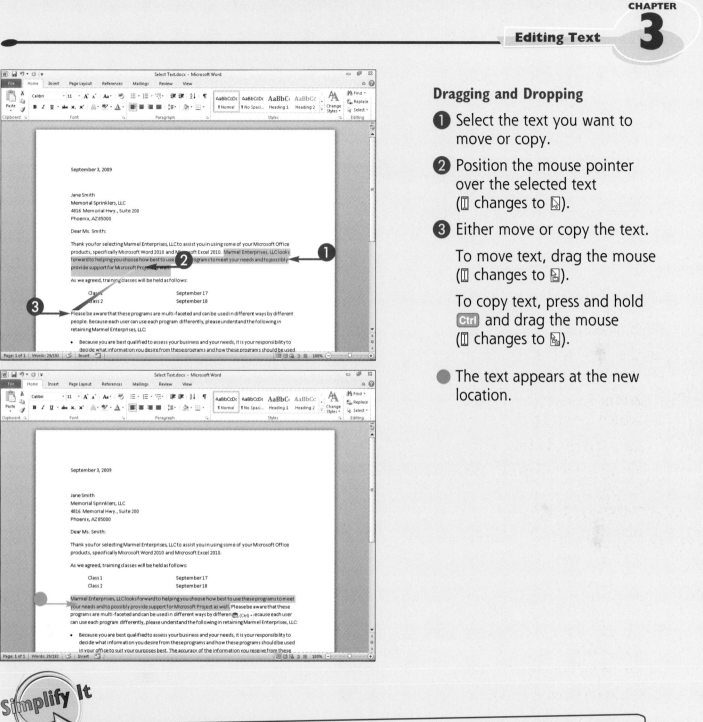

Dragging and Dropping

1️⃣ Select the text you want to move or copy.

2️⃣ Position the mouse pointer over the selected text (⌶ changes to ⍦).

3️⃣ Either move or copy the text.

To move text, drag the mouse (⌶ changes to ⍦).

To copy text, press and hold Ctrl and drag the mouse (⌶ changes to ⍦).

⬤ The text appears at the new location.

Is there a way I can move or copy text using menus?

Yes. You can select the text that you want to move or copy and then right-click it. The context menu and the Mini toolbar appear; click **Cut** or **Copy**. Then place the insertion point at the location where you want the text to appear and right-click again. From the context menu, click **Paste**.

Can I copy or move information other than text?

Yes. You can copy or move any type of element in your Word document: text, pictures, tables, graphics, and so on. Essentially, you can copy or move any element that you can select. You also can copy or move text from one Word document to another; see the section "Share Text Between Documents" later in this chapter.

Share Text Between Documents

When you cut, copy, and paste text, you are not limited to using the text in a single document. You can move or copy text from one document to another or to several other documents. And you can move or copy text from several documents into a single document.

Moving or copying text from one document to another can save you a great deal of time and effort because you do not need to retype text.

Any text that you cut disappears from its original location. Text that you copy continues to appear in its original location.

Share Text Between Documents

① Open the two documents you want to use to share text.

② Select the text you want to move or copy.

Note: *For details on selecting text, see the section "Select Text."*

③ Click ✂ to move text or click 📋 to copy text.

④ Switch to the other document by clicking its button in the Windows taskbar.

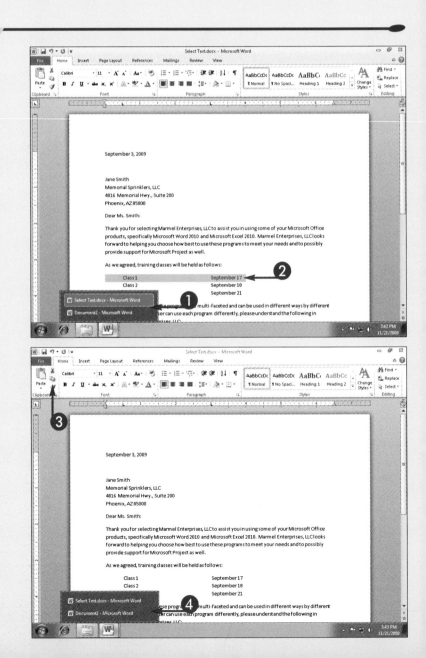

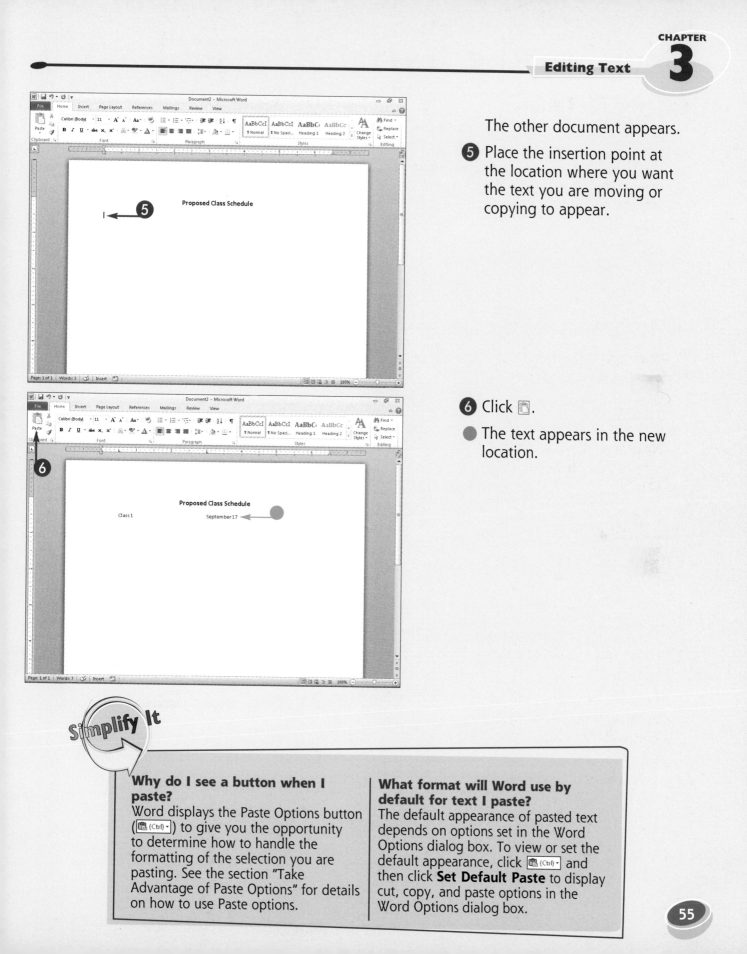

The other document appears.

⑤ Place the insertion point at the location where you want the text you are moving or copying to appear.

⑥ Click 📋.

● The text appears in the new location.

Why do I see a button when I paste?
Word displays the Paste Options button (📋(Ctrl)▾) to give you the opportunity to determine how to handle the formatting of the selection you are pasting. See the section "Take Advantage of Paste Options" for details on how to use Paste options.

What format will Word use by default for text I paste?
The default appearance of pasted text depends on options set in the Word Options dialog box. To view or set the default appearance, click 📋(Ctrl)▾ and then click **Set Default Paste** to display cut, copy, and paste options in the Word Options dialog box.

Move or Copy Several Selections

When you need to move or copy several selections of text or selections of text that do not appear contiguously in your document, you can use the Office Clipboard.

Typically, when you cut or copy a selection of text, Word stores that single selection on the Windows Clipboard, and the Windows Clipboard can hold only one selection at a time. Each time you cut or copy, Windows replaces the previous selection with the new selection.

The Office Clipboard, however, can hold up to the last 24 selections that you cut or copied in any Office program.

Move or Copy Several Selections

1 Click the **Clipboard** ⊡.

● The Office Clipboard pane appears.

Note: If you cut or copied anything prior to this time, an entry appears in the Clipboard pane.

2 Select the text or information you want to move or copy.

3 Click ✂ or ⧉.

● An entry appears in the Clipboard pane.

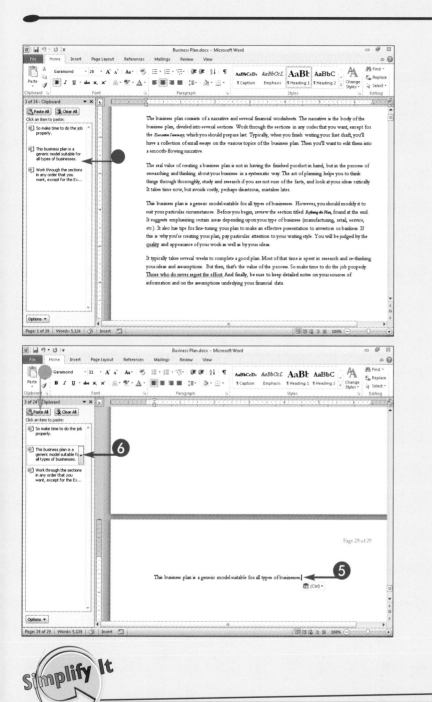

④ Repeat Steps **2** and **3** for each selection you want to move or copy.

● Word adds each entry to the Clipboard pane; the newest entry appears at the top of the pane.

⑤ Click in the document where you want to place text you cut or copied.

⑥ Click a selection in the Clipboard pane to place it in the document.

⑦ Repeat Steps **5** and **6** to paste other items from the Clipboard.

● If you want to place all of the items in one location and the items appear in the Clipboard pane in the order you want them in your document, you can click **Paste All**.

Why does ⏷ appear when I point at an item in the Clipboard pane?
If you click ⏷, a menu appears. From this menu, you can click **Paste** to add the item to your document, or you can click **Delete** to remove the item from the Clipboard pane.

Must I display the Office Clipboard to collect copied elements?
No. Click the **Options** button at the bottom of the Clipboard pane and then click **Collect Without Showing Office Clipboard**. As you cut or copy, a message appears in the lower-right corner of your screen, telling you how many elements are stored on the Office Clipboard. You must display the Office Clipboard to paste any item except the one you last cut or copied.

Take Advantage of Paste Options

When you move or copy information, you can choose the formatting Word applies to the selection at its new location. You can apply the formatting of the selection you copied or cut, you can use the formatting used at the location where you paste the selection; or you can apply formatting.

You also can link a selection you paste to the selection that you copy; in this case, any updates you make to the text at the original location also appear at the new location.

In some cases, you might be able to paste information as graphics that you cannot edit in Word.

Take Advantage of Paste Options

1 Select the text you want to copy or cut.

This example uses an Excel spreadsheet selection, but you can select text in a Word document.

2 Click 📋 or ✂.

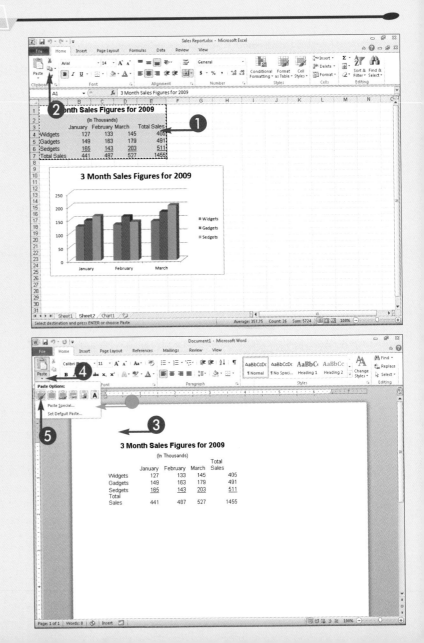

3 Position the insertion point in your Word document where you want to paste the information.

4 Click the **Paste** ⏷.

● Buttons representing paste options appear.

5 To preview the appearance of the selection, point at the Keep **Source Formatting** button (📝).

6 To preview the appearance of the selection, point at the **Use Destination Styles** (⊞) button.

7 To preview the appearance of the selection, point at the **Keep Text Only** button (A).

8 Click a **Paste Options** button to paste the selection and specify its format in your Word document.

Simplify It

What do the various Paste Options buttons mean?

Paste Options Button	Function
▤	Formats the selection you copied or cut.
▤	Formats the selection using the style of the location where you paste the selection.
▤	Uses the formatting of the selection you cut or copied and links the new location to the original location.
▤	Formats the selection using the style of the location where you paste the selection and links the new location to the original location.
▤	Formats the selection as a graphic that you cannot edit in Word.
A	Applies no formatting to the selection; only text appears.

Switch Document Views

You can view a document five ways. Viewing your document in different ways can help you in different ways. For example, if you are focusing on the formatting in your document, you might prefer Draft view, but if you want to see your document the way it will print, you should use Print Layout view. The view you use depends entirely on what you are doing at the time; select the view that best meets your needs. For more on the various views, see the section "Understanding Document Views." The button for the currently selected view appears in orange.

Switch Document Views

1 Click the **View** tab.

2 Click one of the Document Views buttons on the Ribbon:

- 📄 Print Layout
- 📄 Full Screen Reading
- 🌐 Web Layout
- 📄 Outline
- 📄 Draft

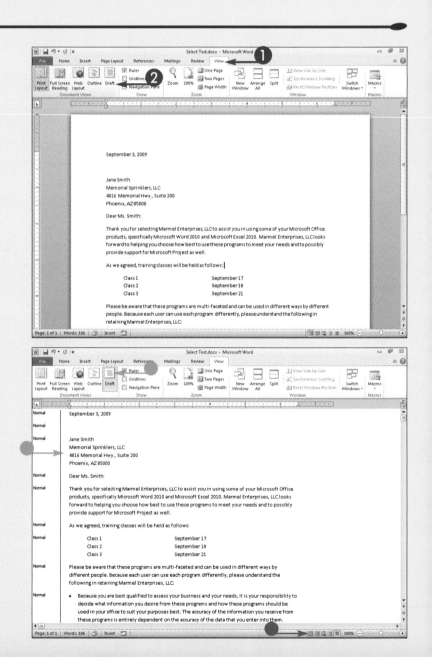

● Word switches your document to the view you selected.

● Buttons for each view also appear at the right edge of the status bar; position the mouse pointer over each button to see its function and click a button to switch views.

Understanding Document Views

When working in your document, you should select any of the five different views that best meets your needs. But, which view is right for you? The purpose of each view is described in this section. You will find that you need different views at different times, often depending on what you are trying to do.

For example, Draft view helps you focus on document formatting, Print Layout helps you focus on the way your document will look when it prints, and Outline view helps you focus on your document's organization.

To switch between views, see the section "Switch Document Views."

Draft View

Draft view is designed for editing and formatting; it does not display your document the way it will print. Instead, you can view elements such as the Style Area on the left side of the screen, but you cannot view the document's margins, headers and footers, or graphics in the location where they will appear.

Web Layout View

Web Layout view is useful when you are designing a Web page.

Print Layout View

Print Layout view presents a "what you see is what you get" view of your document. In Print Layout view, you see elements of your document that affect the printed page, such as margins.

Outline View

Outline view helps you work with the organization of a document. Word indents text styled as headings based on the heading number; you can move or copy entire sections of a document by moving or copying the heading.

Full Screen Reading View

Full Screen Reading view is designed to minimize eye strain when you read a document on-screen. This view removes most toolbars. To return to another view, click the Close button (⊠ Close) in the upper-right corner of the screen.

Zoom In or Out

You can use the Zoom feature to enlarge or reduce the size of the text on-screen. Zooming in enlarges text. Zooming out reduces text, providing more of an overview of your document.

Using the Zoom feature does not change the way your document will print or the pagination in your document. Zooming simply changes the size of the font on-screen. You might zoom in to make your document easier to read while you work on it, and you might zoom out to get a sense of the way text lays out on a page.

Zoom In or Out

1 Click the **View** tab.

2 Click **Zoom**.

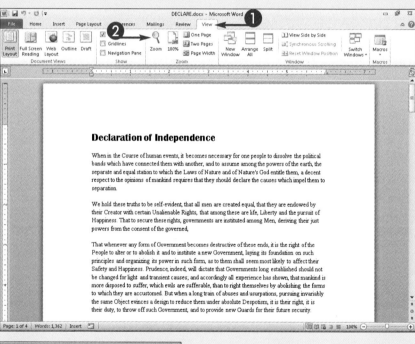

The Zoom dialog box appears.

3 Click a zoom setting.

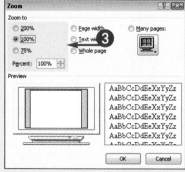

● You can click the **Many pages** down arrow (▼) and select to display multiple pages.

Note: The number of pages you can view depends on the resolution you set for your monitor.

④ Click **OK**.

The document appears on-screen using the new zoom setting.

What do the Page width and Text width options do?

You can select the **Page width** option (◎ changes to ◉) to fit the page, including margins, across the width of the screen, or **Text width** to fit text, excluding margins, across the width of the screen. The Page Width button on the Ribbon serves the same purpose as the Page width option in the Zoom dialog box, and the One Page button and the Two Pages button on the Ribbon are the most common choices when using the Many pages option in the Zoom dialog box.

Can I use the mouse to zoom?

Yes. Drag the Zoom slider in the status bar or click the plus or minus signs at either end of the Zoom slider. Each click of the plus sign zooms in 10 percent; each click of the minus sign zooms out 10 percent.

Insert a Symbol

Using the Symbol feature, you can insert characters into your documents that do not appear on your keyboard. Although you can use ASCII code keyboard combinations to insert symbols, most people do not memorize ASCII codes, and with the Symbol feature, there is

no need to do so. To insert symbols you use occasionally, follow the steps in this section. If you find yourself using a particular symbol frequently, you can assign a keyboard shortcut to it, as described in the tip in this section.

Insert a Symbol

1 Click the location in the document where you want the symbol to appear.

2 Click the **Insert** tab.

3 Click **Symbol**.

A list of commonly used symbols appears. If the symbol you need appears in the list, you can click it and skip the rest of these steps.

4 Click **More Symbols**.

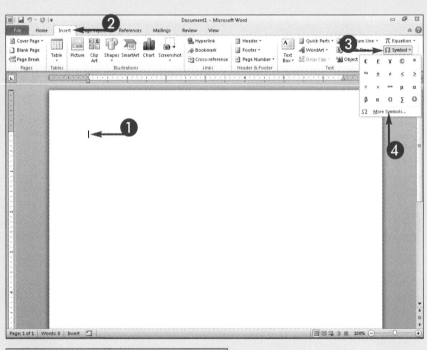

The Symbol dialog box appears.

5 Click here and select the symbol's font.

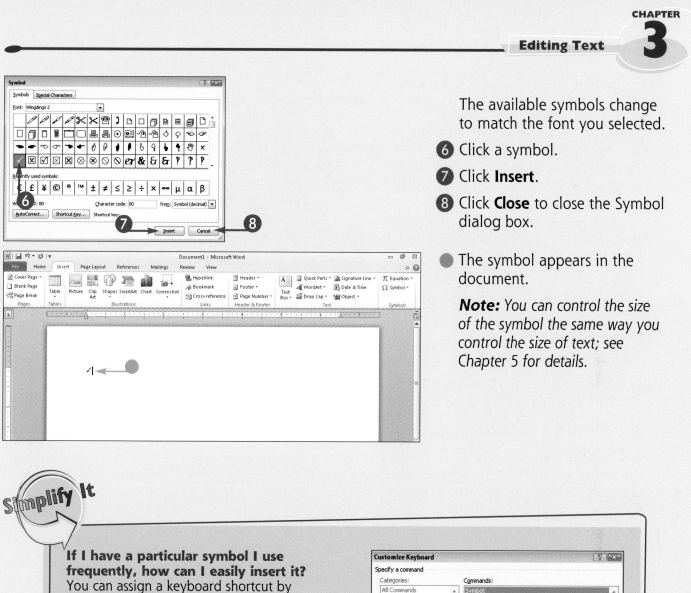

The available symbols change to match the font you selected.

⑥ Click a symbol.

⑦ Click **Insert**.

⑧ Click **Close** to close the Symbol dialog box.

● The symbol appears in the document.

Note: *You can control the size of the symbol the same way you control the size of text; see Chapter 5 for details.*

If I have a particular symbol I use frequently, how can I easily insert it?
You can assign a keyboard shortcut by following these steps:

❶ Complete Steps **1** to **6** in this section and then click **Shortcut Key**.

❷ In the Customize Keyboard dialog box, press Alt or Ctrl and any other key.

❸ Click **Assign**.

❹ Click **Close** in both dialog boxes.

You can now position the insertion point and press the assigned keyboard shortcut to place the symbol.

Set Options for Additional Actions

Word can recognize certain kinds of information and provide time-saving actions associated with this information. For example, you can have Word give you the option of displaying a map to an address you type.

You control the kinds of information Word recognizes and identifies for actions that can save you time. By default, Word does not

recognize any type of information, but you can have Word recognize addresses, dates, financial symbols, Instant Messaging contacts, measurements, people's names, telephone numbers, and times. Or you can opt to not let Word recognize any type of information for additional actions.

Set Options for Additional Actions

1 Click the **File** tab.

The Backstage view appears.

2 Click **Options**.

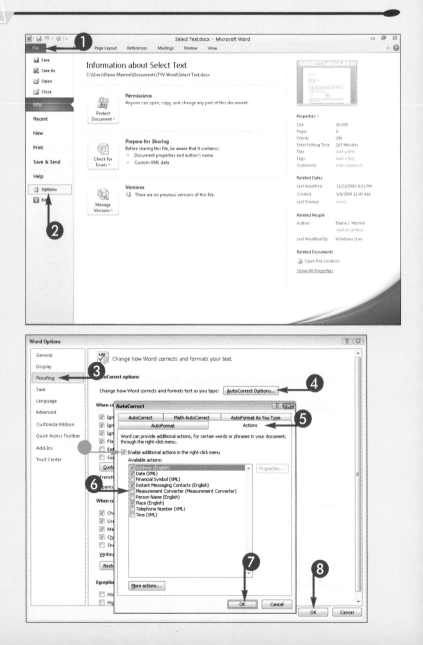

The Word Options dialog box appears.

3 Click **Proofing**.

4 Click **AutoCorrect Options**.

The AutoCorrect dialog box appears.

5 Click the **Actions** tab.

● You can click here (☑ changes to ☐) to turn off smart tag recognition.

6 Click the check box beside an item to turn additional action recognition on (☑) or off (☐).

7 Click **OK** to close the AutoCorrect dialog box.

8 Click **OK** to close the Word Options window.

66

Word saves your preferences.

Using Additional Actions

You can use the Additional Actions feature, formerly called "smart tags," to save time. Using this feature, Word can convert measurements, add a telephone number to Outlook Contacts, or schedule a meeting.

This feature may not be on by default; see the section, "Set Options for Additional Actions." You select the types of information you want

Word to recognize; then, when one of these types of information appears in your document, you can use the Additional Actions menu to display a map to an address or dial a telephone number.

Using Additional Actions

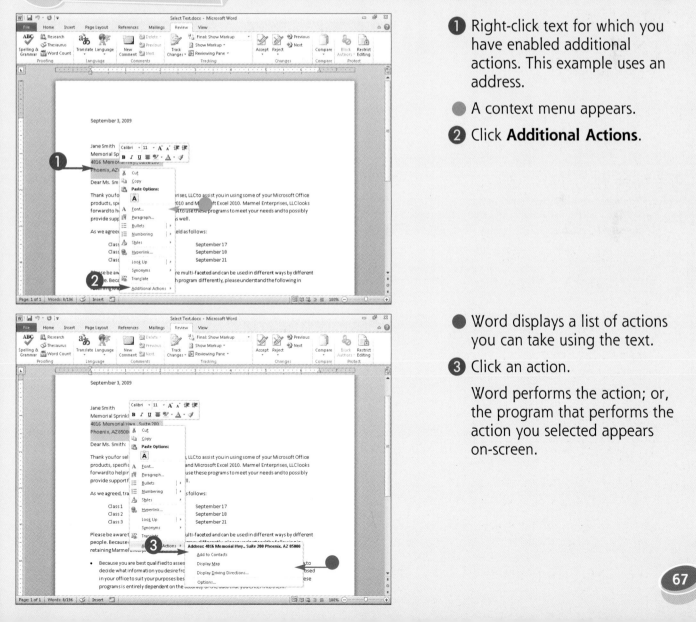

1 Right-click text for which you have enabled additional actions. This example uses an address.

● A context menu appears.

2 Click **Additional Actions**.

● Word displays a list of actions you can take using the text.

3 Click an action.

Word performs the action; or, the program that performs the action you selected appears on-screen.

67

Chapter 4

Proofreading in Word

This chapter shows you how to use a variety of Word features to handle proofreading tasks. You can search through text to find something in particular, as well as search for particular text to replace it. And Word contains features to help you resolve spelling and grammar issues.

Many people work in environments where several people review a particular document before it becomes the final version. In cases like these, you can take advantage of Word features that help you track revisions made by each reviewer and then combine those revisions into one final document.

Search for Text

Occasionally, you need to search for a word or phrase in a document. You might, for example, need to make sure that a particular word or phrase is used consistently throughout a document. You can use Word's Navigation pane to search for all occurrences simultaneously. Or you can use the Find and Replace window to search for each single occurrence. Using the Find and Replace window, you can highlight each occurrence in yellow.

This section shows you how to use both methods to search for text and focuses on finding text; see the next section, "Substitute Text" for information on finding and replacing text.

Search for Text

Search for All Occurrences

1 Click the **Home** tab.

2 Click **Find**.

● The Navigation Pane appears.

3 Type the word or phrase for which you want to search.

● Word highlights all occurrences of the word or phrase in yellow.

4 Click **Close (X)** to clear the search and results.

5 Click **Close (X)** to close the Navigation Pane.

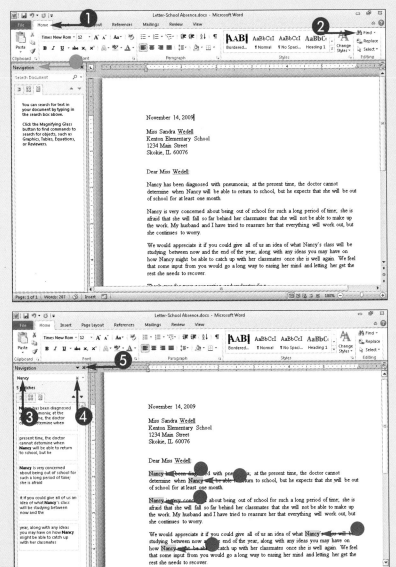

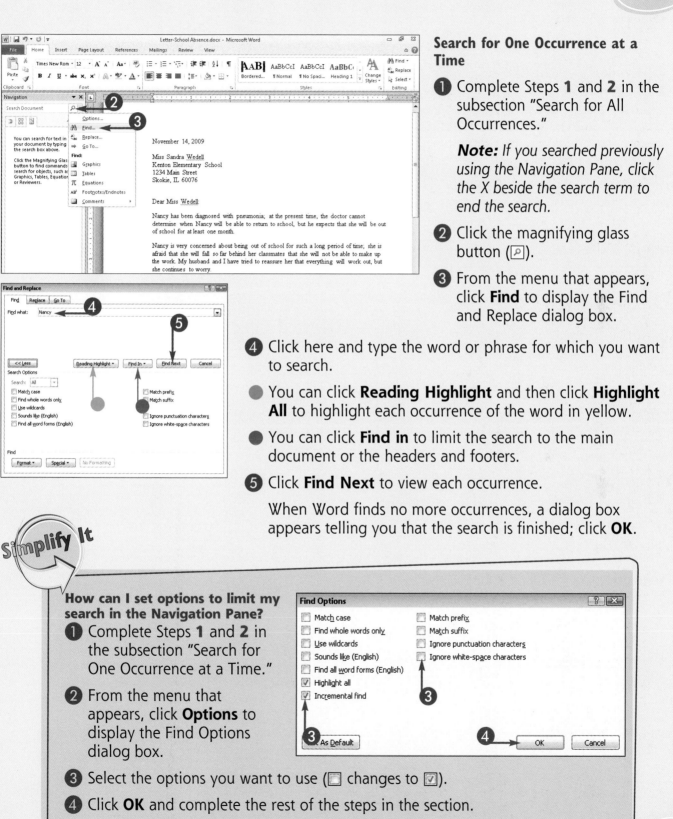

Search for One Occurrence at a Time

① Complete Steps **1** and **2** in the subsection "Search for All Occurrences."

Note: *If you searched previously using the Navigation Pane, click the X beside the search term to end the search.*

② Click the magnifying glass button (🔍).

③ From the menu that appears, click **Find** to display the Find and Replace dialog box.

④ Click here and type the word or phrase for which you want to search.

● You can click **Reading Highlight** and then click **Highlight All** to highlight each occurrence of the word in yellow.

● You can click **Find in** to limit the search to the main document or the headers and footers.

⑤ Click **Find Next** to view each occurrence.

When Word finds no more occurrences, a dialog box appears telling you that the search is finished; click **OK**.

Simplify It

How can I set options to limit my search in the Navigation Pane?

① Complete Steps **1** and **2** in the subsection "Search for One Occurrence at a Time."

② From the menu that appears, click **Options** to display the Find Options dialog box.

③ Select the options you want to use (☐ changes to ☑).

④ Click **OK** and complete the rest of the steps in the section.

Substitute Text

Often, you want to find a word or phrase because you need to substitute some other word or phrase for it. Using Word's Find and Replace window, you can substitute a word or phrase for all occurrences of the original word or phrase, or you can selectively substitute.

When you perform a search, you can specify parameters that, for example, force Word to find whole words only or match the case of the text.

And you are not limited to searching for and replacing text. You can search for and replace formatting such as boldface or italics and special characters such as paragraph marks, line breaks, or tabs.

Substitute Text

1 Click the **Home** tab.

2 Click **Replace**.

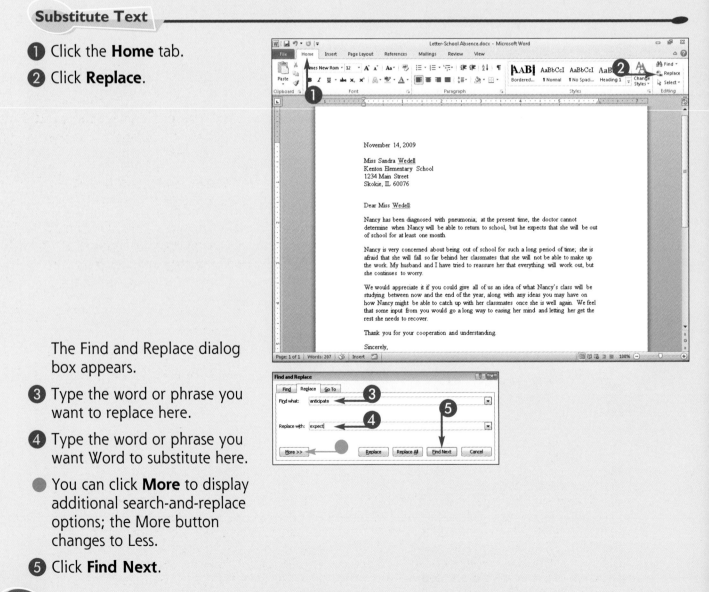

The Find and Replace dialog box appears.

3 Type the word or phrase you want to replace here.

4 Type the word or phrase you want Word to substitute here.

● You can click **More** to display additional search-and-replace options; the More button changes to Less.

5 Click **Find Next**.

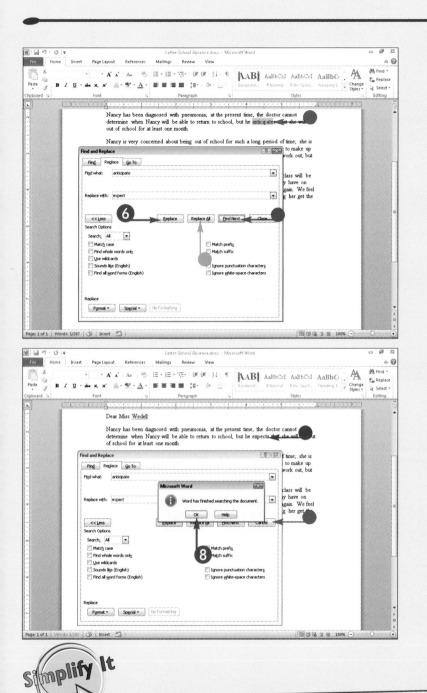

● Word highlights the first occurrence of the word or phrase that it finds.

● If you do not want to change the highlighted occurrence, you can click **Find Next** to ignore it.

⑥ Click **Replace**.

○ To change all occurrences in the document, you can click **Replace All**.

● Word replaces the original word or phrase with the word or phrase you specify as the substitute.

⑦ Repeat Steps **5** and **6** as needed.

⑧ When Word finds no more occurrences, a dialog box appears telling you that the search is finished; click **OK**.

● The Cancel button changes to Close.

⑨ Click **Close** to close the Find and Replace dialog box.

Simplify It

Can I find italic text and change it to boldface text?
Yes. Follow Steps **1** and **2** and click **More** to expand the window. Follow Steps **3** and **4**, but, instead of typing text, click **Format** and then click **Font**. In the Font style list of the Font dialog box that appears, click **Italic** for Step **3** and **Bold** for Step **4**. Then complete Steps **5** to **9**.

Can I search for and replace special characters such as tabs or paragraph marks?
Yes. Follow Steps **1** and **2** and click **More** to expand the window. Then follow Steps **3** and **4**, but instead of typing text, click **Special** to display a menu of special characters. For Step **3**, select the special character you want to find. For Step **4**, select the special character you want to substitute. Then complete Steps **5** to **9**.

Automatically Correct Mistakes

Using the AutoCorrect feature, Word automatically corrects hundreds of common typing and spelling mistakes as you work. You can also add your own set of mistakes and the corrections to the list Word references.

In addition to correcting mistakes, you can use AutoCorrect to replace just a few characters with a complete, fairly lengthy phrase. For example, if your company name is Marmel Enterprises, LLC, you can create an AutoCorrect entry that substitutes your company name each time you type mll. Be sure you do not use a word for the characters Word should substitute.

Automatically Correct Mistakes

1 Click the **File** tab.

The Backstage view appears.

2 Click **Options**.

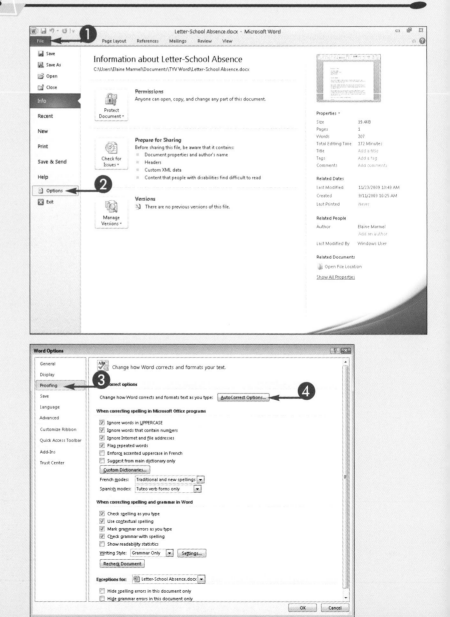

The Word Options dialog box appears.

3 Click **Proofing** to display proofing options.

4 Click **AutoCorrect Options**.

The AutoCorrect dialog box appears.

● The corrections Word already makes automatically appear in this area.

⑤ Click here and type the word you typically mistype or misspell.

⑥ Click here and type the correct version of the word.

⑦ Click **Add**.

● Word adds the entry to the list to automatically correct.

You can repeat Steps **5** to **7** for each automatic correction you want to add.

⑧ Click **OK** to close the AutoCorrect dialog box.

⑨ Click **OK** to close the Word Options dialog box.

How does the automatic correction work?
You do not need to do anything unusual — just type. If you mistype or misspell a word stored as an AutoCorrect entry, Word corrects the entry when you press Spacebar, Tab, or Enter.

What should I do if Word automatically replaces an entry that I do not want replaced?
Position the insertion point at the beginning of the AutoCorrected word and click the **AutoCorrect Options** button (🗷 ▾) that appears. From the list of choices displayed, click **Change back to**. To make Word permanently stop correcting an entry, follow Steps **1** to **4**, click the stored AutoCorrect entry in the list, and then click **Delete**.

Automatically Insert Frequently Used Text

Using the Quick Parts feature, you can store and then insert phrases you use frequently that include formatting. The Quick Parts feature is particularly useful for phrases that take up more than one line, such as a name, title, and company name that appears at the bottom of a letter.

Quick Parts were known as AutoText entries in versions of Word prior to Word 2007. Any AutoText entries you created appear in Word 2010, but unless you remember their names, you can insert them only using the AutoText Gallery. For Word 2010, Quick Parts are faster and easier to use.

Automatically Insert Frequently Used Text

Create a Quick Part Entry

1. Type the text that you want to store, including all formatting that should appear each time you insert the entry.

2. Select the text you typed.

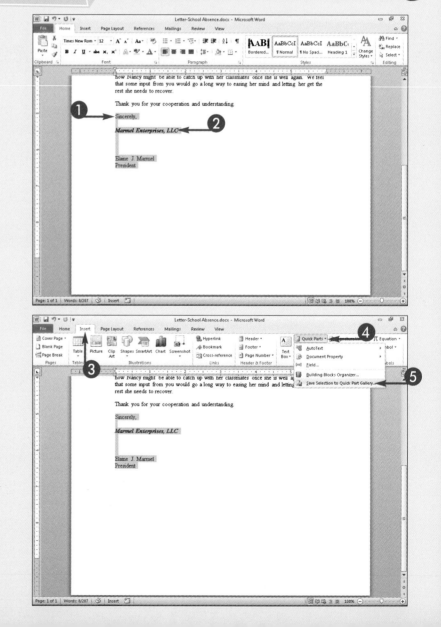

3. Click the **Insert** tab.

4. Click **Quick Parts**.

5. Click **Save Selection to Quick Part Gallery**.

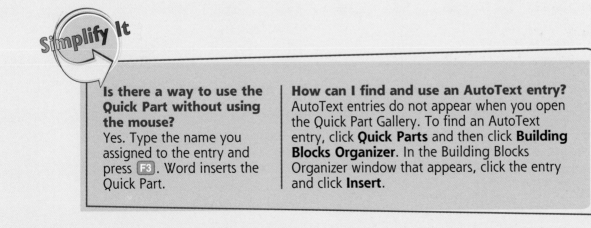

The Create New Building Block dialog box appears.

⑥ Type a name that you want to use as a shortcut for the entry.

⑦ Click **OK**.

Word stores the entry on the Quick Part Gallery.

Insert a Quick Part Entry

① Position the insertion point where you want the Quick Part entry to appear.

② Click **Quick Parts**.

All building blocks you define as Quick Parts appear on the Quick Part Gallery.

③ Click the entry.

Word inserts the Quick Part entry.

Is there a way to use the Quick Part without using the mouse?
Yes. Type the name you assigned to the entry and press F3. Word inserts the Quick Part.

How can I find and use an AutoText entry?
AutoText entries do not appear when you open the Quick Part Gallery. To find an AutoText entry, click **Quick Parts** and then click **Building Blocks Organizer**. In the Building Blocks Organizer window that appears, click the entry and click **Insert**.

Check Spelling and Grammar

The Spelling and Grammar Checker enables you to search for and correct all spelling and grammar mistakes in your document.

As you work, Word underlines words that are misspelled or misused, as well as grammar errors. On-screen, Word places a red squiggly underline beneath spelling errors, a green squiggly underline beneath grammar errors, and a blue squiggly line under correctly spelled but misused words. You can correct these errors one by one or you can use the Spelling and Grammar Checker to do the job for your entire document at one time.

Check Spelling and Grammar

1 Click the **Review** tab.

2 Click **Spelling & Grammar**.

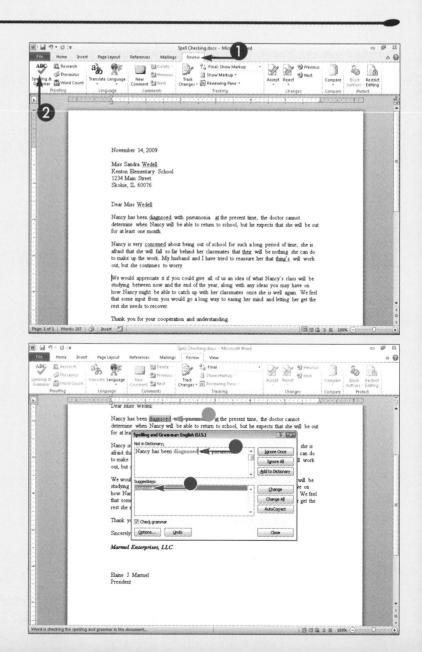

● Word selects the first spelling or grammar mistake and displays the Spelling and Grammar window.

Note: *If your document contains no errors, this window does not appear.*

● This area displays the spelling or grammar mistake.

● This area displays suggestions to correct the error.

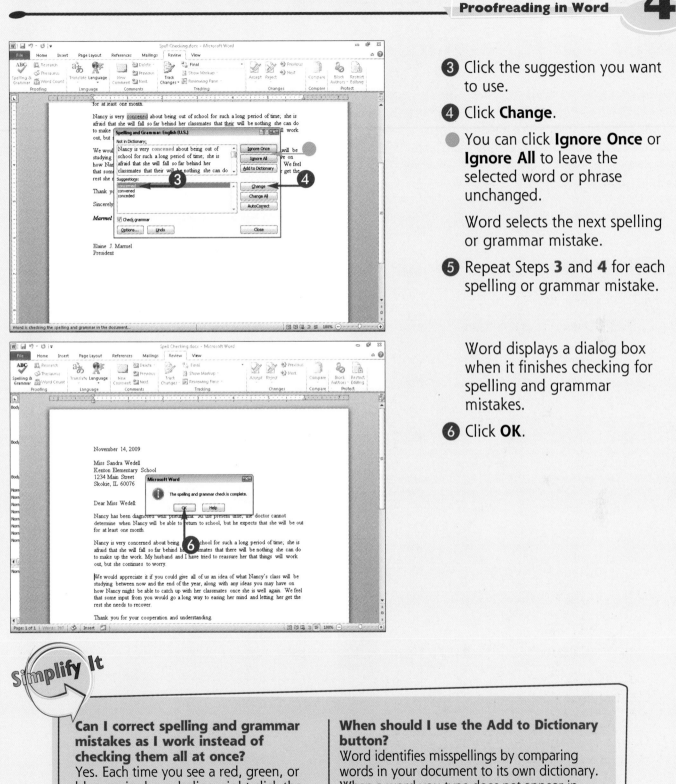

③ Click the suggestion you want to use.

④ Click **Change**.

● You can click **Ignore Once** or **Ignore All** to leave the selected word or phrase unchanged.

Word selects the next spelling or grammar mistake.

⑤ Repeat Steps **3** and **4** for each spelling or grammar mistake.

Word displays a dialog box when it finishes checking for spelling and grammar mistakes.

⑥ Click **OK**.

Can I correct spelling and grammar mistakes as I work instead of checking them all at once?
Yes. Each time you see a red, green, or blue squiggly underline, right-click the word or phrase. Word displays a menu of suggestions; you can click one to correct the error.

When should I use the Add to Dictionary button?
Word identifies misspellings by comparing words in your document to its own dictionary. When a word you type does not appear in Word's dictionary, Word flags the word as misspelled. If the word is a term you use regularly, click **Add to Dictionary** so that Word stops flagging the word as a misspelling.

Disable Grammar and Spell Checking

By default, Word automatically checks spelling and grammar by displaying red and green squiggly lines whenever it identifies a spelling or grammar mistake, and a blue squiggly line whenever it identifies a misused word. If the squiggly underlines annoy or distract you, you can turn off automatic spelling and grammar checking.

Turning off automatic spelling and grammar checking does not take away your ability to check grammar and spelling. Instead, it simply does not alert you while you work. Later, when you are ready to address spelling and grammar issues, you can do so using the steps in the section, "Check Spelling and Grammar."

Disable Grammar and Spell Checking

1 Click the **File** tab.

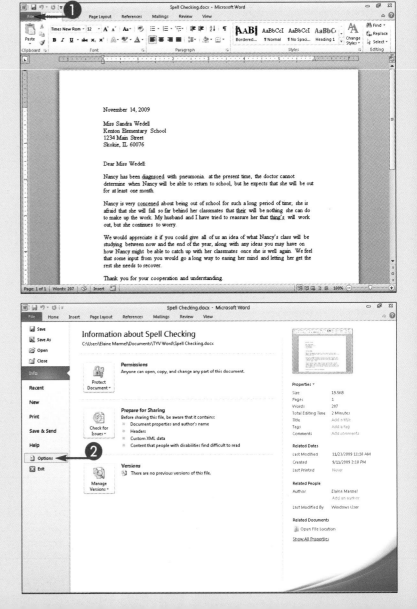

The Backstage view appears.

2 Click **Options**.

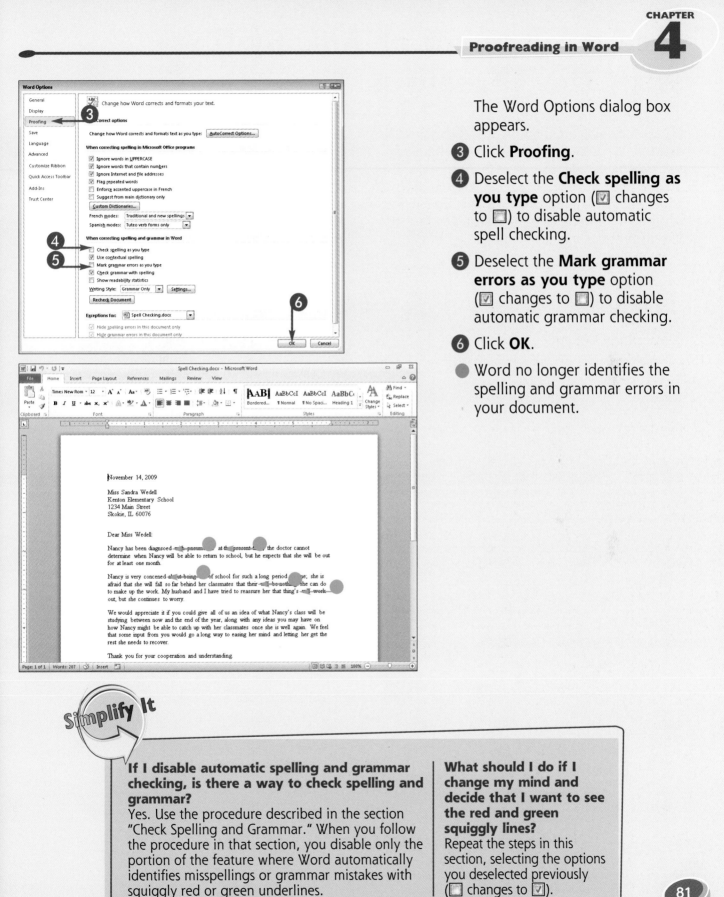

The Word Options dialog box appears.

③ Click **Proofing**.

④ Deselect the **Check spelling as you type** option (☑ changes to ☐) to disable automatic spell checking.

⑤ Deselect the **Mark grammar errors as you type** option (☑ changes to ☐) to disable automatic grammar checking.

⑥ Click **OK**.

● Word no longer identifies the spelling and grammar errors in your document.

Simplify It

If I disable automatic spelling and grammar checking, is there a way to check spelling and grammar?
Yes. Use the procedure described in the section "Check Spelling and Grammar." When you follow the procedure in that section, you disable only the portion of the feature where Word automatically identifies misspellings or grammar mistakes with squiggly red or green underlines.

What should I do if I change my mind and decide that I want to see the red and green squiggly lines?
Repeat the steps in this section, selecting the options you deselected previously (☐ changes to ☑).

Find a Synonym or Antonym with the Thesaurus

Using the thesaurus, you can search for a more suitable word than the word you originally chose. The thesaurus can help you find a synonym — a word with a similar meaning — for the word you originally chose, as well as an antonym, which is a word with an opposite meaning.

When you use the thesaurus, Word lists all forms of the word. For example, if you check the thesaurus for the word *present*, Word displays the adjectives *current* and *near*, the nouns *gift* and *now*, and a variety of verbs, including *give*, *stage*, *pose*, *portray*, *appear*, and *impart*.

Find a Synonym or Antonym with the Thesaurus

1 Click the word for which you want to find an opposite or substitute.

2 Click the **Review** tab.

3 Click **Thesaurus**.

The Research task pane appears.

● The word you selected appears here.

● Click here to display a list of resources you can use to search for information.

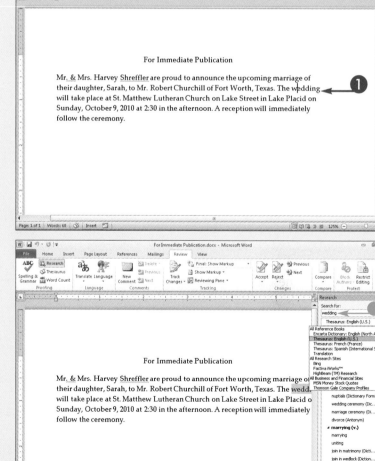

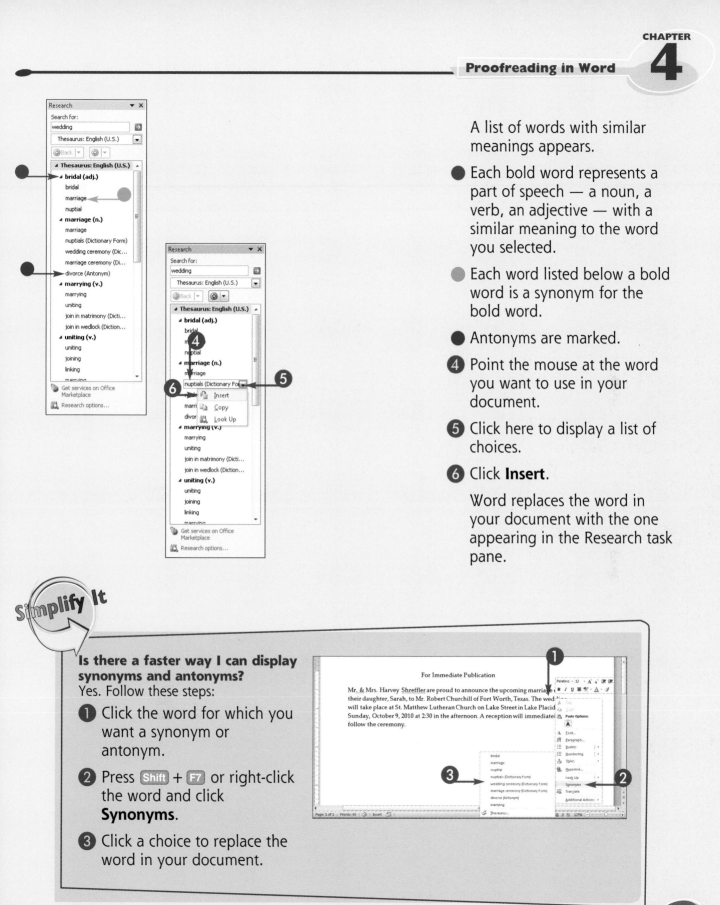

A list of words with similar meanings appears.

● Each bold word represents a part of speech — a noun, a verb, an adjective — with a similar meaning to the word you selected.

● Each word listed below a bold word is a synonym for the bold word.

● Antonyms are marked.

④ Point the mouse at the word you want to use in your document.

⑤ Click here to display a list of choices.

⑥ Click **Insert**.

Word replaces the word in your document with the one appearing in the Research task pane.

Simplify It

Is there a faster way I can display synonyms and antonyms?
Yes. Follow these steps:

① Click the word for which you want a synonym or antonym.

② Press Shift + F7 or right-click the word and click **Synonyms**.

③ Click a choice to replace the word in your document.

Add Comments to a Document

You can add comments to clarify information in your documents. For example, you can use a comment to explain a statement, add a note of clarification, or remind you to take an action.

Many people also use comments while reviewing a document. Comments are not part of the main text of the document; in Print Layout view, they appear in comment balloons, and in Draft view, they appear in the Reviewing Pane. In Print Layout, the comment balloons automatically appear, but in Draft view, you must display the Reviewing Pane to see them. In addition, comments do not print unless you specifically choose to print them.

Add Comments to a Document

Add a Comment

① On the status bar, click the **Full Screen Reading** button (▣), the **Web Layout** button (▣), or the **Print Layout** button (▣) to view your document.

You alternatively can click ▣, ▣, or ▣ on the View tab.

② Select the text about which you want to comment.

③ Click the **Review** tab.

④ Click **New Comment**.

● A comment balloon appears in the markup area on the right side of the document.

● The comment balloon is attached to the text you selected, which is highlighted in the color of the balloon.

Note: *In the comment, Word inserts the initials stored in the Personalize section of the Word Options dialog box along with a comment number.*

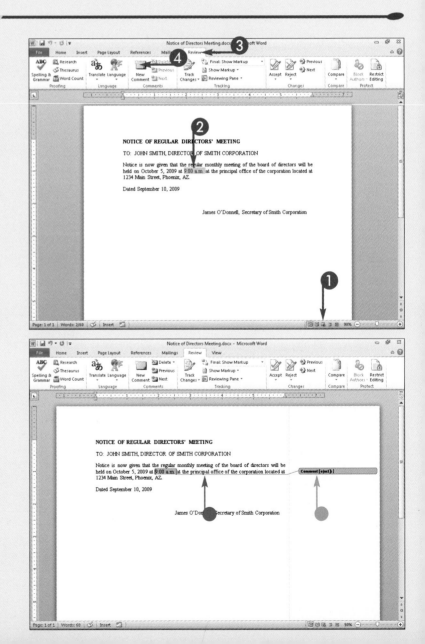

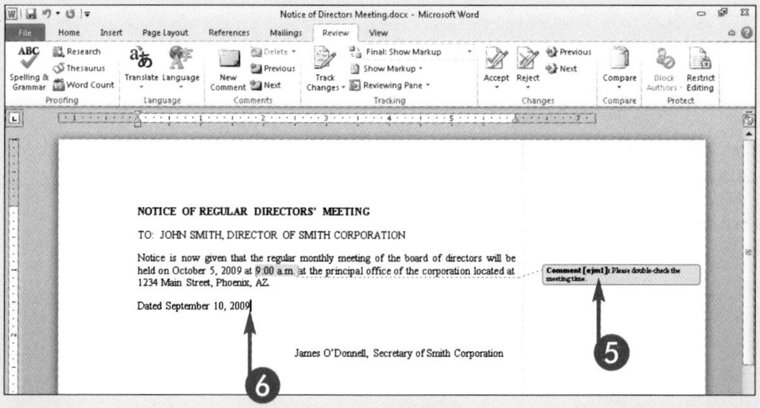

5 Type the text you want to store in the comment.

6 Click outside the comment balloon to save your comment.

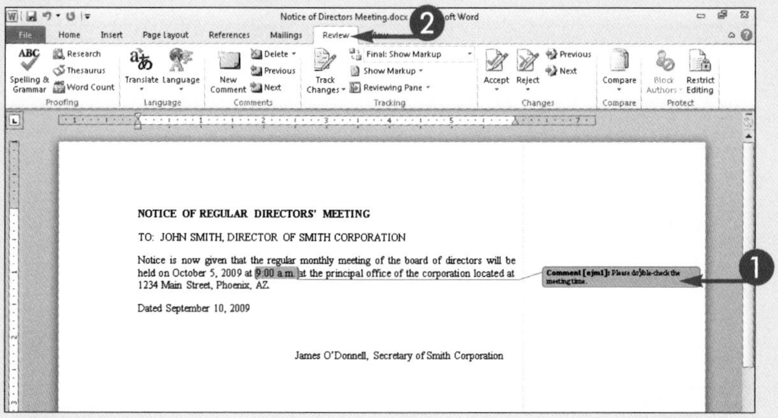

Delete a Comment

1 Click anywhere in the comment balloon you want to delete.

2 On the Review tab, click **Delete**.

Word deletes the comment balloon and removes the highlighting from the associated text.

Simplify It

Can I insert a comment in Draft view or Outline view?
Yes. Do the following:

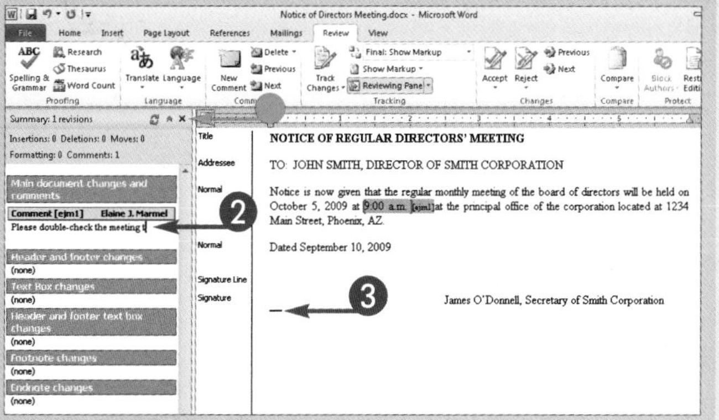

1 Follow Steps **1** to **4** in this section, selecting **Draft** view (🔲) or **Outline** view (🔲) in Step **1**.

A pane containing the insertion point appears on the left side of the screen.

2 Type your comment.

3 To continue working, click in the document.

● To hide the pane, click the **Close** button (☒).

Track Document Changes During Review

Word can track the editing and formatting changes that you or other people make to your document. This feature is particularly useful when more than one person works on the same document and you want to be able to quickly and easily identify changes made to the document.

When Word tracks document revisions, it tracks additions and deletions as well as formatting changes. Additions appear as underlined text, while deletions are marked with strikethrough. Word also tracks who makes each change so that you can easily identify who did what to a document.

Track Document Changes During Review

1 Click 📄.

The document appears in Print Layout view.

2 Click the **Review** tab.

3 Click **Track Changes**.

● The Track Changes button appears pressed.

4 Make changes to the document as needed.

● A vertical bar appears in the left margin beside lines containing changes.

● Deleted text changes appear with strikethrough formatting.

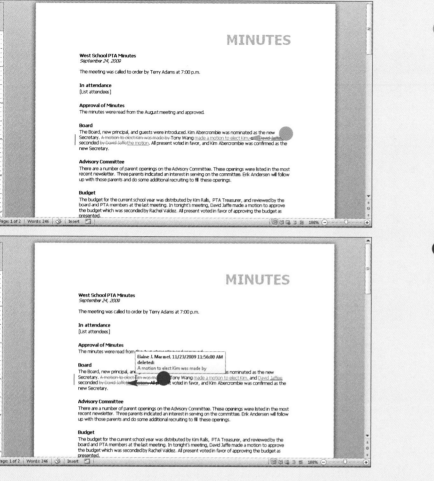

● Added text appears underlined and in a color other than black.

Each reviewer's changes appear in a different color.

● You can view details about a change and who made it by positioning the mouse pointer over a change.

You can stop tracking changes by repeating Steps **2** and **3**.

Note: *To review changes and accept or reject them, see the section "Review Tracked Changes."*

Simplify It

Can I print revisions?
Yes. Follow the steps.

❶ Click the **File** tab.

   The Backstage view appears.

❷ Click **Print**.

❸ Click the button below **Settings**.

❹ Click **List of Markup**.

❺ Click **Print**.

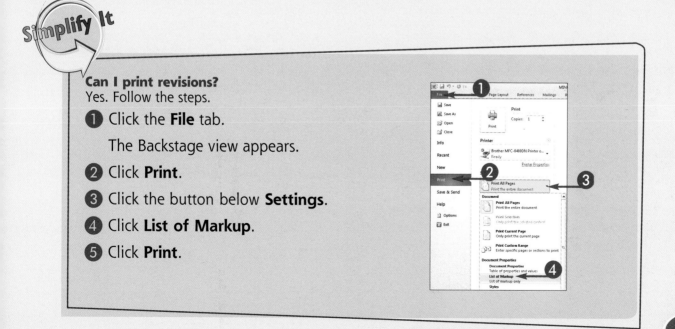

Review Tracked Changes

When you review a document containing tracked changes, you do not need to manually remove any of the revision marks that Word includes to identify additions and deletions in the document. Instead, you decide whether to accept or reject the changes. As you accept or reject changes, Word removes the revision marks.

By default, when you view a document containing tracked changes, Word displays the original document and the changes appear in revision marks — additions are underlined and deletions are marked with strikethrough. If you find the revision marks distracting, you can hide them.

Review Tracked Changes

1 Open a document in which changes were tracked.

2 Click the **Review** tab.

3 Click **Reviewing Pane**.

● For each change, Word displays the reviewer's name, the date and time of the change, and the details of the change.

● You can click ⊠ to close the pane.

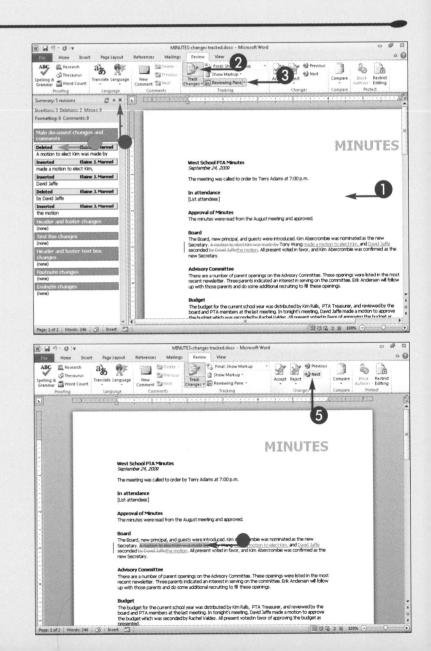

4 Press Ctrl + Home to place the insertion point at the beginning of the document.

5 Click **Next** to review the first change.

● Word highlights the change.

You can click **Next** again to skip over the change without accepting or rejecting it.

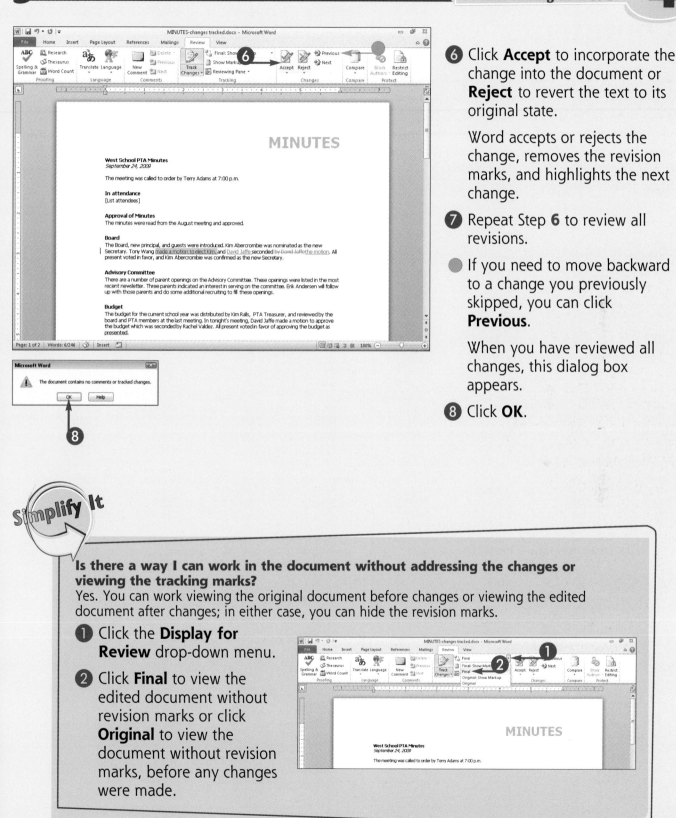

6 Click **Accept** to incorporate the change into the document or **Reject** to revert the text to its original state.

Word accepts or rejects the change, removes the revision marks, and highlights the next change.

7 Repeat Step **6** to review all revisions.

● If you need to move backward to a change you previously skipped, you can click **Previous**.

When you have reviewed all changes, this dialog box appears.

8 Click **OK**.

Simplify It

Is there a way I can work in the document without addressing the changes or viewing the tracking marks?
Yes. You can work viewing the original document before changes or viewing the edited document after changes; in either case, you can hide the revision marks.

1 Click the **Display for Review** drop-down menu.

2 Click **Final** to view the edited document without revision marks or click **Original** to view the document without revision marks, before any changes were made.

Combine Reviewers' Comments

You can combine two versions of the same document. This feature is particularly useful when you send two different copies of the same document to two reviewers and each reviewer works on the document simultaneously instead of sequentially. The reviewers send back changes to you in two documents and you can combine them into one document.

If more than two people review a document, you can combine versions of the document two at a time. That is, you can combine Reviewer 1's version with Reviewer 2's version and save the combined version. Then you can combine that version with Reviewer 3's version, and so on.

Combine Reviewers' Comments

1 Click the **Review** tab.

2 Click **Compare**.

3 Click **Combine**.

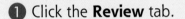

The Combine Documents dialog box appears.

4 Click the **Open** button (🖼) for the Original document.

The Open dialog box appears.

5 Navigate to the folder containing the original file you want to combine.

6 Click the file.

7 Click **Open**.

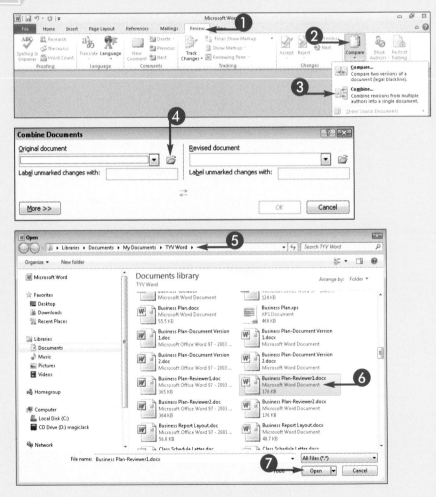

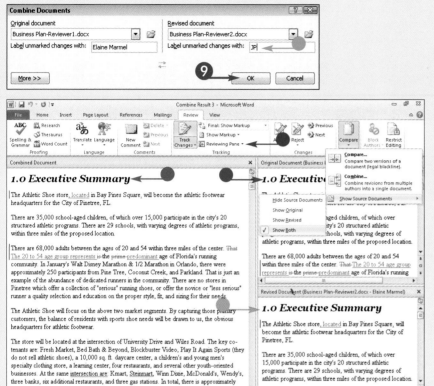

The Combine Documents dialog box reappears.

⑧ Repeat Steps **4** to **7**, clicking 📁 for the Revised document.

⬤ You can type a label for changes to each document in these boxes.

⑨ Click **OK**.

Word displays three panes.

⬤ The left pane contains the results of combining both documents.

⬤ The top-right pane displays the document you selected in Step **6**.

⬤ The bottom-right pane displays the document you selected in Step **8**.

⬤ You can display information about each revision by clicking **Reviewing Pane**.

Simplify It

What happens when I click the More button?

Word displays a series of settings you can control. You can specify the comparisons you want to make and you can identify how to show changes. For example, you can control whether Word displays changes in the original document, the revised document, or a new document.

Two reviewers reviewed same document but they forgot to track changes; can I somehow see their changes?

You can compare the documents with the original or with each other. Follow the steps in this section, but, in Step **3**, click **Compare**. Word again displays three panes; the results of comparing the two documents appears in the left pane, while the document you select in Step **6** appears in the top-right pane, and the document you select in Step **8** appears in the bottom-right pane.

Chapter 5

Formatting Text

You can format text for emphasis and for greater readability. And although the individual types of formatting are discussed separately, you can perform each of the tasks in this chapter on a single selection of text.

Change the Font

You can change the typeface that appears in your document by changing the font. Changing the font can help readers better understand your document.

For example, serif fonts contain short lines stemming from the bottoms of the letters and are most effective in regular text, because they provide a line that guides the reader's eyes.

Sans serif fonts do not contain short lines stemming from the bottoms of the letters and are most useful for headlines or section headings in a document, because headlines and headings are typically larger in size than regular text and the eye does not need any guidance.

Change the Font

① Select the text that you want to change to a different font.

If you drag to select, the Mini toolbar appears faded in the background, and you can use it by moving ☐ toward the Mini toolbar.

● To use the Ribbon, you can click the **Home** tab.

② Click here to display a list of the available fonts on your computer.

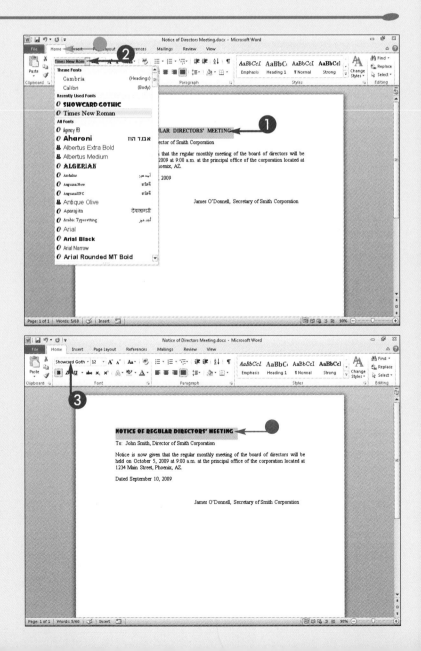

Word displays a sample of the selected text in any font at which you point the mouse.

Note: *See Chapter 1 for details on Live Preview and the Mini toolbar.*

③ Click the font you want to use.

● Word assigns the font you selected to the text you selected.

You can click anywhere outside the selection to continue working.

Change Text Size

You can increase or decrease the size of the text in your document. If you increase the size of text, you make it easier to read, but, at the same time, less text fits on a single page. Therefore, increasing the size of the text in your document might make the document longer.

If you decrease the size of text, you can fit more text on a page. However, if you make the text too small, you run the risk of making it difficult to read.

When selecting a size for your text, consider the audience who will be reading your document.

Change Text Size

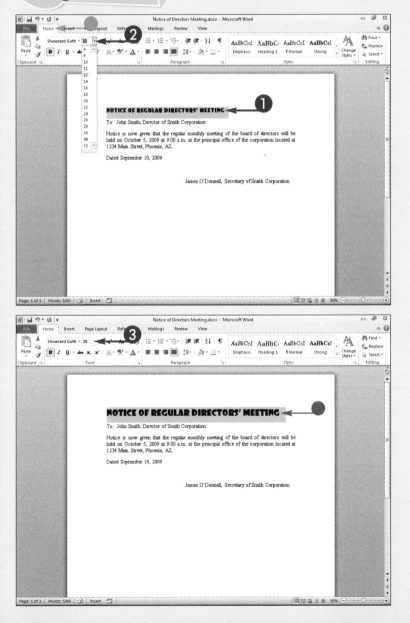

① Select the text to which you want to assign a new size.

If you drag to select, the Mini toolbar appears faded in the background, and you can use it by moving ▱ toward the Mini toolbar.

● To use the Ribbon, click the **Home** tab.

② Click here to display a list of the possible sizes for the current font.

Word displays a sample of the selected text in any font size at which you point the mouse.

Note: *See Chapter 1 for details on* Live Preview *and the Mini toolbar.*

③ Click the size you want to use.

● Word changes the size of the selected text.

You can click anywhere outside the selection to continue working.

Emphasize Information with Bold, Italic, or Underline

You can apply italics, boldface, or underlining to text in your document for emphasis. Italics, boldface, and underlining capture the reader's eye, helping you emphasize concepts and important points in your document.

Although there is nothing wrong with emphasizing text, be aware that doing so excessively negates its effect. If you mark every other word in your document with italics, underlining, or boldface, your reader will mentally adjust and ignore all emphasis. Emphasis is like shouting: People who shout all the time are often ignored because it becomes ordinary and doesn't give anyone reason to pause and listen carefully.

Emphasize Information with Bold, Italic, or Underline

① Select the text that you want to emphasize.

● If you drag to select, the Mini toolbar appears faded in the background, and you can use it by moving ▷ toward the Mini toolbar.

Note: *See Chapter 1 for details on the Mini toolbar.*

● If you want to use the Ribbon, click the **Home** tab.

② Click the **Bold** button (**B**), the **Italic** button (*I*), or the **Underline** button (U) on the Ribbon or the Mini toolbar.

● Word applies the emphasis you selected.

This example shows the text after italics is selected.

You can click anywhere outside the selection to continue working.

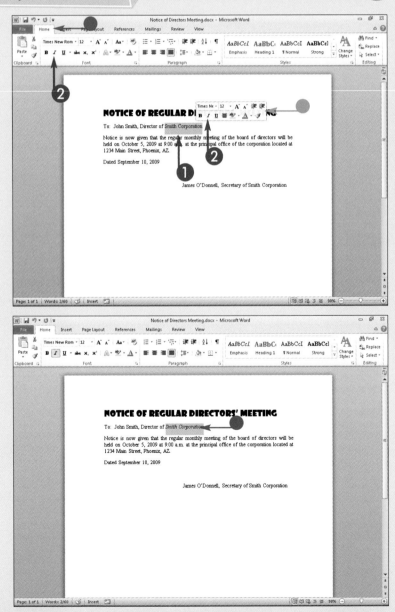

Change Text Case

You can change the case of selected text instead of retyping it with a new case applied.

Word supports five different types of text case treatment. Uppercase displays text in capital letters, while lowercase displays text in lowercase letters. If you use sentence case,

Word capitalizes only the first word of each sentence. You can also opt to capitalize each word; this action works well for headings. Finally, Word can toggle the case of a selection. For example, if the selection is all lowercase, Word can change it to all uppercase.

Change Text Case

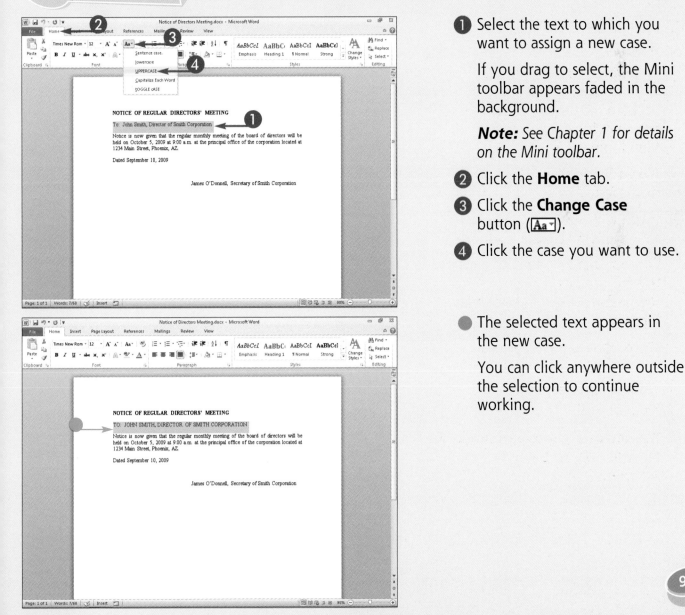

① Select the text to which you want to assign a new case.

   If you drag to select, the Mini toolbar appears faded in the background.

   Note: See Chapter 1 for details on the Mini toolbar.

② Click the **Home** tab.

③ Click the **Change Case** button (⌐Aa⌐).

④ Click the case you want to use.

● The selected text appears in the new case.

   You can click anywhere outside the selection to continue working.

Change Text Color

You can change the color of selected text for emphasis. Applying color to text is effective when you view your document on-screen, save it as a PDF or an XPS file, or print it using a color printer.

Color captures the reader's eye, helping you emphasize concepts and important points in your document.

Although there is nothing wrong with emphasizing text, be aware that doing it excessively negates its effect. If you make every other word a different color in your document, then you will distract your reader, who in turn will mentally adjust and ignore all color.

Change Text Color

① Select the text that you want to change to a different color.

● If you drag to select, the Mini toolbar appears faded in the background, and you can use it by moving ▷ toward the Mini toolbar.

● To use the Ribbon, click the **Home** tab.

② Click the **Font Color** button (△) on the Ribbon or on the Mini toolbar and point at a color.

Word displays a sample of the selected text.

Note: *See Chapter 1 for details on Live Preview and the Mini toolbar.*

③ Click a color.

● Word assigns the color to the selected text.

You can click anywhere outside the selection to continue working.

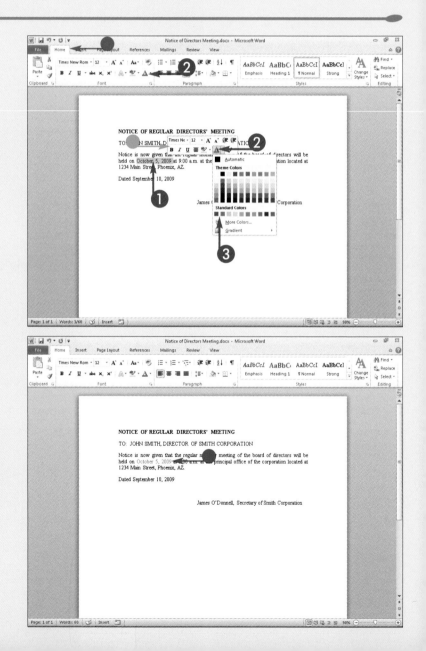

Apply Highlighting to Text

You can use color to create highlights in a document to draw attention to the text. Highlights are effective when you view the document on-screen or when you print it using a color printer.

Highlighting captures the reader's eye, helping you emphasize concepts and important points in your document.

Although there is nothing wrong with emphasizing text, be aware that doing it excessively negates its effect. If you highlight every other word or use many different colors, you will distract your reader, who in turn will mentally adjust and ignore all highlights.

Apply Highlighting to Text

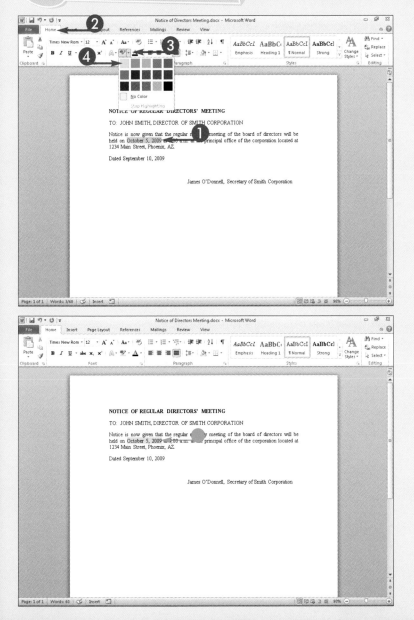

① Select the text that you want to highlight.

If you drag to select, the Mini toolbar appears faded in the background, and you can use it by moving ⍵ toward the Mini toolbar.

② To use the Ribbon, click the **Home** tab.

③ Click ⊡ beside the **Text Highlight Color** button (⟨ab⟩⌄⟩) on the Ribbon or the Mini toolbar and point at a color.

Word displays a sample of the selected text highlighted in any color at which you point the mouse.

Note: *See Chapter 1 for details on Live Preview and the Mini toolbar.*

④ Click a color.

● Word highlights the selected text using the color you select.

Copy Text Formatting

To save time, you can copy formatting that you apply to text in one portion of your document to another portion of your document.

Suppose, for example, that you have five paragraphs of text. You want the first and the last paragraphs to share one set of formatting, and you want the middle three paragraphs to share a different set of formatting.

Instead of formatting all five paragraphs, you can establish the formatting for the first paragraph and then simply copy the formatting to the last paragraph. Similarly, you can format the second paragraph and copy that formatting to the third and fourth paragraphs.

Copy Text Formatting

1 Select the text containing the formatting that you want to copy.

● If you drag to select, the Mini toolbar appears faded in the background, and you can use it by moving ⬚ toward the Mini toolbar.

● To use the Ribbon, click the **Home** tab.

2 Click the **Format Painter** button (⬚).

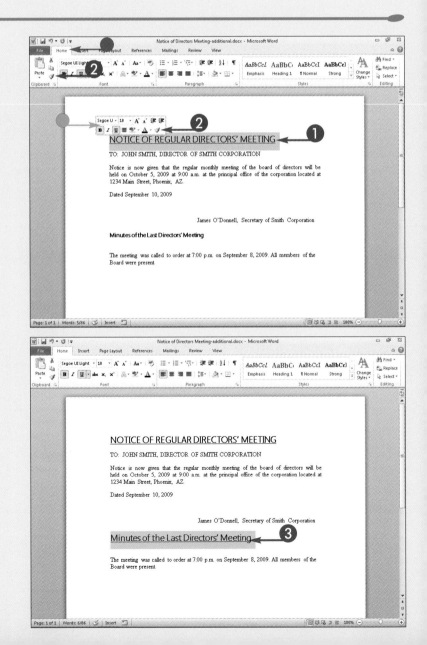

The mouse pointer changes to ⬚ when you move the mouse over your document.

3 Select the text to which you want to assign formatting.

The newly selected text changes to the format used for the original selection.

You can click anywhere outside the selection to continue working.

Remove Text Formatting

You can quickly and easily remove formatting that you have applied to text in your document. This feature is particularly effective if you have applied a lot of formatting that you want to remove. It is also effective if you find that you apply several different types of

formatting — perhaps color and italics and underlining — and then decide that you really only want one of the formats. Removing all the formatting and reapplying only one format might be faster than removing only those formats you do not want to use.

Remove Text Formatting

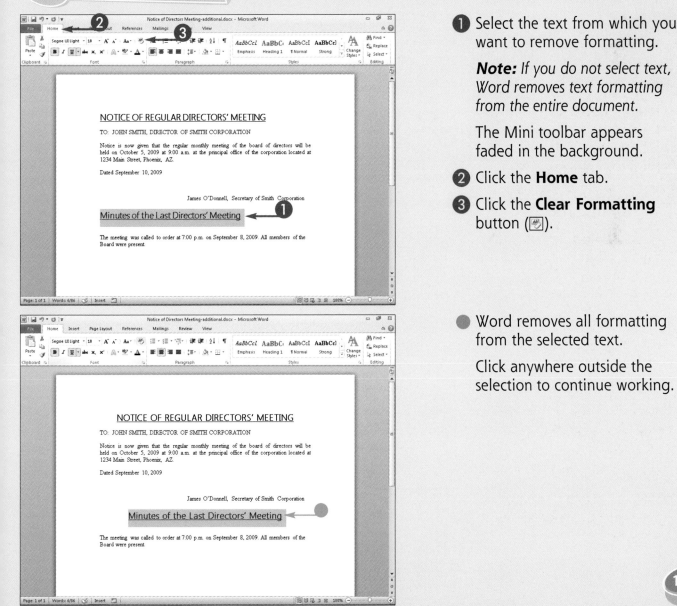

① Select the text from which you want to remove formatting.

Note: *If you do not select text, Word removes text formatting from the entire document.*

The Mini toolbar appears faded in the background.

② Click the **Home** tab.

③ Click the **Clear Formatting** button (⟐).

● Word removes all formatting from the selected text.

Click anywhere outside the selection to continue working.

Set the Default Font for All New Documents

You can change the default font that Word uses for all new documents you create. The default font that ships with Word is Calibri, 11 point, and each new document you create uses Calibri, 11 point. But suppose that you do not like Calibri or that you prefer to use a font size of 12 points instead of 11 points. You can change the font and the font size every time you create a new document, but changing the default font saves you a lot of work.

Changing the default font does not affect documents you have already created.

1 Click the **Home** tab.

2 Right-click the Normal style.

3 Click **Modify**.

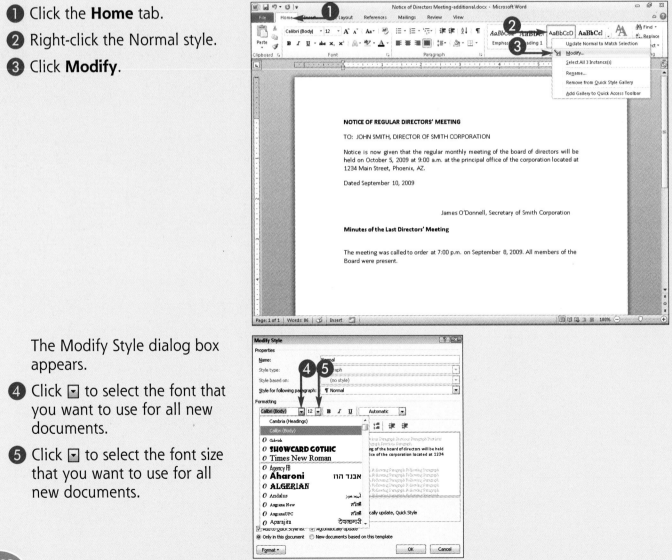

The Modify Style dialog box appears.

4 Click ▣ to select the font that you want to use for all new documents.

5 Click ▣ to select the font size that you want to use for all new documents.

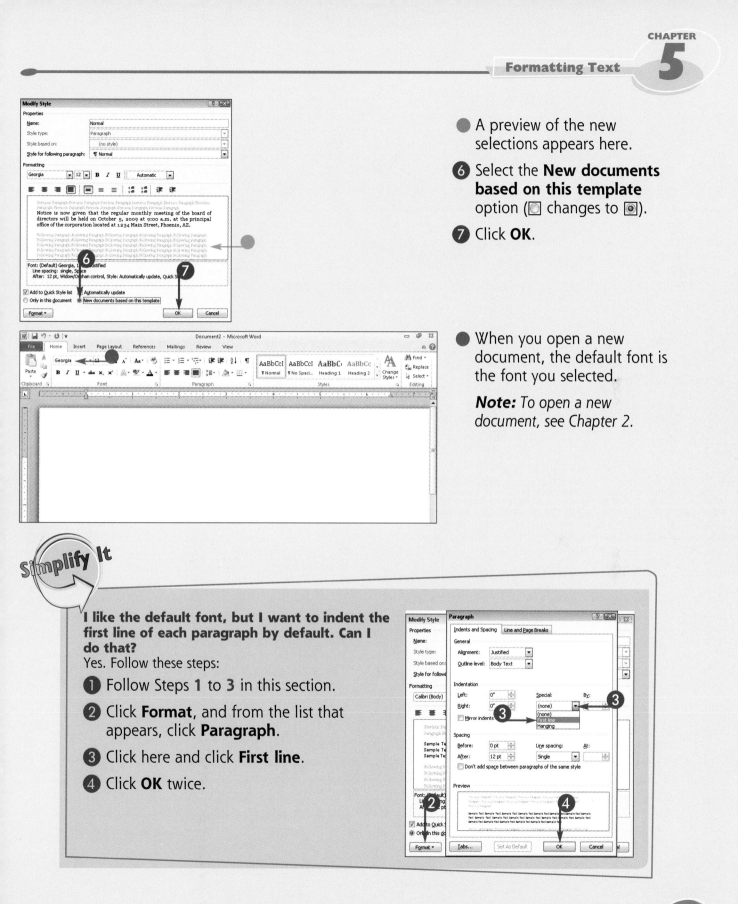

A preview of the new selections appears here.

⑥ Select the **New documents based on this template** option (◯ changes to ◉).

⑦ Click **OK**.

● When you open a new document, the default font is the font you selected.

Note: To open a new document, see Chapter 2.

Simplify It

I like the default font, but I want to indent the first line of each paragraph by default. Can I do that?

Yes. Follow these steps:

① Follow Steps **1** to **3** in this section.

② Click **Format**, and from the list that appears, click **Paragraph**.

③ Click here and click **First line**.

④ Click **OK** twice.

Chapter 6

Formatting Paragraphs

Instead of formatting individual words in your document, you can apply changes to entire paragraphs to help certain sections of your text stand out. You can change the alignment of text in a paragraph, and set line spacing both within and between paragraphs. You can create bulleted or numbered lists to enhance the appearance of the document.

As you work with paragraph formatting, you might find it useful to display formatting marks and the horizontal and vertical rulers Word supplies, particularly when you decide to indent paragraphs or set tabs to help you align text.

Change Text Alignment

You can change the alignment of various paragraphs in your document to enhance the document's appearance.

You can align a paragraph's text with the left margin or with the right margin. Or you can center text in the paragraph horizontally between both margins. If you prefer right and left margins that are smooth and even, consider justifying paragraphs so that their text aligns with both the left and right margins. Just keep in mind that justifying text adds extra spaces between words. To align text vertically, see Chapter 7. The example in this section centers a headline between the left and right margins.

Change Text Alignment

① Click anywhere in the paragraph that you want to align.

② Click the **Home** tab.

③ Click an alignment button.

The **Align Left** button (≡) aligns text with the left margin, the **Center** button (≡), centers text between the left and right margins, the **Align Right** button (≡) aligns text with the right margin, and the **Justify** button (≡) aligns text between the left and right margins.

Word aligns the text.

● This text is aligned with the left margin.

● This text is centered between both margins.

● This text is aligned with the right margin.

● This text is justified between both margins.

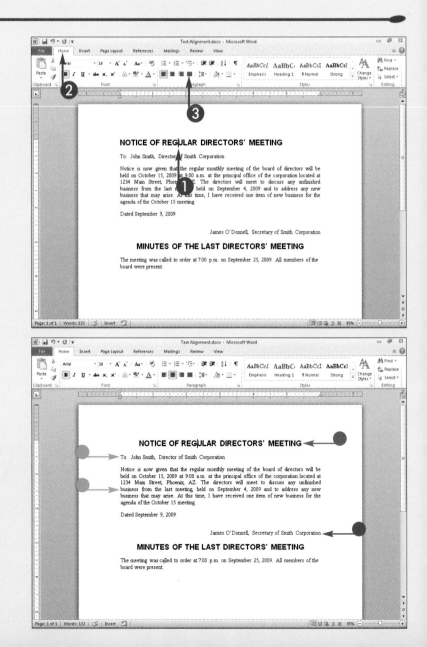

Set Line Spacing Within a Paragraph

You can change the amount of blank space Word places between the lines of text within a paragraph. For example, when you use single spacing, Word does not include any extra blank space between the lines of a paragraph. If you set line spacing to 1.5 or 2, Word leaves a half line or a full line of blank space between the

lines of the paragraph. Word 2010 uses a different default line spacing than Word 2003 and earlier.

Word can measure line spacing in inches, but it is typically easiest to measure in points, specified as pts. 12 pts equal approximately one line of space.

Set Line Spacing Within a Paragraph

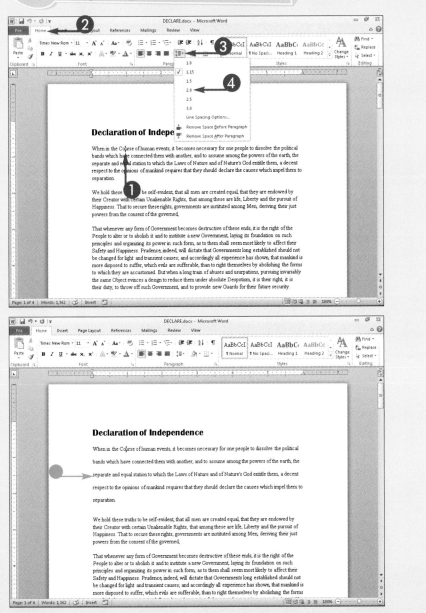

1 Click in the paragraph for which you want to change line spacing.

2 Click **Home**.

3 Click the **Line Spacing** button (⌑).

4 Click a number.

1 represents single spacing, the default in Word 97–2003; **1.15** is the default spacing in Word 2010; **1.5** places ½ blank line between lines of text; **2** represents double spacing; **2.5** places 1½ blank lines between lines of text; and **3** represents triple spacing.

● Word applies the line spacing you specified to the selected text.

Set Line Spacing Between Paragraphs

You can control the amount of blank space Word places between paragraphs of text. By default, Word leaves 10 points of blank space after each paragraph, but you can leave as much blank space between paragraphs as you want. The amount of blank space you leave between paragraphs does not affect the amount of blank space you place between lines within a paragraph. For example, you can set double spacing between paragraphs while maintaining single spacing within each paragraph. You also do not need to leave the same amount of blank space between all paragraphs in your document.

Set Line Spacing Between Paragraphs

① Select the paragraph or paragraphs for which you want to define spacing.

② Click the **Home** tab.

③ Click the **Paragraph** 🔲.

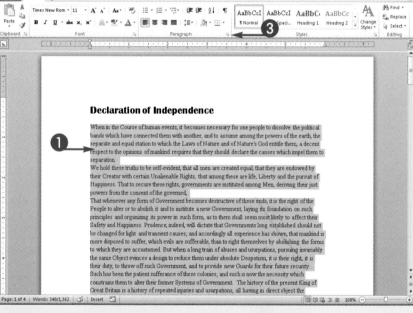

The Paragraph dialog box appears.

④ Click here to increase or decrease the space before the selected paragraph.

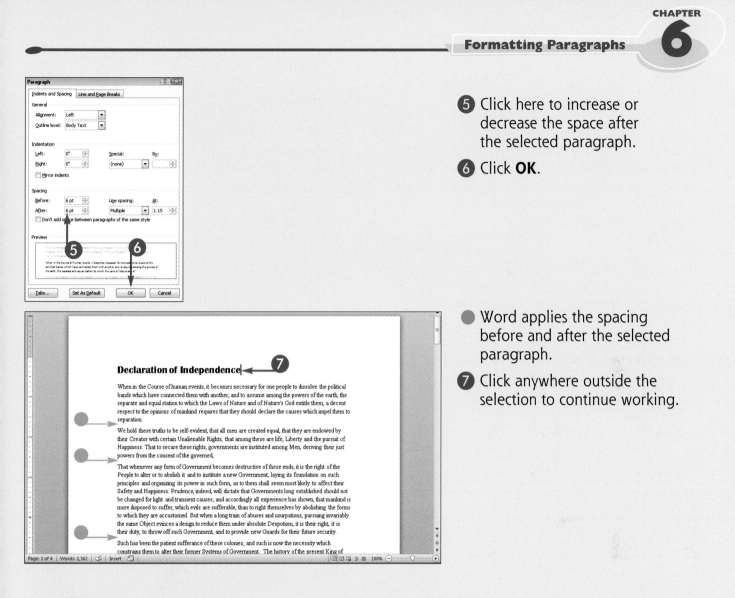

⑤ Click here to increase or decrease the space after the selected paragraph.

⑥ Click **OK**.

● Word applies the spacing before and after the selected paragraph.

⑦ Click anywhere outside the selection to continue working.

What does the Don't add space between paragraphs of the same style check box do?
As described later in this chapter, you can use styles to assign predefined sets of formatting information, such as font and paragraph information. By default, Word assigns the Normal style to each paragraph of text. You can use the Don't add space between paragraphs of the same style check box to use the same spacing both within a paragraph and between paragraphs to which you have assigned the same style.

How many points should I use before and after paragraphs to leave one blank line between paragraphs?
Assign 6 points before and after each paragraph. The 6 points of space at the bottom of Paragraph 1 plus the 6 points of space at the top of Paragraph 2 equal 12 points, or one line space. A point is 1/72 of an inch. A 72-point line of text is approximately 1 inch high. Measure 1 inch of text vertically; in most cases, six lines of text fill 1 vertical inch of space. One line equals about 1/6 inch, and 1/6 inch equals 12 points of vertical line space.

Create a Bulleted or Numbered List

You can use bullets or numbers to call attention to lists that you present in your documents. Using bulleted lists or numbered lists helps your reader understand the material you are presenting, particularly when your list consists of more than three items.

Use numbers when the items in your list follow a particular order. Use bullets when the items in your list do not follow any particular order.

Word also makes it easy for you to create numbered lists that resemble outline lists; Word calls these types of lists *multilevel lists*.

Create a Bulleted or Numbered List

Create a List from Existing Text

① Select the text to which you want to assign bullets or numbers.

② Click the **Home** tab.

③ Click the **Numbering** button (▤▾) or the **Bullets** button (▤▾).

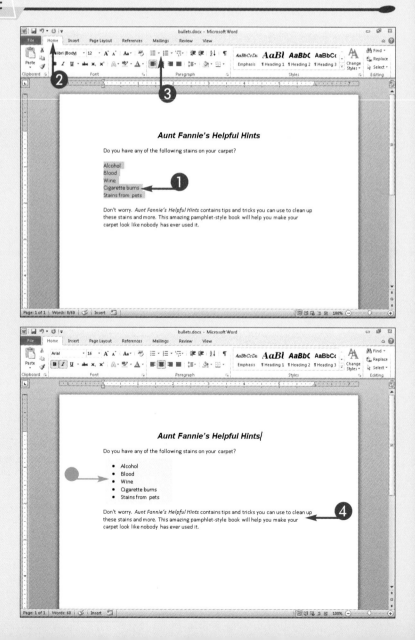

● Word applies numbers or bullets to the selection.

This example uses bullets.

④ Click anywhere outside the selection to continue working.

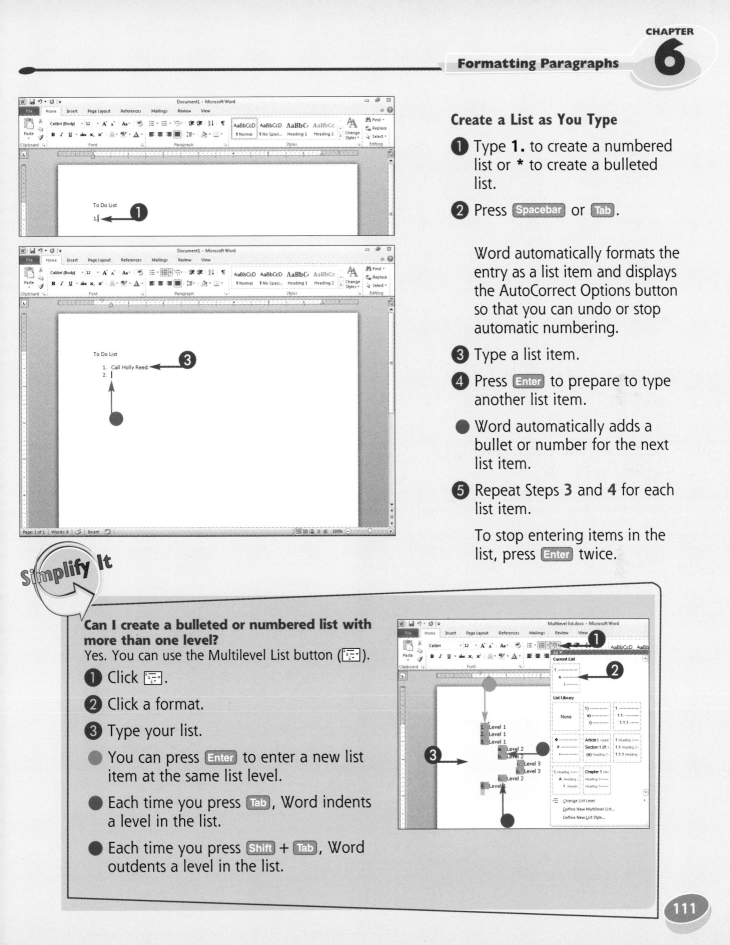

Create a List as You Type

1 Type **1.** to create a numbered list or ***** to create a bulleted list.

2 Press Spacebar or Tab.

Word automatically formats the entry as a list item and displays the AutoCorrect Options button so that you can undo or stop automatic numbering.

3 Type a list item.

4 Press Enter to prepare to type another list item.

● Word automatically adds a bullet or number for the next list item.

5 Repeat Steps **3** and **4** for each list item.

To stop entering items in the list, press Enter twice.

Simplify It

Can I create a bulleted or numbered list with more than one level?
Yes. You can use the Multilevel List button (⌐⊟⌐).

1 Click ⌐⊟⌐.

2 Click a format.

3 Type your list.

● You can press Enter to enter a new list item at the same list level.

● Each time you press Tab, Word indents a level in the list.

● Each time you press Shift + Tab, Word outdents a level in the list.

Display Formatting Marks

You can display formatting marks that do not print but help you identify formatting in your document. Displaying formatting marks can be particularly useful when Word flags a phrase as misspelled or as a grammar error and you do not see a problem. For example, if you forget to include a space at the end of a sentence, Word flags the problem as a spelling error.

Similarly, if you place two spaces between words in the middle of a sentence, Word flags the phrase as a grammar error.

Word can display formatting marks that represent spaces, tabs, paragraphs, hidden text, and optional hyphens.

Display Formatting Marks

① Open any document.

② Click the **Home** tab.

③ Click the **Show/Hide** button (¶).

Word displays all formatting marks in your document.

● Single dots (·) appear each time you press Spacebar.

● Paragraph marks (¶) appear each time you press Enter.

● Arrows (→) appear each time you press Tab.

● Hidden text appears underlined with dots.

● Optional hyphens, inserted by pressing Ctrl + -, appear as ⌐.

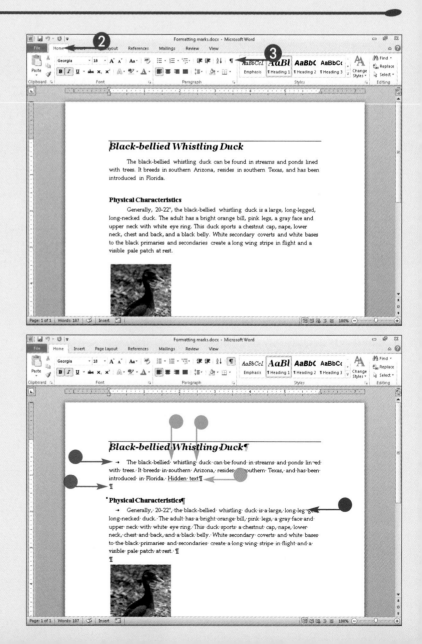

Hide or Display the Ruler

Word contains horizontal and vertical rulers that appear just below the Ribbon and on the left side of the Word screen. You can hide or display these rulers to help you identify the position of the insertion point or the alignment text.

The horizontal ruler is not just a visual aid; it is an interactive tool. You can use the horizontal ruler to indent paragraphs or set tabs in your document. It even identifies the type of tab that appears at a particular position; see the sections "Indent Paragraphs" and "Set Tabs" for more information.

Hide or Display the Ruler

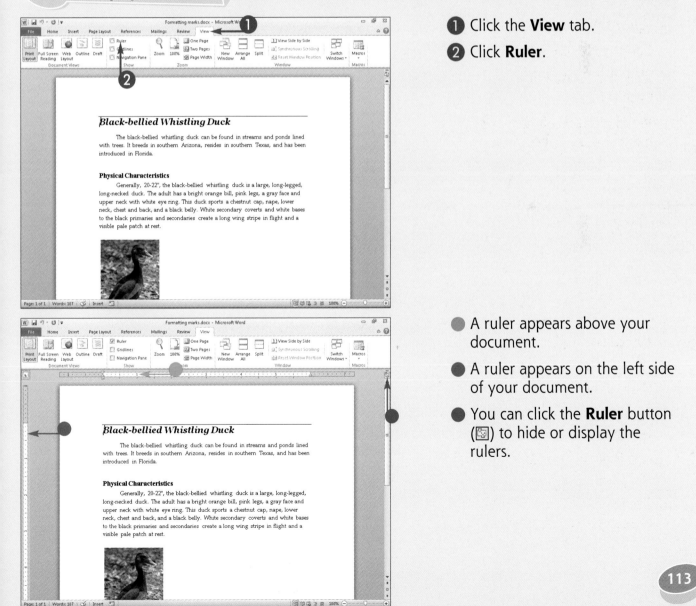

① Click the **View** tab.

② Click **Ruler**.

● A ruler appears above your document.

● A ruler appears on the left side of your document.

● You can click the **Ruler** button (▦) to hide or display the rulers.

Indent Paragraphs

Although margin settings typically determine the blank space that appears on each side of a paragraph, you can indent paragraphs in your document from the left margin, the right margin, or both margins. This technique is particularly useful if you want to call attention to the information in a particular paragraph.

You are not limited to indenting from the left and right margins. You also can indent only the first line of a paragraph or all lines *except* the first line of the paragraph. When you indent all lines except the first line of a paragraph, you create a *hanging indent*.

Indent Paragraphs

1 Select the text that you want to indent.

2 Click the **Home** tab.

3 Click the **Paragraph** ▣.

The Paragraph dialog box appears.

4 Click here to specify the number of inches to indent the left and right edge of the paragraph.

● The effects of your settings appear here.

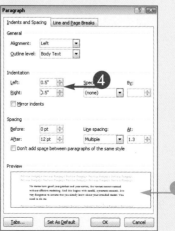

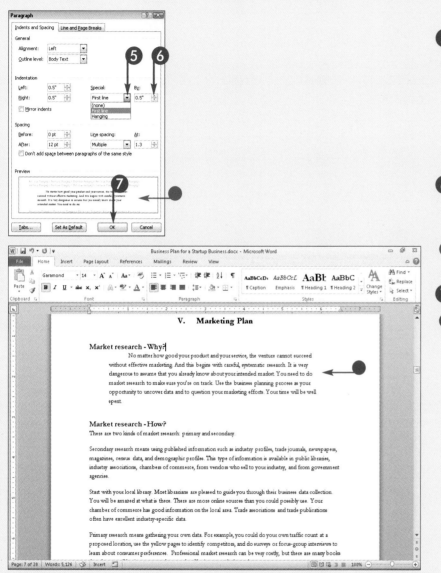

5 Click here and select an indenting option.

First line indents only the first line of the paragraph, and **Hanging** indents all lines *except* the first line of the paragraph.

6 Click here to set the amount of the first line or hanging indent.

● The effects of your settings appear here.

7 Click **OK**.

● Word applies your settings to the selected paragraph.

You can click anywhere outside the selection to continue working.

Simplify It

Can I set paragraph indentations without using a dialog box?

Yes. You can use buttons in the ruler. On the ruler, drag the **Left Indent** button (☐) to indent all lines from the left margin, drag the **Hanging Indent** button (☐) to create a hanging indent, or drag the **First Line Indent** button (☐) to indent the first line only. On the right side of the ruler, drag the **Right Indent** button (☐) to indent all lines from the right margin.

What do the Decrease Indent button and the Increase Indent button do?

The **Increase Indent** button (☷) indents all lines from the left margin. The **Decrease Indent** button (☷) decreases the indent of all lines from the left margin.

Set Tabs

When you want to align information in columns, you can use tabs. Using tabs ensures that information lines up properly within a column, particularly when you use proportional fonts. Proportional fonts allot a different amount of space to each character in the font set; therefore, adding spaces between two columns of information rarely results in the

second column aligning properly. Tabs, however, solve that problem.

Word enables you to set left, center, right, decimal, or bar tabs to line up columnar information. By default, Word places tabs every .5 inch across the page between the left and right margins.

Set Tabs

Add a Tab

1. Click here until the type of tab you want to add appears.

⊞ Left tab

⊞ Center tab

⊞ Right tab

⊞ Decimal tab

⊞ Bar tab

2. Select the lines to which you want to add a tab.

3. Click the ruler where you want the tab to appear.

Word displays a tab at the location you clicked on each selected line.

Emergency Contact Phone List

Police   555-1212

Fire

Ambulance

Doctor

Veterinarian

Using a Tab

1 Click to the left of the information you want to appear at the tab.

2 Press **Tab**.

3 Type your text.

The text appears at the tab.

Move a Tab

1 Click the line using the tab or select the lines of text affected by the tab.

2 Drag the tab to the left or right.

● A vertical line marks its position as you drag.

When you click and drag a tab, the text moves with the tab.

Emergency Contact Phone List

Police   555-1212

Fire

Ambulance

Doctor

Veterinarian

Simplify It

How can I delete a tab?
Follow these steps:

1 Click in or select the paragraphs containing the tab.

2 Drag the tab off the ruler.

● When you delete a tab, text aligned at the tab moves to the first preset tab on the line.

Emergency Contact Phone List

Police 555-1212

Fire

Ambulance

Doctor

Veterinarian

continued

Set Tabs
(continued)

In addition to aligning text to the left, right, or center of a tab or using bar or decimal tabs, you can add leader characters between the end of one column and the beginning of the next column. Leader characters help your reader's eyes follow information across a page. For example, you often find leaders between the columns in a table of contents to help a reader find the page number associated with a particular topic.

Word enables you to use periods (called *dot leaders*), dashes, or underscore characters as leader characters. This example uses use dot leader tabs.

Set Tabs *(continued)*

Add Leader Characters to Tabs

1 Follow Steps **1** to **3** in the subsection "Add a Tab" to create a tab stop.

2 Select the text containing the tab to which you want to add dot leaders.

3 Click the **Home** tab.

4 Click the **Paragraph** .

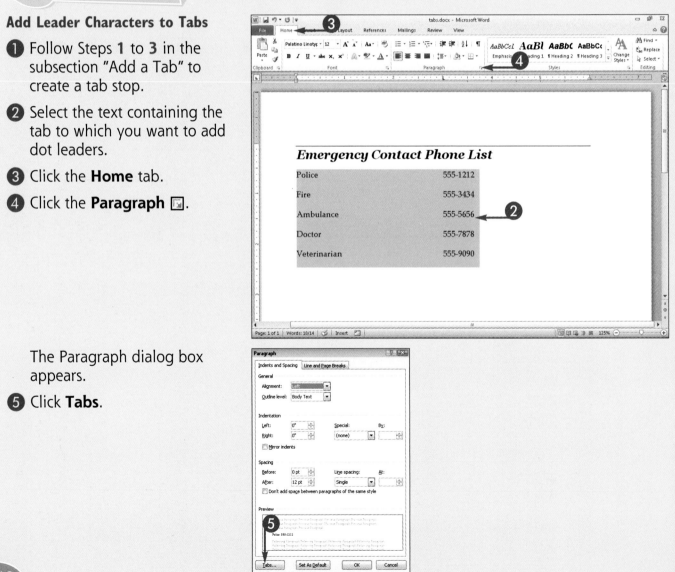

The Paragraph dialog box appears.

5 Click **Tabs**.

The Tabs dialog box appears.

6 Click the tab setting to which you want to add leaders.

7 Select a leader option (◎ changes to ◉).

8 Click **OK**.

● Word adds leading characters from the last character before the tab to the first character at the tab.

Click anywhere outside the selection to continue working.

Emergency Contact Phone List

Police..555-1212

Fire...555-3434

Ambulance...555-5656

Doctor..555-7878

Veterinarian.......................................555-9090

Simplify It

Can I set tabs using the Tabs dialog box instead of the ruler?

Yes. Follow these steps:

1 Follow Steps **2** to **5** on this page to display the Tabs dialog box.

2 Click here and type a tab stop position.

3 Click here and select a tab alignment option (◎ changes to ◉).

4 Click **Set**.

5 Repeat Steps **2** to **4** for each tab stop you want to set.

6 Click **OK** to have the tabs you set appear on the ruler.

Chapter 7

Formatting Pages

In addition to applying formatting to text and paragraphs, you can apply formatting to pages of your Word document. For example, you can adjust margins for your entire document or parts of it. And, although Word automatically inserts page breaks when your page fills with text, you can insert page breaks at locations you specify to control the vertical alignment of the text. You also can change the orientation of pages from portrait to landscape, break your document into sections, and use document headers and footers.

Adjust Margins

You can adjust the right, left, top, and bottom margins of your document. By default, Word sets all margins — left, right, top, and bottom — to 1 inch. But you might want to make those margins larger or smaller to affect the amount of text that appears on the page. Be aware that most printers require that top and bottom margins be at least .5 inches and left and right margins be at least .25 inches. Therefore, you will not be able to specify a smaller margin; for example, one that is .15 inches.

When you adjust margins, Word sets the margins from the position of the insertion point to the end of the document.

Adjust Margins

① Click anywhere in the document or section where you want to change margins.

② Click the **Page Layout** tab.

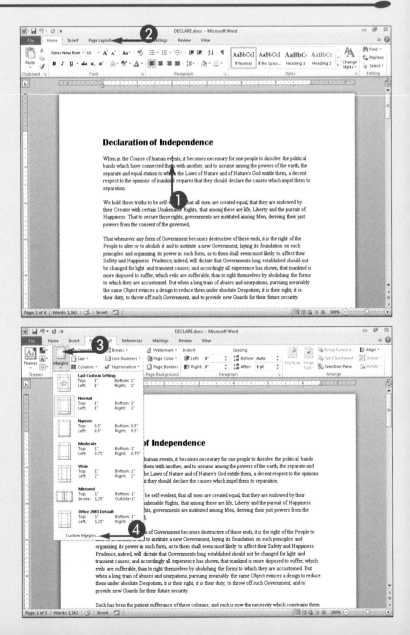

③ Click **Margins**.

The Margins Gallery appears.

If the margins you want to use appear in the Margins Gallery, click them and skip the rest of these steps; otherwise, proceed with Steps **4** to **9**.

④ Click **Custom Margins**.

The Page Setup dialog box appears, displaying the Margins tab.

⑤ Drag the mouse pointer over any margin setting.

⑥ Type a new margin setting.

⑦ Repeat Steps **5** and **6** for each margin setting.

⑧ Click **OK**.

Word saves your changes and applies them to your document.

Declaration of Independence

When in the Course of human events, it becomes necessary for one people to dissolve the political bands which have connected them with another, and to assume among the powers of the earth, the separate and equal station to which the Laws of Nature and of Nature's God entitle them, a decent respect to the opinions of mankind requires that they should declare the causes which impel them to separation.

We hold these truths to be self-evident, that all men are created equal, that they are endowed by their Creator with certain Unalienable Rights, that among these are life, Liberty and the pursuit of Happiness. That to secure these rights, governments are instituted among Men, deriving their just powers from the consent of the governed,

That whenever any form of Government becomes destructive of these ends, it is the right of the People to alter or to abolish it and to institute a new Government, laying its foundation on such principles and organizing its power in such form, as to them shall seem most likely to affect their Safety and Happiness. Prudence, indeed, will dictate that Governments long established should not be changed for light and transient causes; and accordingly all experience has shown, that mankind is more disposed to suffer, which evils are sufferable,

Simplify It

Can I change the margins for just one part of my document?
Yes, you can if you divide your document into sections using section breaks. You can set distinct margins for each section of a document. See the section "Insert a Section Break" for more information.

Can I use the mouse to change margins?
In Print Layout view, Word displays margins in blue on the ruler. Select the text you want to change. To reposition the left margin, point the mouse at ☐ on the ruler and drag to the right or left. To adjust the right margin, drag ◩ to the right or left. To adjust top and bottom margins, move the mouse into the ruler area on the left side of the window, between the white and blue portions of the ruler. ◩ changes to ⬍. Drag ⬍ up or down to reposition the margin.

Insert a Page Break

You can insert a page break to force Word to start text on a new page. By default, Word automatically starts a new page when the current page becomes filled with text. But suppose that you want to create a cover page for a report and include only the cover page information on that page. You can type the cover page information and then insert a page break to limit the information on the page to just the cover page.

You can insert a page break using either the mouse or the keyboard.

Insert a Page Break

Using the Mouse

1 Position the insertion point immediately before the text that you want to appear on a new page.

2 Click the **Insert** tab.

3 Click **Page Break**.

● Word inserts a page break and moves all text after the page break onto a new page.

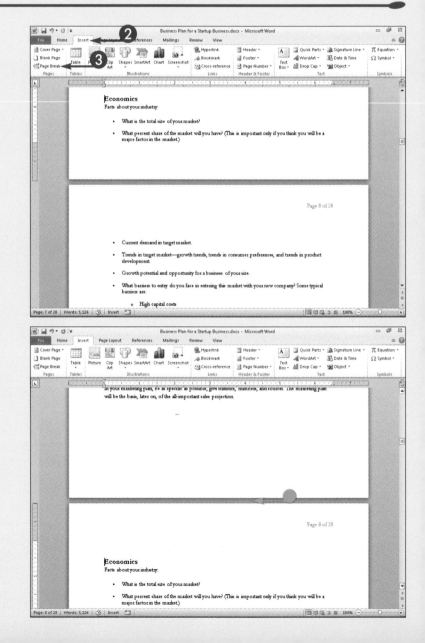

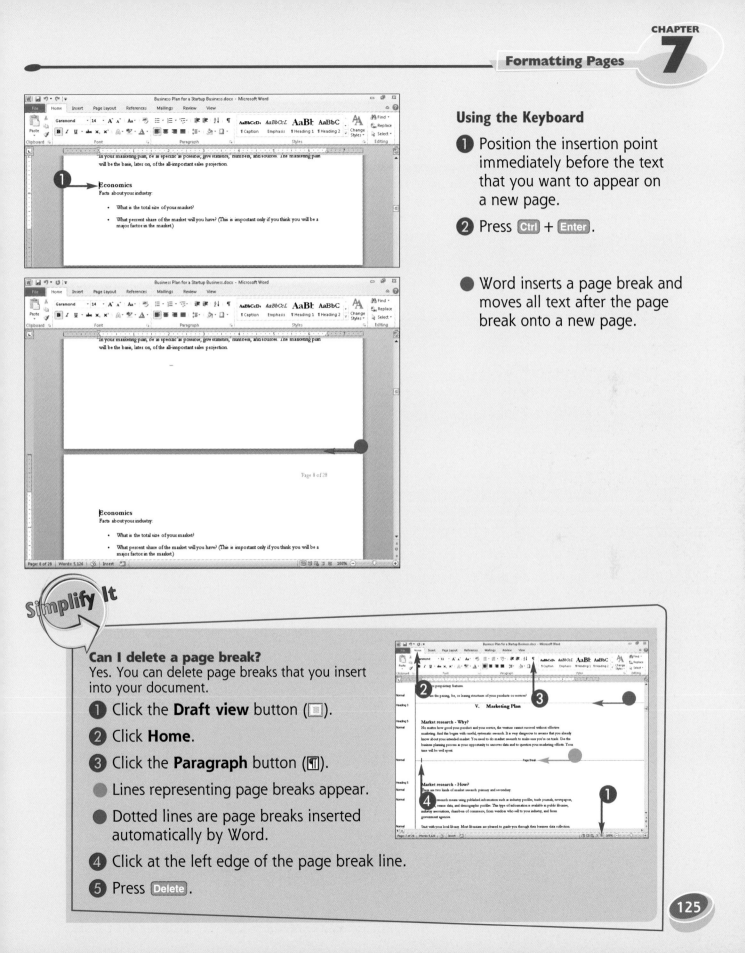

Using the Keyboard

① Position the insertion point immediately before the text that you want to appear on a new page.

② Press Ctrl + Enter.

● Word inserts a page break and moves all text after the page break onto a new page.

Simplify It

Can I delete a page break?
Yes. You can delete page breaks that you insert into your document.

① Click the **Draft view** button (▣).

② Click **Home**.

③ Click the **Paragraph** button (¶).

● Lines representing page breaks appear.

● Dotted lines are page breaks inserted automatically by Word.

④ Click at the left edge of the page break line.

⑤ Press Delete.

Align Text Vertically on the Page

You can align text between the top and bottom margins of a page if the text on the page does not fill the page. For example, centering text vertically often improves the appearance of short business letters or report cover pages. When you center text vertically on the page, Word evenly distributes the blank lines on the page between the top and bottom of the page.

By default, Word applies vertical alignment to your entire document, but you can limit the alignment if you divide the document into sections. See the section "Insert a Section Break" for more information.

Align Text Vertically on the Page

1 In the document you want to align, click the **Page Layout** tab.

2 Click the **Page Setup** ⬛.

The Page Setup dialog box appears.

3 Click the **Layout** tab.

4 Click the **Vertical alignment** ⬇ and select a vertical alignment choice.

● To align all pages from the insertion point to the end of the document, click the **Apply to** ⬇ and select **This point forward**.

5 Click **OK**.

● Word applies vertical alignment.

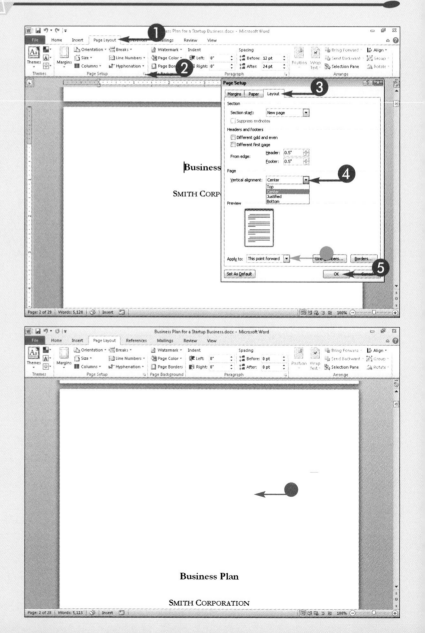

Change Page Orientation

You can change the direction that text prints from the standard portrait orientation of 8½ inches × 11 inches to landscape orientation of 11 inches × 8½ inches. When you use portrait orientation, less text fits between the left and the right margins on the page than when you use landscape orientation.

To remember the difference between the orientations, think of paintings. Leonardo da Vinci painted his famous *Mona Lisa* portrait with the canvas oriented vertically. Georges Seurat painted his famous *Sunday Afternoon on the Island of La Grande Jatte* landscape with the canvas oriented horizontally.

Change Page Orientation

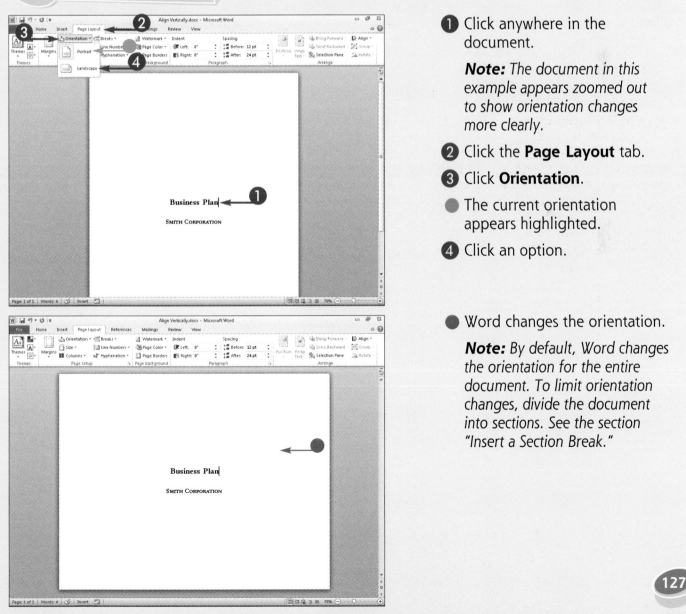

1 Click anywhere in the document.

Note: *The document in this example appears zoomed out to show orientation changes more clearly.*

2 Click the **Page Layout** tab.

3 Click **Orientation**.

● The current orientation appears highlighted.

4 Click an option.

● Word changes the orientation.

Note: *By default, Word changes the orientation for the entire document. To limit orientation changes, divide the document into sections. See the section "Insert a Section Break."*

Insert a
Section Break

You can break your document into sections by inserting section breaks at various locations. Section breaks help you use different sets of page-formatting settings in different portions of your document.

For example, suppose that your document contains three different parts and you want to establish different margins for the second part,

but want the margins for the first and third parts to be the same. In this case, you insert section breaks before the second and third parts and then establish margin settings for them.

You can also use section breaks when headers, footers, vertical page alignment, and other page-formatting settings vary in your document.

Insert a Section Break

1. Click in the location where you want to start a new section in your document.

2. Click the **Page Layout** tab.

3. Click **Breaks**.

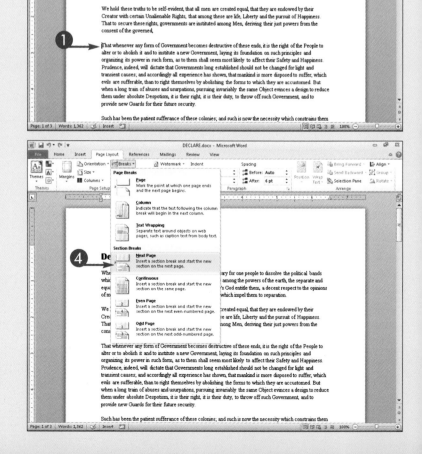

The Breaks Gallery appears.

4. Click an option to select the type of section break you want to insert.

● Word inserts the type of break you selected.

5 Click ▤ to display the document in Draft view.

● A section break line appears.

You can remove the section break by clicking the section break line and pressing the **Delete** key on your keyboard.

Simplify It

How does Word handle printing when I insert a section break?
Section breaks are formatting marks that do not print; instead, the effects of the section break are apparent when you print. For example, if you insert a Next Page section break as shown in the example in this section, Word starts the text that immediately follows the section break on a new page.

What happens if I select Even page or Odd page?
Word starts the next section of your document on the next even or odd page. If you insert an Even page section break on an odd page, Word leaves the odd page blank. Similarly, if you insert an Odd page section break on an even page, Word leaves the even page blank.

Add Page Numbers to a Document

You can have Word automatically print page numbers on the pages of your document. As you edit your document to add or remove text, Word adjusts the document and the page numbers accordingly.

Page numbers appear on-screen only in Print Layout view. If you display page numbers at the top or bottom of the page, Word stores page numbers in the header or footer area. You also can display the page number in the left or right margins at the top or the bottom of a page. And, you can display the page number at the current location of the insertion point.

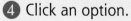

1 Click the **Insert** tab.

2 Click **Page Number**.

Page number placement options appear.

3 Click a placement option.

A gallery of page number alignment and formatting options appears.

4 Click an option.

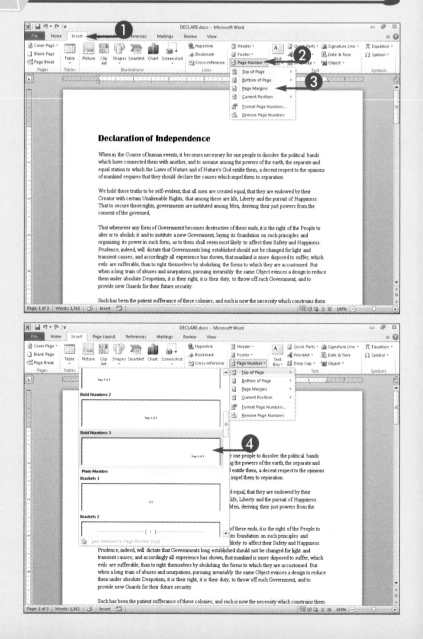

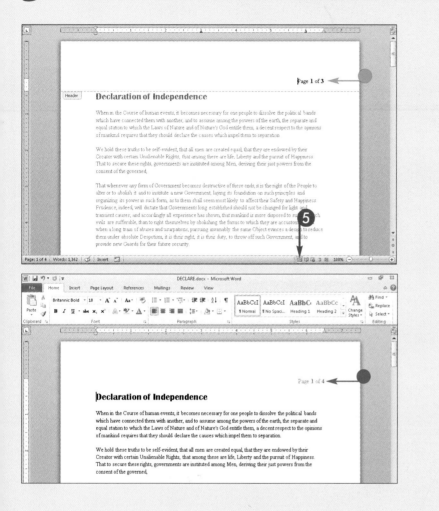

● The page number appears in the header or footer.

⑤ Click the **Print Layout** button (▣) to display the document in Print Layout view and continue working on the document.

● The page number appears in the location and formatting you selected.

Note: The page number appears gray and is unavailable for editing in Print Layout view. To work with the page number, you must open the header. See the section "Add a Header or Footer" later in this chapter.

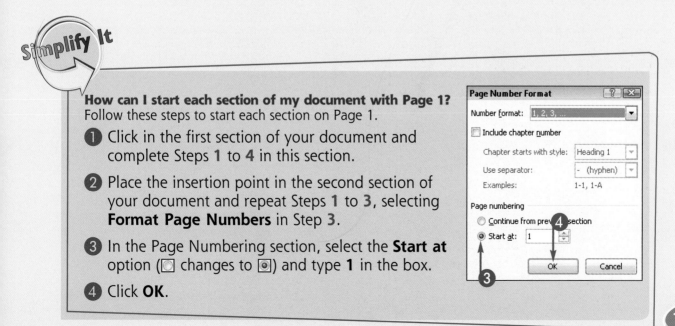

Simplify It

How can I start each section of my document with Page 1?
Follow these steps to start each section on Page 1.

① Click in the first section of your document and complete Steps **1** to **4** in this section.

② Place the insertion point in the second section of your document and repeat Steps **1** to **3**, selecting **Format Page Numbers** in Step **3**.

③ In the Page Numbering section, select the **Start at** option (◌ changes to ◉) and type **1** in the box.

④ Click **OK**.

Add a Header
or Footer

You can use headers at the top of the page and footers at the bottom of the page to add information that you want to appear on each page of your document. For example, you might include your document's title in the header or the footer area. You might also include page numbers and the total number of pages, and you can include information such as the date and time.

This section shows how to add a footer, but you can use the steps in this section to add a header by substituting "header" everywhere that "footer" appears.

Add a Header or Footer

① Click the **Insert** tab.

② Click **Footer**.

The Footer Gallery appears.

③ Click a footer style.

Note: *The headers and footers that appear in the Header Gallery and the Footer Gallery are building blocks that also appear in the Building Blocks Organizer.*

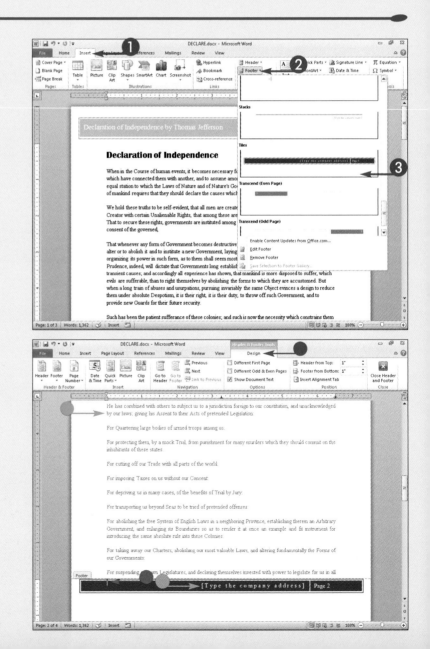

● The text in your document appears dimmed.

● The insertion point appears in the Footer area.

● Header & Footer Tools appear on the Ribbon.

● Some footers contain information prompts.

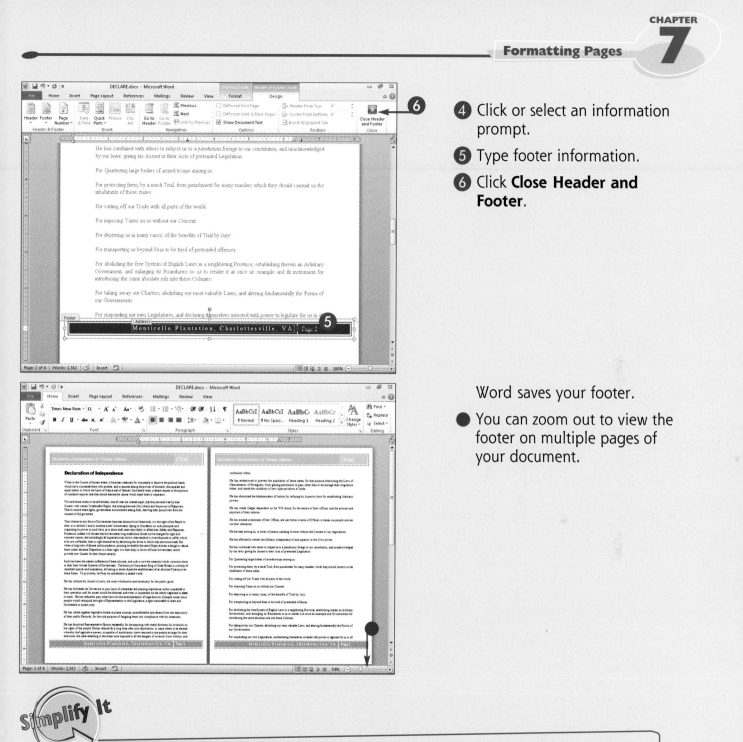

④ Click or select an information prompt.

⑤ Type footer information.

⑥ Click **Close Header and Footer**.

Word saves your footer.

● You can zoom out to view the footer on multiple pages of your document.

Can I change the style of header or footer?
Yes. If you closed the header or footer pane, perform Steps **1** to **3**, clicking **Edit Header** or **Edit Footer** in Step **3**. Then click **Header** or **Footer** at the left side of the Ribbon to redisplay the Header Gallery or Footer Gallery and make a different selection.

Can I format text in a header or footer?
Yes. You can apply boldface, italics, underlining, and other character formatting the same way that you apply them in the body of a document. And, the Header area and the Footer area each contain two predefined tabs so that you can center or right-align text you type.

Using Different Headers or Footers Within a Document

You can use different headers or footers in different portions of your document. For example, if you break your document into chapters, you might want to use different headers or footers in each chapter so that you can include each chapter's title in the header or footer. If you plan to use more than one

header or footer, insert section breaks before you begin. See the section "Insert a Section Break" for details.

This section shows how to create different headers in your document, but you can use the steps to create different footers by substituting "footer" everywhere that "header" appears.

Using Different Headers or Footers Within a Document

① Click in the first section for which you want to create a header.

② Click the **Insert** tab.

③ Click **Header**.

The Header Gallery appears.

④ Click a header.

Word inserts the header.

● The text in your document appears dimmed.

● The insertion point appears in the Header-Section 1 box.

⑤ Type any necessary text in the header.

⑥ Click **Next**.

Word moves the insertion point into the header for Section 2.

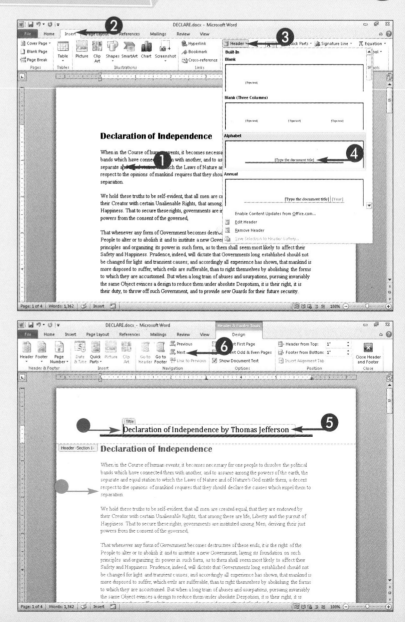

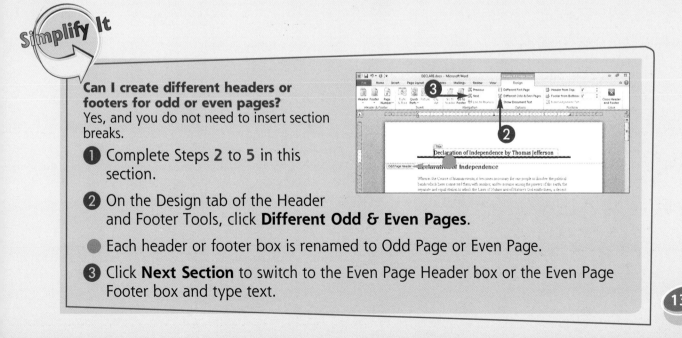

● The Header-Section 2 box appears.

● Word identifies the header or footer as "Same as Previous."

⑦ Click **Link to Previous** to deselect it and unlink the headers of the two sections.

Word removes the "Same as Previous" marking from the right side of the header box.

⑧ Repeat Steps **2** to **5** to insert a new header in the second section.

⑨ Repeat Steps **6** to **8** for each section for which you want a different header.

● You can zoom out to preview the different headers.

● Word displays two different headers in the document.

⑩ Click **Close Header and Footer**.

Simplify It

Can I create different headers or footers for odd or even pages?
Yes, and you do not need to insert section breaks.

❶ Complete Steps **2** to **5** in this section.

❷ On the Design tab of the Header and Footer Tools, click **Different Odd & Even Pages**.

● Each header or footer box is renamed to Odd Page or Even Page.

❸ Click **Next Section** to switch to the Even Page Header box or the Even Page Footer box and type text.

Chapter 8

Printing Documents

Once your document looks the way you want it to look, you are ready to distribute it. You can preview a document before you print it to look for and correct layout errors and formatting inconsistencies.

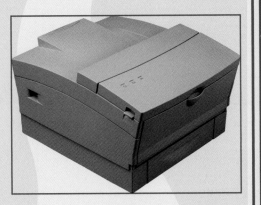

In addition to printing documents, you also learn in this chapter how to print single envelopes and labels and to print on different sizes of paper.

Regardless of what you are printing — a document, labels, or envelopes — Word enables you to change your document's margins, specify the pages to print, select a printer, and set other print options just before you print.

Preview and Print a Document

If your computer is connected to a printer that is turned on, you can preview your document to look for layout errors and other possible formatting inconsistencies and print it to produce a paper copy of it.

Previewing before you print can be very helpful; for example, you might discover that you forgot to vertically center the information on the cover page of your report.

Before you print, you also have the option to change the margins for your document, specify which pages to print, select a printer, specify the paper size on which you want to print, and set other printing options.

Preview and Print a Document

1 Open the document you want to print.

2 Click the **File** tab.

To print only selected text, select that text.

The Backstage view appears.

3 Click **Print**.

● A preview of your document appears here.

4 Click these arrows to page through your document.

5 To magnify an area of a page, drag the Zoom slider.

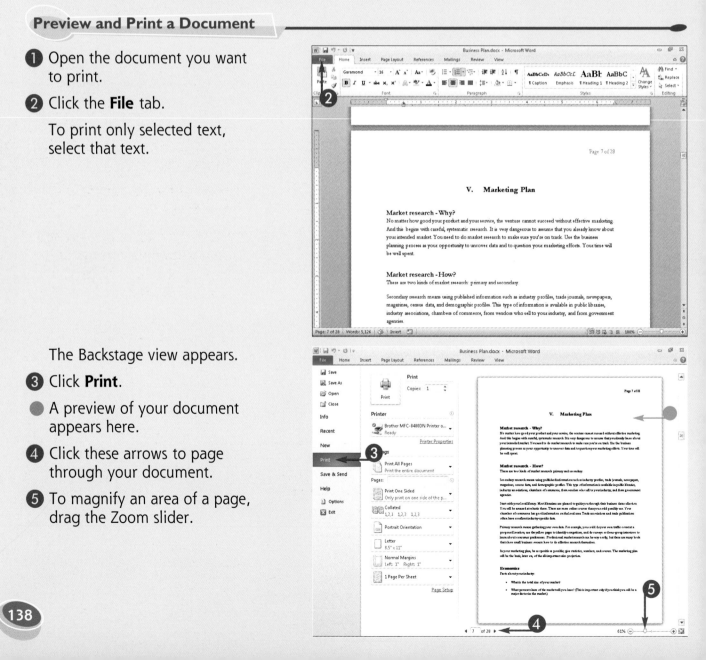

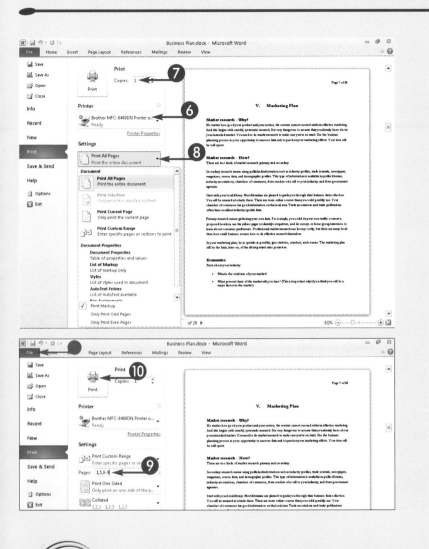

6 Click here to select a printer.

7 To print more than one copy, type the number of copies to print here.

8 Click the Settings button to print the entire document, text you selected, only the current page, or document elements such as document properties or a list of styles used in the document.

9 To print noncontiguous pages, type the pages you want to print, such as **1,5,6-9**, in the Pages box.

10 To print the document, click the **Print** button.

● If you change your mind and do not want to print, click the **File** tab to return to the document window.

![Simplify It]

What other print options can I set?
In the Other Settings section, click buttons to select options:

Option	Purpose
Print One Sided Only print on one side of the pa...	Determine whether to print on one or both sides of the paper.
Collated 1,2,3 1,2,3 1,2,3	When printing multiple copies, specify whether to collate the copies or print multiple copies of each page at the same time.
Portrait Orientation	Choose to print in Portrait or Landscape orientation.
Letter 8.5" x 11"	Select a paper size.
Normal Margins Left: 1" Right: 1"	Select page margins.
1 Page Per Sheet	Specify the number of pages to print on a single sheet of paper.

Print on Different Paper Sizes

You can print one part of your document on one size of paper and another part on a different size of paper. For example, you may want to print one portion of your document on legal-sized paper and another on letter-sized paper.

To print on different sizes of paper, you must divide your document into sections. Then you can identify the paper size for each section. In addition to specifying paper size for each section, you also can set page formatting options for each section. To learn how to insert section breaks, see Chapter 7.

Print on Different Paper Sizes

1 After dividing your document into sections, place the insertion point in the section you want to print on a different paper size.

2 Click the **Page Layout** tab.

3 Click the **Page Setup** dialog box launcher (⬚).

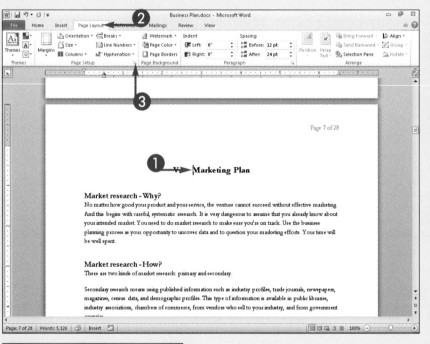

The Page Setup dialog box appears, displaying the Margins tab.

4 Click the **Paper** tab.

5 Click here and select the paper size you want to use.

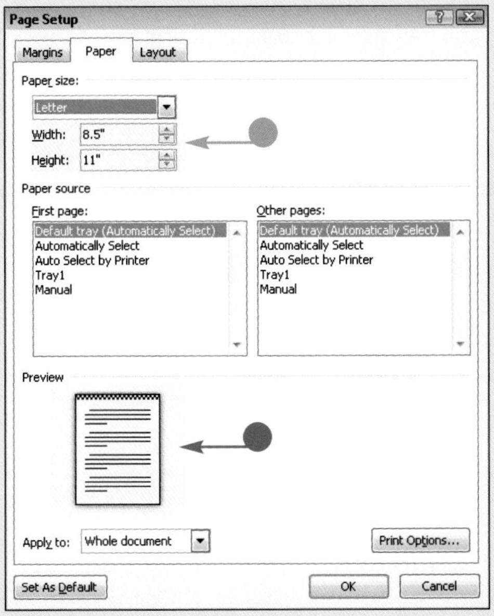

● The height and width of the paper size you selected appear here.

● A preview of your selection appears here.

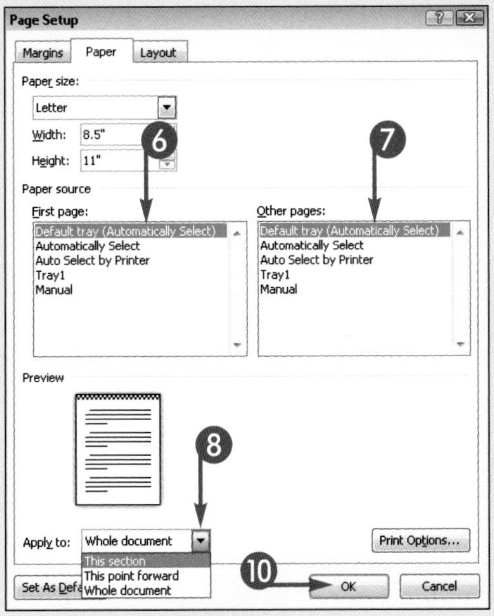

⑥ Click here to select a paper tray for the first page in the section.

⑦ Click here to select a paper tray for the rest of the section.

⑧ Click the **Apply to** ▾ and click **This section**.

⑨ Repeat these steps for other sections of the document.

⑩ Click **OK** to save your changes.

Simplify It

What happens when I click Print Options in the Page Setup dialog box?
The Display tab of the Word Options dialog box appears. In the Printing Options section, you can select check boxes to control the printing of various Word elements.

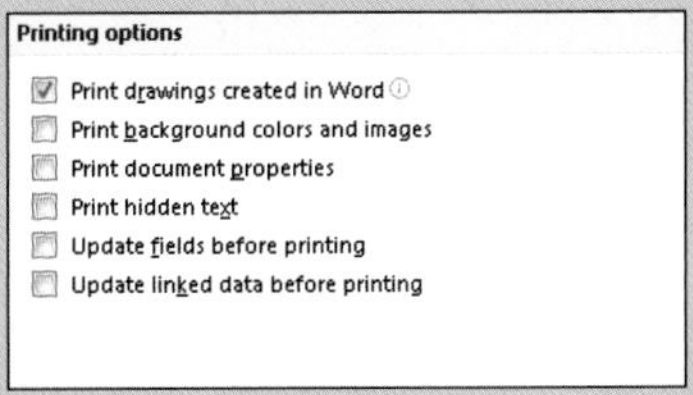

Print an Envelope

If your printer supports printing envelopes, Word can print a delivery address and a return address on an envelope for you. If you include an *inside address* — the address of the letter's recipient, found in most business letters — in your document, Word suggests that delivery address for the envelope.

You also can save your return address when you create an envelope so that you do not need to supply it each time you print envelopes.

Consult your printer manual to determine if your printer supports printing envelopes.

Print an Envelope

① Click the **Mailings** tab.

② Click **Envelopes**.

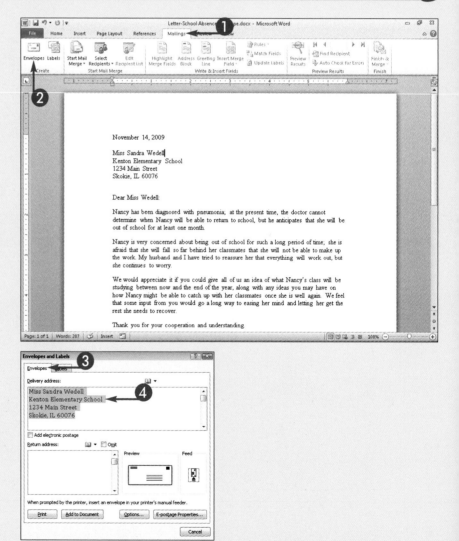

The Envelopes and Labels dialog box appears.

③ Click the **Envelopes** tab.

Note: *If Word finds an address near the top of your document, it enters that address in the Delivery address box.*

④ You can type a delivery address.

You can remove an existing address by pressing Delete on your keyboard.

142

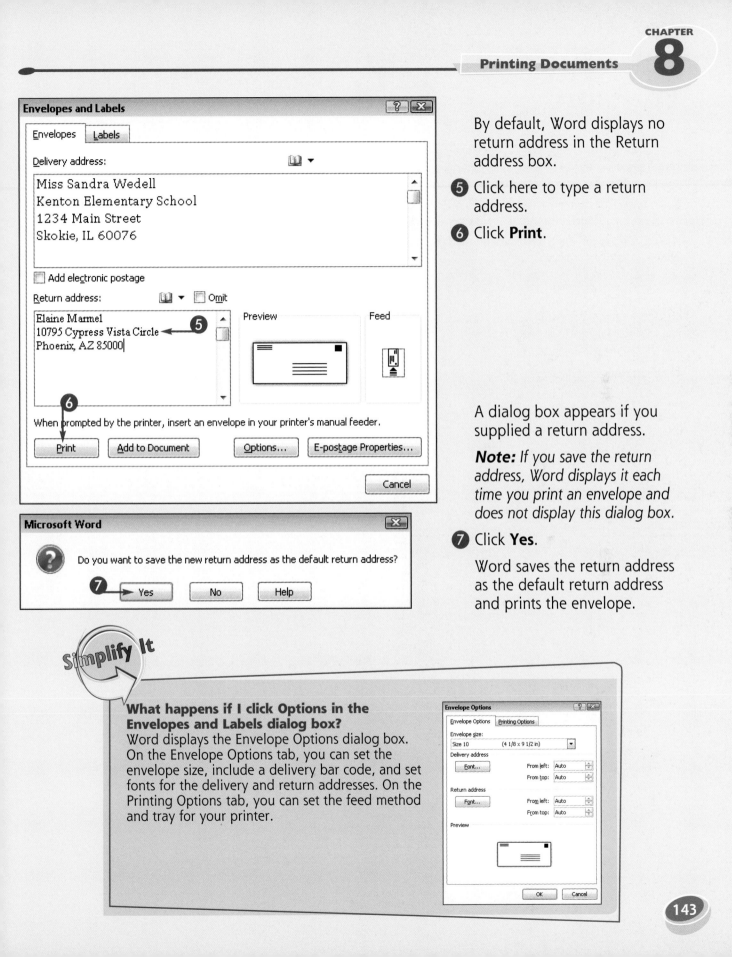

By default, Word displays no return address in the Return address box.

⑤ Click here to type a return address.

⑥ Click **Print**.

A dialog box appears if you supplied a return address.

Note: If you save the return address, Word displays it each time you print an envelope and does not display this dialog box.

⑦ Click **Yes**.

Word saves the return address as the default return address and prints the envelope.

Simplify It

What happens if I click Options in the Envelopes and Labels dialog box?
Word displays the Envelope Options dialog box. On the Envelope Options tab, you can set the envelope size, include a delivery bar code, and set fonts for the delivery and return addresses. On the Printing Options tab, you can set the feed method and tray for your printer.

143

Set Up Labels to Print

You can format a Word document so that you can use it to type labels. For example, you can create address, name tag, and file folder labels. Word supports a variety of label products from well-known label manufacturers.

This section demonstrates how to create a blank page of address labels onto which you can type address label information. You also can use the information in this section to print a single address label. If you need to create a group of mailing labels — for example, to send holiday greeting cards — use Word's Mail Merge feature, described in Chapter 12.

Set Up Labels to Print

1 Click the **Mailings** tab.

2 Click the **Labels** tab.

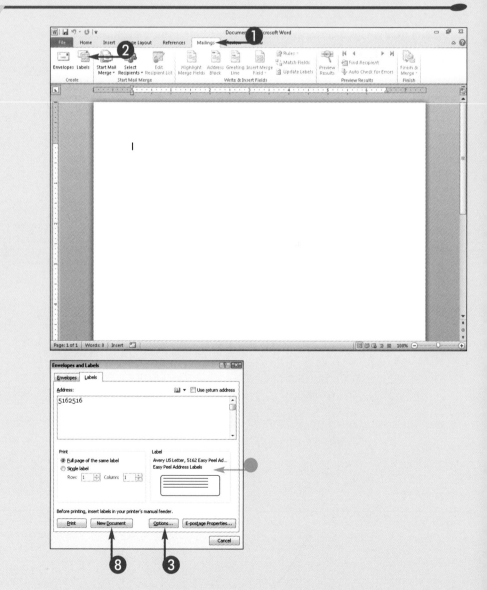

The Envelopes and Labels dialog box appears.

● This area shows the label currently selected.

3 Click **Options**.

The Label Options dialog box appears.

④ In this area, select the type of printer and printer tray to print labels (⊙ changes to ⊚).

⑤ Click here to select the maker of your labels.

⑥ Click the product number of your labels.

⑦ Click **OK**.

⑧ Click **New Document** in the Envelopes and Labels dialog box.

⑨ If you do not see gridlines to separate labels, click **Design**.

⑩ Click the **Borders** ▾.

⑪ Click **View Gridlines**.

⑫ Type a label.

⑬ Press `Tab` to move to the next label and type an address.

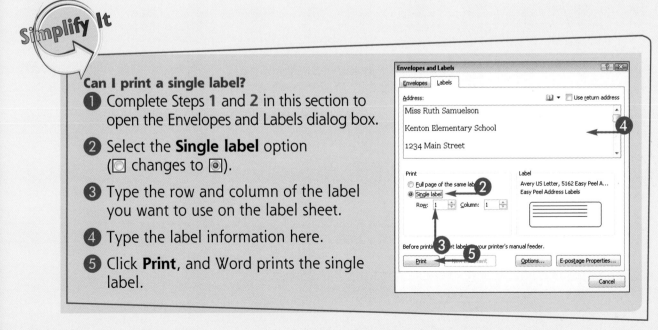

Simplify It

Can I print a single label?

① Complete Steps **1** and **2** in this section to open the Envelopes and Labels dialog box.

② Select the **Single label** option (⊙ changes to ⊚).

③ Type the row and column of the label you want to use on the label sheet.

④ Type the label information here.

⑤ Click **Print**, and Word prints the single label.

Chapter 9

Creating Tables and Charts

Do you want to keep the information in your Word document easy to read? The solution may very well be to add a table to contain your data. In this chapter, you learn how to create and work with tables in Word and to include a chart of table data in a Word document.

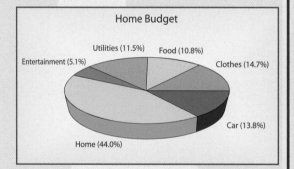

You can change the height of rows and the width of columns, and you can add and delete rows or columns from a table. You can combine table cells and you can split one table into multiple tables.

You can format tables in several ways, and you can also include formulas.

Create a Table

You can create a table and type text into it. Tables are well suited for organizing and displaying large amounts of columnar data consisting of text, numbers, or both. For example, Column 1 might contain a word, Column 2 a definition of the word, and Column 3 an antonym for the word. Or, you might incorporate a table in which each column contains one month's worth of sales data for three products.

The initial table you create may not contain the number of rows and columns you ultimately need, but you can always add rows or columns to your table later.

Create a Table

Set up a Table

1 Click in your document where you want the table to appear.

2 Click the **Insert** tab.

3 Click **Table**.

● Word displays a table grid.

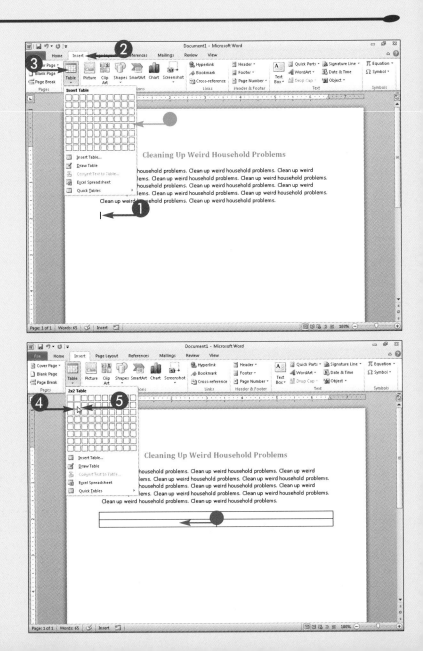

4 Slide the mouse pointer across the squares that represent the number of rows and columns you want in your table.

● Live Preview draws a sample of the table on-screen.

5 Click the square representing the lower-right corner of your table.

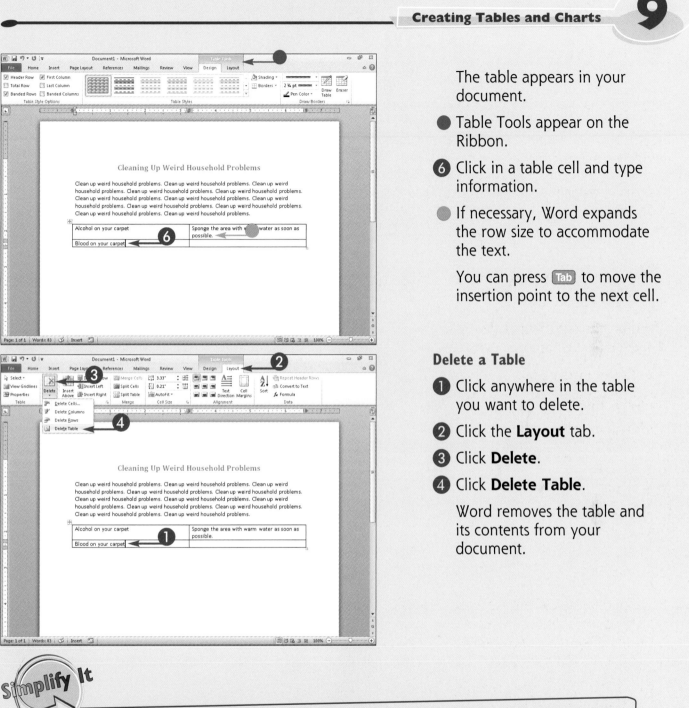

The table appears in your document.

● Table Tools appear on the Ribbon.

❻ Click in a table cell and type information.

● If necessary, Word expands the row size to accommodate the text.

You can press Tab to move the insertion point to the next cell.

Delete a Table

❶ Click anywhere in the table you want to delete.

❷ Click the **Layout** tab.

❸ Click **Delete**.

❹ Click **Delete Table**.

Word removes the table and its contents from your document.

Simplify It

Can I add rows to the bottom of the table?
Yes. You can easily add rows to the bottom of a table by placing the insertion point in the last cell of the table and pressing the Tab key.

What, exactly, is a table cell?
A *cell* is the term used to refer to the square that appears at the intersection of a row and a column. In spreadsheet programs, columns are named with letters, rows are named with numbers, and a cell is named using the column letter and row number. For example, the cell at the intersection of Column A and Row 2 is called A2.

Change the Row Height or Column Width

You can change the height of rows or the width of columns to accommodate your table information. Be aware that Word automatically adjusts the height of a row to accommodate the text you type, but you can adjust the row height to suit your purposes. On the other hand, Word does not automatically adjust the width of a column; instead, Word wraps the text in the column. To control a column's width, you must manually change it.

Make sure that you are working from Print Layout or Web Layout view; you can use the buttons on the status bar to switch views if necessary.

Change the Row Height or Column Width

Change the Row Height

1 Click the **Print Layout** button (▦) or the **Web Layout** button (▣).

2 Position the mouse pointer over the bottom of the row you want to change (▯ changes to ÷) and drag the row edge up to shorten or down to lengthen the row height.

● A dotted line marks the proposed bottom of the row.

3 When the row height suits you, release the mouse button.

● Word adjusts the row height.

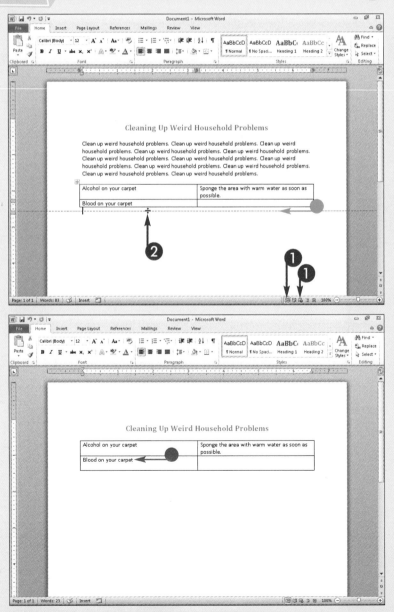

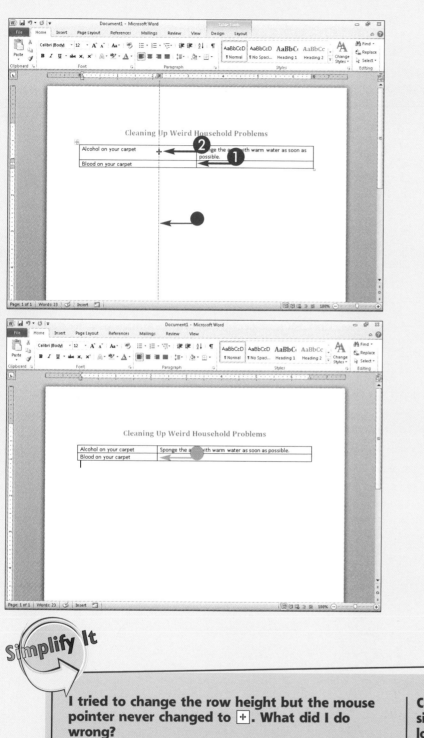

Change the Column Width

1 Position the mouse pointer over the right side of the column you want to change (⬚ changes to ⊞).

2 Drag the column edge right to widen or left to narrow the column width.

● A dotted line marks the proposed right side of the column.

3 Release the mouse.

● Word adjusts the column width.

Note: *For any column except the rightmost column, changing a column's width also changes the width of the column to its right, but the overall table size remains constant. When you change the width of the rightmost column, you change the width of the entire table.*

S🔍mplify It

I tried to change the row height but the mouse pointer never changed to ⬍. What did I do wrong?
You can change row height only when displaying your document in either Print Layout view or Web Layout view. Make sure you select one of those views by clicking the **Print Layout** view button (▦) or the **Web Layout** view button (▣). See Chapter 3 for more on understanding and switching between document views.

Can I easily make a column the size that accommodates the longest item in it?
Yes. You double-click the right edge of the column. Word widens or narrows the column based on the longest entry in the column. When you use this technique, Word also adjusts the overall table size.

Add or Delete a Row

You can easily add rows to accommodate more information or remove rows of information you do not need.

By default, if you place the insertion point in the last cell of a table and press the Tab key, Word automatically creates a new row in your table. But you are not limited to adding rows at the bottom of a table. You can insert rows wherever you need them in a table. Word determines where to insert the new row using the insertion point as a guide.

When you delete a row, Word deletes all the information that appears in that row.

Add or Delete a Row

Add a Row

1 Click in the row below where you want a new row to appear.

2 Click the **Layout** tab.

3 Click **Insert Above**.

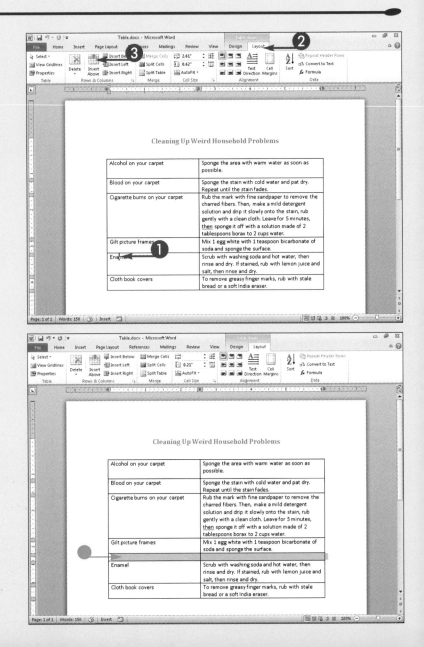

● Word inserts a row and selects it.

You can click in the row to add information to the table.

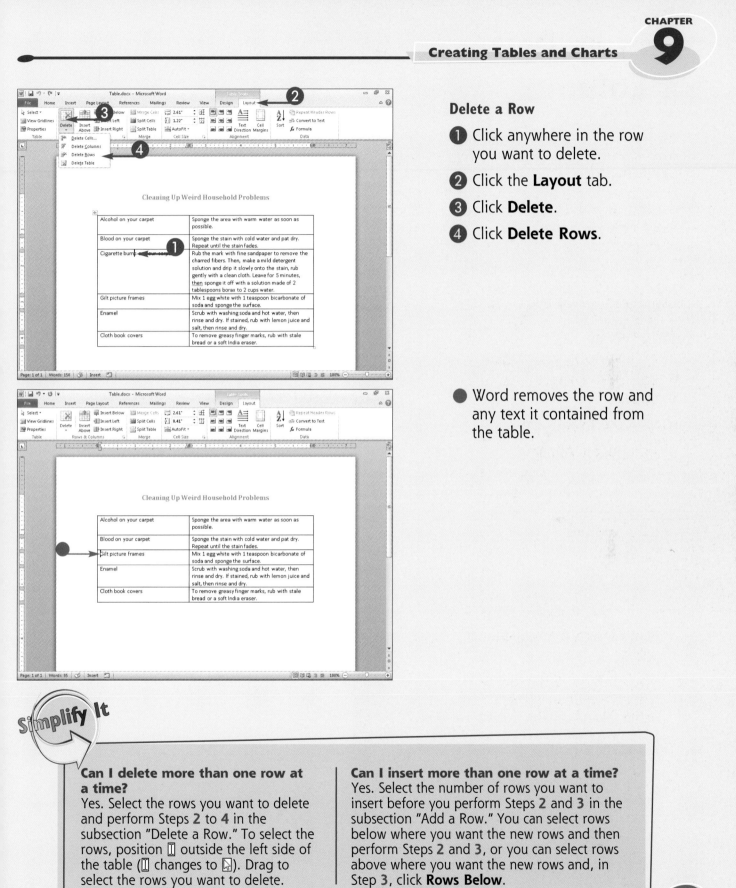

Delete a Row

1. Click anywhere in the row you want to delete.

2. Click the **Layout** tab.

3. Click **Delete**.

4. Click **Delete Rows**.

● Word removes the row and any text it contained from the table.

Can I delete more than one row at a time?
Yes. Select the rows you want to delete and perform Steps **2** to **4** in the subsection "Delete a Row." To select the rows, position ⌶ outside the left side of the table (⌶ changes to ⇗). Drag to select the rows you want to delete.

Can I insert more than one row at a time?
Yes. Select the number of rows you want to insert before you perform Steps **2** and **3** in the subsection "Add a Row." You can select rows below where you want the new rows and then perform Steps **2** and **3**, or you can select rows above where you want the new rows and, in Step **3**, click **Rows Below**.

Add or Delete a Column

You can add or delete columns to change the structure of a table to accommodate more or less information. You can add columns at any place in a table, not just at the left or right edge of the table. When you delete a column, Word deletes all the information that appears in that column.

When you add a column to a table, Word decreases the width of the other columns to create space for the new column within your document's margins while retaining the overall size of the table.

Add or Delete a Column

Add a Column

1 Click in the column to the left of the column you want to add.

2 Click the **Layout** tab.

3 Click **Insert Right**.

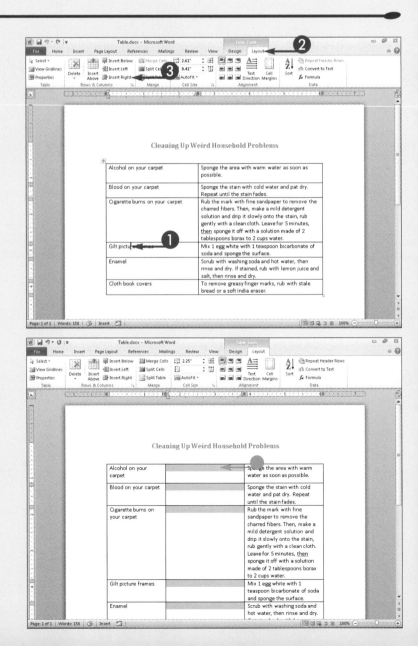

● Word inserts a new column in the table to the right of the column you clicked in Step **1** and selects the new column.

You can click in the column to add text to it.

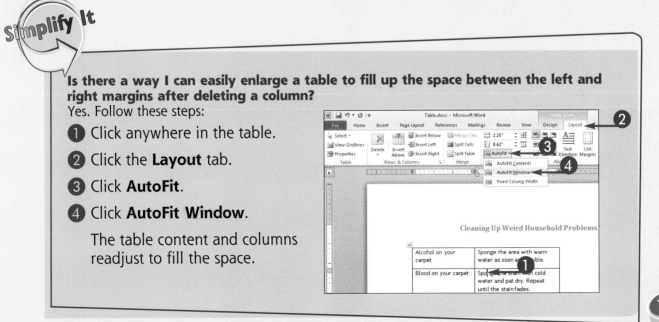

Delete a Column

1 Click anywhere in the column you want to delete.

2 Click the **Layout** tab.

3 Click **Delete**.

4 Click **Delete Columns**.

● Word removes the column and any text it contained from the table.

● The insertion point appears in the column to the right of the one you deleted.

Word does not resize existing columns to use the space previously occupied by the deleted column.

Simplify It

Is there a way I can easily enlarge a table to fill up the space between the left and right margins after deleting a column?

Yes. Follow these steps:

1 Click anywhere in the table.

2 Click the **Layout** tab.

3 Click **AutoFit**.

4 Click **AutoFit Window**.

The table content and columns readjust to fill the space.

Move
a Table

No table is permanently located where you insert it. If you find, after creating a table, that it really belongs in another location in your document, you can easily move all of the contents of a table to a new place in your document. There is no need to re-create the table and retype any information.

To move a table, you need to work in either Print Layout or Web Layout view. To switch to either of these views, you can use the View shortcut buttons at the right edge of the status bar.

Move a Table

① Click or ▣

② Position the mouse pointer over the table.

● A handle (⊞) appears in the upper-left corner of the table.

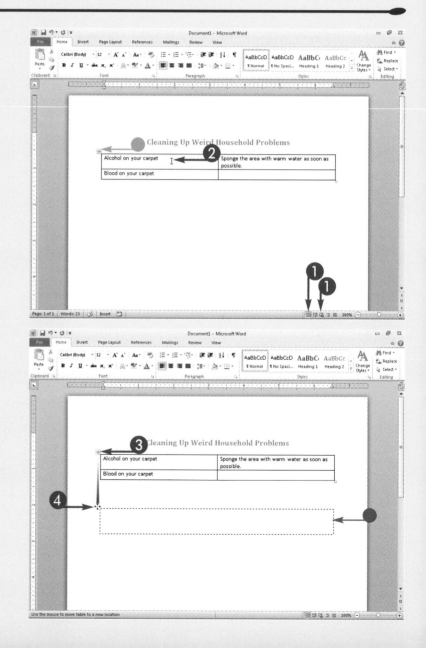

③ Position the mouse pointer over the handle (▯ changes to ▨).

④ Drag the table to a new location.

● A dashed line represents the proposed table position.

⑤ Release the mouse button.

The table appears in the new location.

To copy the table, perform these steps but press Ctrl in Step **3**.

Resize
a Table

When you create a table, you initially specify the table's size. However, you are not restricted to the size you establish when you create your table. If you find that your table dimensions do not suit your purpose, you can resize the table. For example, you may want to resize a table to make it longer and narrower.

To resize a table, you need to work in either Print Layout or Web Layout view. To switch to either of these views, you can use the View shortcut buttons at the right edge of the status bar.

Resize a Table

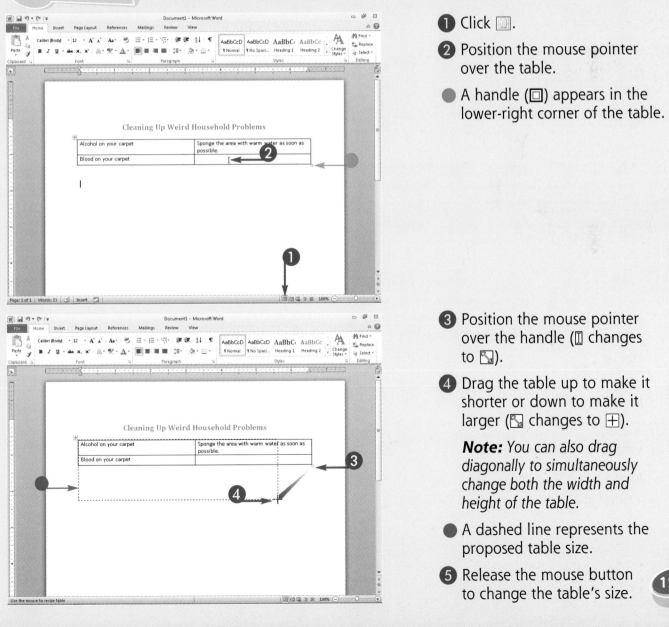

① Click ▦.

② Position the mouse pointer over the table.

● A handle (▢) appears in the lower-right corner of the table.

③ Position the mouse pointer over the handle (▯ changes to ◤).

④ Drag the table up to make it shorter or down to make it larger (◤ changes to ⊞).

Note: *You can also drag diagonally to simultaneously change both the width and height of the table.*

● A dashed line represents the proposed table size.

⑤ Release the mouse button to change the table's size.

157

Set Cell Margins

You can set margins in table cells to make table information more legible. When you increase cell margins, you increase the amount of space that appears between the information in a cell and the cell's border, adding white space between the text and the cell border.

Because cell margins affect all table cells, adding margin space can effectively double the space between cells. For example, if you set the top and bottom margins to .1 inches, Word displays .2 inches of space between Rows 1 and 2 — .1 inch for the bottom of Row 1 and .1 inch for the top of Row 2.

Set Cell Margins

1 Click anywhere in the table.

2 Click the **Layout** tab.

3 Click **Cell Margins**.

The Table Options dialog box appears.

4 Type margin settings here.

5 Click **OK**.

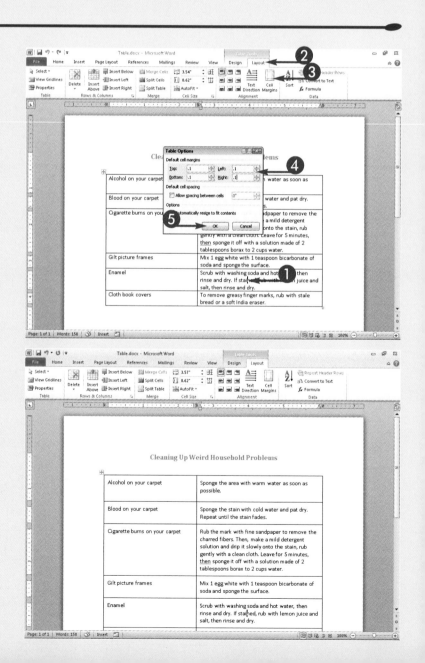

Word applies cell margin settings.

Add Space Between Cells

You can set spacing between table cells to separate table cells and make table information easier to read and more attractive.

When you add space between cells, Word adds the space outside each cell. Adding space between cells does not change the amount of white space that appears between text and each cell's border; instead, the added white space appears between cell borders.

Note that you can add space between cells and change cell margins as described in the section, "Set Cell Margins." If you increase cell margins and add space between cells, you increase the amount of white space both within and between cells.

Add Space Between Cells

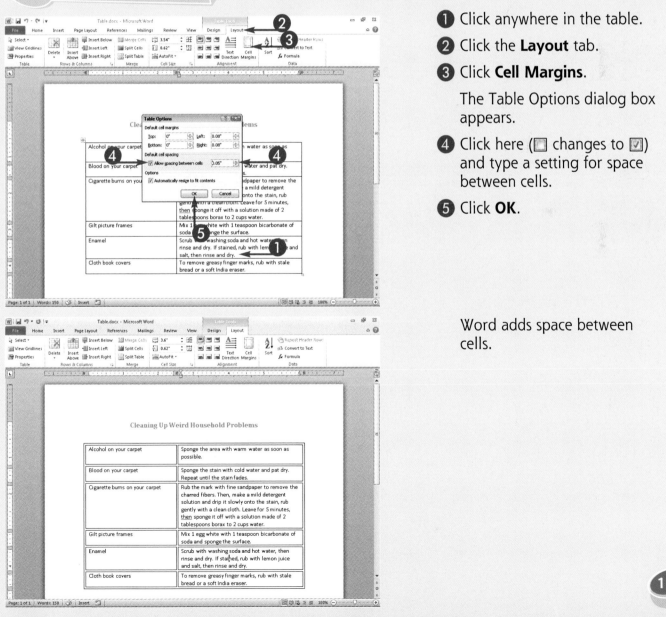

① Click anywhere in the table.

② Click the **Layout** tab.

③ Click **Cell Margins**.

The Table Options dialog box appears.

④ Click here (☐ changes to ☑) and type a setting for space between cells.

⑤ Click **OK**.

Word adds space between cells.

Combine Cells

You can combine two or more cells to create one large cell. Suppose, for example, that your table contains three columns and you want to display the table's title in the first row and center the title over the total width of the table. If you place the title in the first cell in Row 1, you cannot center the title across the table's width. But if you combine the cells in Row 1, you create one cell that spans the width of your table. Any information you place in that cell can then be aligned over the width of the table.

Combine Cells

1 Position the mouse pointer inside the first cell you want to merge (⌶ changes to ▪).

2 Drag ▪ across the cells you want to merge to select them.

3 Click the **Layout** tab.

4 Click **Merge Cells**.

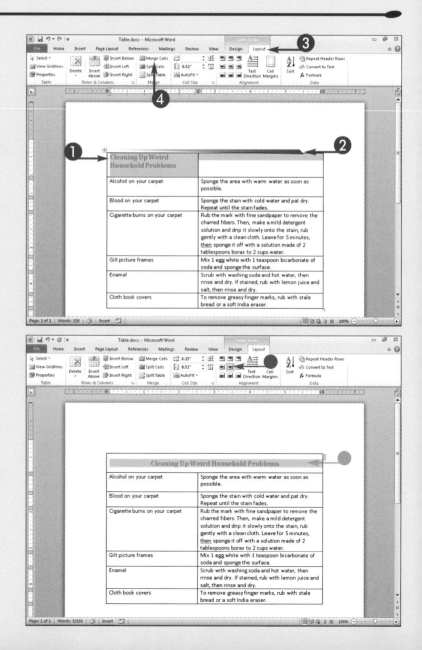

● Word combines the cells into one cell and selects that cell.

● For a table title, you can click the **Align Center** button (▤) to center text in the cell both horizontally and vertically.

5 Click anywhere to cancel the selection.

Split
a Table

You can split one table into two tables. Suppose that you enter a significant amount of information into a table and then discover that you need to insert new text in paragraph format between two portions of the table. You could delete the rows that need to appear after your paragraph, but then you would need to re-create that information. Instead of deleting rows so that you can insert text in paragraph form, you can split the table. When you split a table, Word creates two tables with one blank line between them, and the blank line is not a table row.

Split a Table

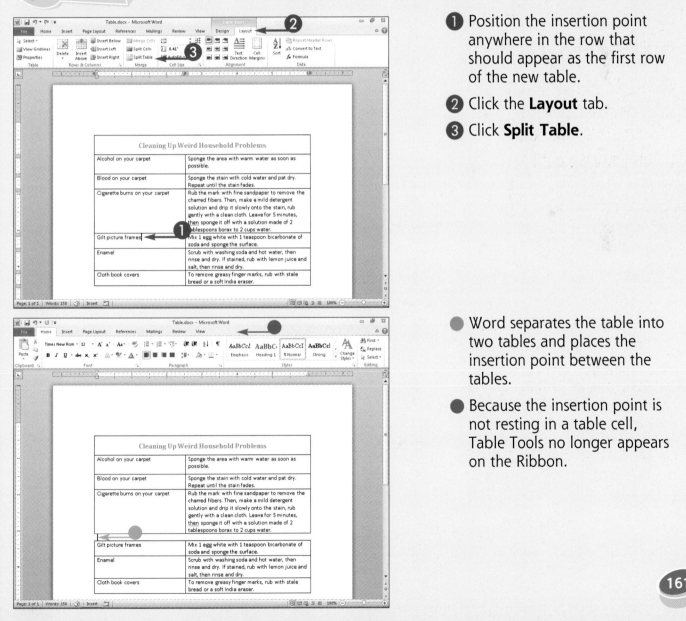

① Position the insertion point anywhere in the row that should appear as the first row of the new table.

② Click the **Layout** tab.

③ Click **Split Table**.

● Word separates the table into two tables and places the insertion point between the tables.

● Because the insertion point is not resting in a table cell, Table Tools no longer appears on the Ribbon.

161

Add a Formula to a Table

You can place a formula in a cell and let Word automatically do the math for you. For example, you can add numbers, average numbers, or find the largest or smallest number in table cells you specify. You also can round values in cells and count the number of cells that contain numbers. Word contains a fairly long list of formulas and suggests a formula for the situation.

You can accept the suggested formula, as this example does, or you can select a different formula as needed.

Add a Formula to a Table

① In a table containing numbers, click in a cell that should contain the sum of a row or a column.

② Click the **Layout** tab.

③ Click **Formula**.

The Formula dialog box appears, suggesting a formula.

● You can click here to select a number format.

● You can click here to select a different formula.

④ Click **OK**.

● Word places the formula in the cell containing the insertion point and displays the calculated result of the formula.

If you change any of the values in the row or column that the formula sums, you can click in the cell containing the formula and press F9 to update the formula result.

Align Text in Cells

For uniformity, you can align table entries within cells. You can choose from nine possible alignments.

You can align entries with the top of each cell and then align them left or right, or center them between the cell margins.

You can center entries between the top and bottom cell margins and then align them left or right or center them between the cell margins.

Finally, you can align entries with the bottom of each cell and then align them left or right or center them between the cell margins.

By default, Word aligns entries at the top left edge of each cell.

Align Text in Cells

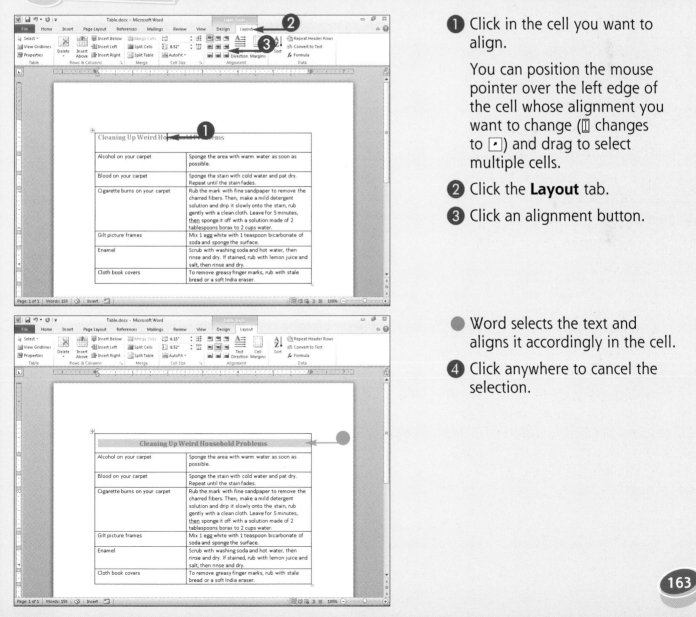

① Click in the cell you want to align.

You can position the mouse pointer over the left edge of the cell whose alignment you want to change (⌶ changes to ▪) and drag to select multiple cells.

② Click the **Layout** tab.

③ Click an alignment button.

● Word selects the text and aligns it accordingly in the cell.

④ Click anywhere to cancel the selection.

Format a Table

You can apply any number of predefined table styles to a table to format it quickly and easily, creating a professional-looking table. Word has styles that apply formatting to every other column, every other row, the left column, and the top row.

Be aware that many of the predefined table styles use color; to get the full effect, you need a color printer or need to present your table information on a color monitor. Color table styles can be particularly effective if you are presenting your information to a large group using overhead projection.

Format a Table

1 Click anywhere in the table.

2 Click the **Design** tab.

3 Click ⊡ in the Table Styles group.

The Table Style Gallery appears.

4 Position the mouse pointer over a table style.

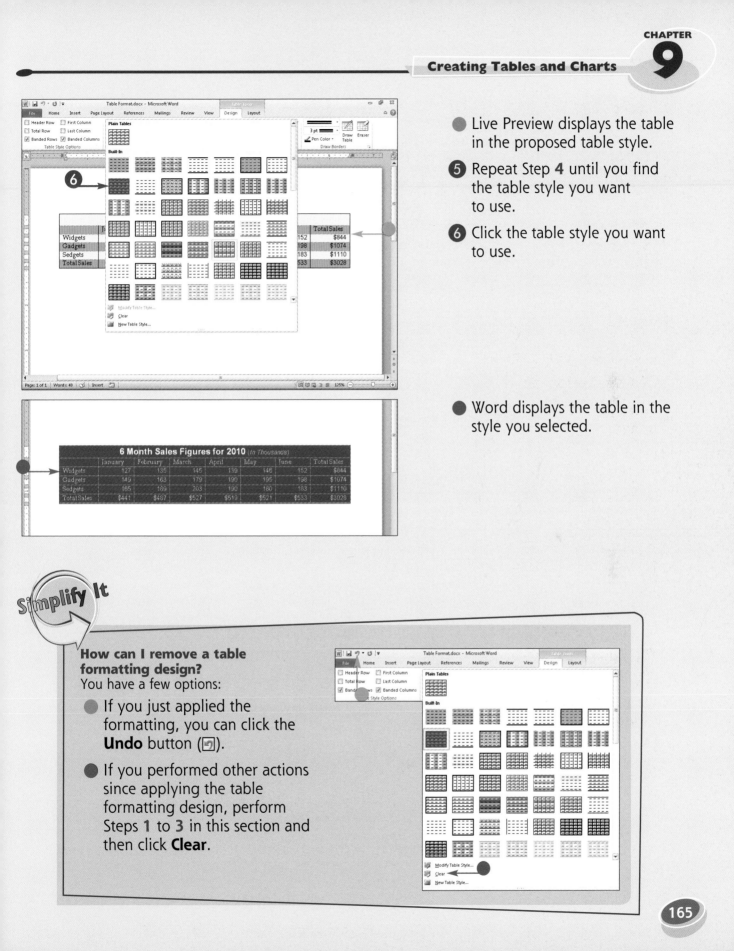

● Live Preview displays the table in the proposed table style.

⑤ Repeat Step **4** until you find the table style you want to use.

⑥ Click the table style you want to use.

● Word displays the table in the style you selected.

6 Month Sales Figures for 2010 (*In Thousands*)

	January	February	March	April	May	June	Total Sales
Widgets	127	135	145	139	146	152	$844
Gadgets	149	163	179	190	195	198	$1074
Sedgets	165	189	203	190	180	183	$1110
Total Sales	$441	$487	$527	$519	$521	$533	$3028

Simplify It

How can I remove a table formatting design?
You have a few options:

● If you just applied the formatting, you can click the **Undo** button (🔄).

● If you performed other actions since applying the table formatting design, perform Steps **1** to **3** in this section and then click **Clear**.

Add a Chart

You can create a chart in a Microsoft Word 2010 document. And although it might not sound intuitive, Word uses Microsoft Excel 2010 to do so.

It is common to present both a chart and a table containing the chart's underlying data. Although this example inserts a chart in a document that contains a table displaying the underlying chart data, the table is independent of the chart. You supply all data for the chart in Excel and you do not need to present chart data in a table or use any information found in Word.

Add a Chart

1 Click in the document where you want a chart to appear.

2 Click the **Insert** tab.

3 Click **Chart**.

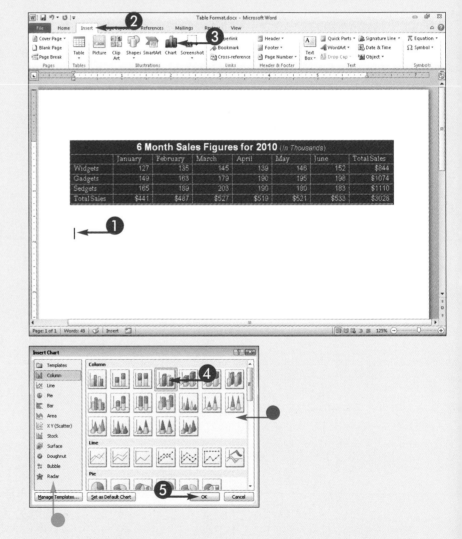

The Insert Chart window appears.

4 Click a chart type.

● Categories of chart types appear here.

● Chart types organized by category appear here.

5 Click **OK**.

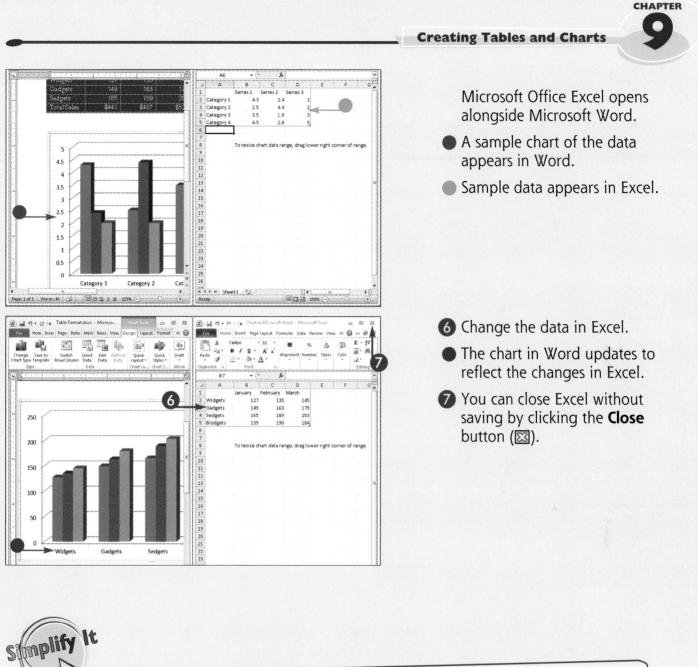

Microsoft Office Excel opens alongside Microsoft Word.

● A sample chart of the data appears in Word.

● Sample data appears in Excel.

⑥ Change the data in Excel.

● The chart in Word updates to reflect the changes in Excel.

⑦ You can close Excel without saving by clicking the **Close** button (⊠).

Simplify It

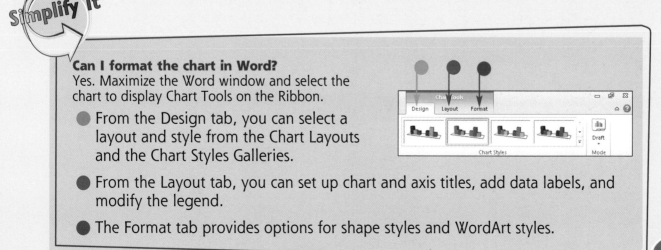

Can I format the chart in Word?
Yes. Maximize the Word window and select the chart to display Chart Tools on the Ribbon.

● From the Design tab, you can select a layout and style from the Chart Layouts and the Chart Styles Galleries.

● From the Layout tab, you can set up chart and axis titles, add data labels, and modify the legend.

● The Format tab provides options for shape styles and WordArt styles.

Chart Concepts

When creating a chart, you have a wide variety of choices. You can create column charts, line charts, pie charts, bar charts, area charts, XY charts, stock charts, surface charts, doughnut charts, bubble charts, and radar charts. Each chart type serves a different purpose and communicates different information to the reader. The type of chart you use depends on the information you are trying to convey to your reader. And you are not limited to the first chart type you select; if you discover that you have not selected the optimal chart type, try a different one.

Column Charts
A column chart shows data changes over a period of time and can compare different sets of data. A column chart contains vertically oriented bars.

Line Charts
Line charts help you see trends. A line chart connects many related data points; by connecting the points with a line, you see a general trend.

Pie Charts
Pie charts demonstrate the relationship of a part to the whole. Pie charts are effective when you are trying to show, for example, the percentage of total sales for which the Midwest region is responsible.

Bar Charts
Bar charts typically compare different sets of data and can also show data changes over time. A bar chart closely resembles a column chart, but the bars are horizontally oriented.

Area Charts
Area charts show data over time, but an area chart helps you see data as broad trends, rather than individual data points.

XY Charts

Statisticians often use an XY chart, also called a scatter chart, to determine whether a correlation exists between two variables. Both axes on a scatter chart are numeric, and the axes can be linear or logarithmic.

Stock Charts

Also called High-Low, Open-Close charts, stock charts are used for stock market reports. This chart type is very effective to display data that fluctuates over time.

Surface Charts

Topographic maps are surface charts, using colors and patterns to identify areas in the same range of values. A surface chart is useful when you want to find the best-possible combination between two sets of data.

Doughnut Charts

Like a pie chart, a doughnut chart shows the relationship of parts to a whole. Although a pie chart contains only one data series, a doughnut chart typically contains more than one data series. The doughnut chart is round like a pie chart, but each series in the doughnut chart appears as a separate ring in the circle.

Bubble Charts

A bubble chart is a specific type of XY chart that compares sets of three values. The size of the bubble indicates the value of a third variable. You can arrange data for a bubble chart by placing the X values in one column and entering corresponding Y values and bubble sizes in the adjacent columns.

Radar Charts

You can use a radar chart to compare data series that consist of several variables. Each data series on a radar chart has its own axis that "radiates" from the center of the chart — hence the name radar chart. A line connects each point in the series.

Chapter 10

Working with Graphics

You can spruce up documents by inserting a variety of graphics; the technique to insert graphics varies, depending on the type of graphic.

When you edit, however, some techniques are common to all types of graphics and others vary by graphic type. When a technique applies to all types of graphics, this chapter uses the generic term *graphic*. For editing techniques that apply to pictures, clip art, and screenshots, this chapter calls these graphics *pictures*. Similarly, for editing techniques that apply to WordArt, shapes, and text boxes this chapter calls these graphics *drawings*. Diagrams fall into a category by themselves.

Add
WordArt

WordArt is decorative text that you can add to a document as an eye-catching visual effect. You choose from different WordArt text styles and Word inserts a graphic that applies the style to text or numbers. You can create WordArt text as you create a WordArt graphic, or you can apply a WordArt style to existing text.

When you apply a WordArt style to existing text, Word places the WordArt graphic at the location of the existing text. Word places a new WordArt graphic in the upper-left corner of your document, and you can move it the same way you move any graphic.

Add WordArt

1 Click in the document where you want to add WordArt or select existing text and apply WordArt to it.

2 Click the **Insert** tab.

3 Click **WordArt**.

● The WordArt Gallery appears.

4 Click the WordArt style you want to apply.

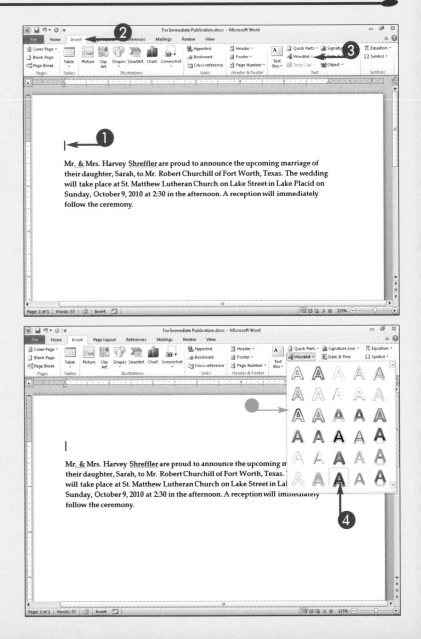

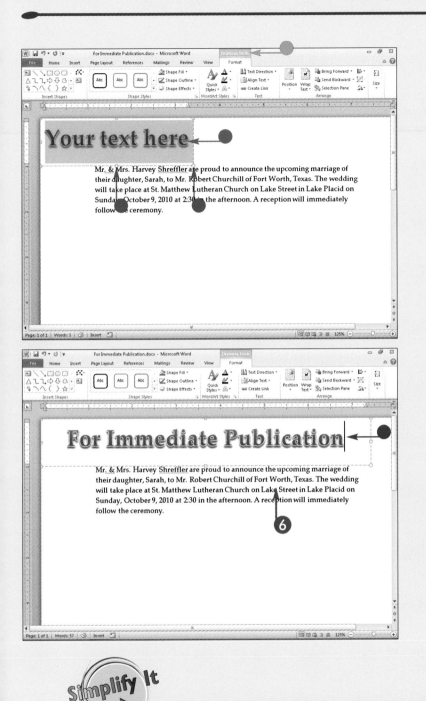

● If you selected text in Step **1**, your text appears selected in the WordArt style you applied; otherwise, the words "Your Text Here" appear selected in the upper-left corner of your document.

● Handles (🔲 and 🔘) surround the WordArt graphic.

● Drawing Tools appear on the Ribbon; you can use these tools to format WordArt, shapes, and text boxes.

⑤ If necessary, type text.

● Word converts the text to a WordArt graphic.

⑥ Click anywhere to continue working.

Note: You can move the WordArt; see the section, "Move or Resize a Graphic."

Note: You can change the size of the WordArt font by selecting the WordArt text and, on the Home tab, selecting a different font size from the Font list in the Font group.

Can I edit the WordArt drawing?
Yes. Click inside the WordArt drawing. Handles (🔲 and 🔘) appear around the WordArt. Edit the text the way you would edit any text, deleting and changing as needed.

Can I delete a WordArt drawing?
Yes, but be aware that deleting the drawing also deletes the text. Click near the edge of the drawing or, if you click inside the drawing, click any handle (🔲 or 🔘) to select the drawing. Then press Delete.

Add a Picture

You can include a picture file graphic stored on your computer in a Word document. Pictures can add elements of interest to a document and help retain a reader's attention by breaking up the monotony of continuous text.

You can use pictures from a variety of sources, including pictures you have taken with your

own digital camera. If you use pictures that you find on the Internet or pictures containing people, be aware that they might be copyrighted and you must secure permission to use them to avoid being in violation of copyright laws.

Add a Picture

1 Click in your document where you want to add a picture.

2 Click the **Insert** tab.

3 Click **Picture**.

The Insert Picture dialog box appears.

● The folder you are viewing appears here.

● You can click here to navigate to commonly used locations where pictures may be stored.

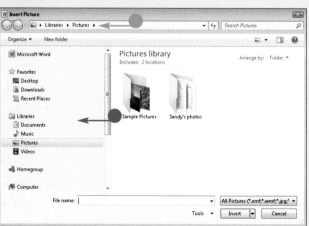

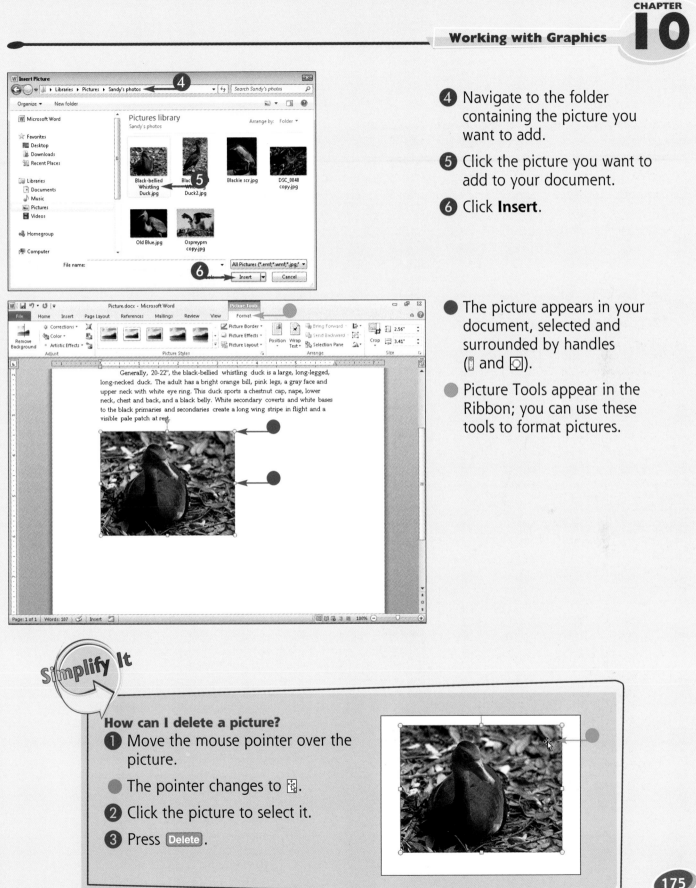

④ Navigate to the folder containing the picture you want to add.

⑤ Click the picture you want to add to your document.

⑥ Click **Insert**.

● The picture appears in your document, selected and surrounded by handles (⬚ and ⬚).

● Picture Tools appear in the Ribbon; you can use these tools to format pictures.

Simplify It

How can I delete a picture?
① Move the mouse pointer over the picture.

● The pointer changes to ⬚.

② Click the picture to select it.

③ Press **Delete**.

Add a Screenshot

You can insert into a Word document an image, called a *screenshot*, of another document open in Word or of a document open in another program. A screenshot is a picture of whatever appears on your screen. Word's screenshot feature enables you to capture the images of other documents open in other programs, even if they are not Office programs, or of other documents that are open in Word. Using Word's screenshot feature, you cannot capture an image of the currently open Word document or of your desktop, but you find a workaround in this section.

Add a Screenshot

① Open a document.

● This example shows a chart in Excel.

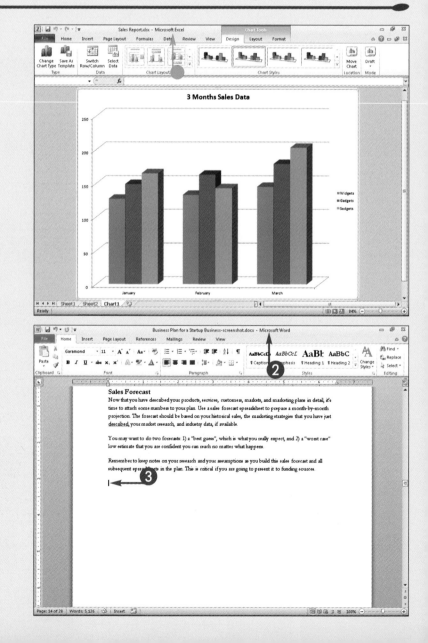

② Open the Word document in which you want to insert a screenshot of the document you opened in Step **1**.

③ Position the insertion point where you want the screenshot to appear.

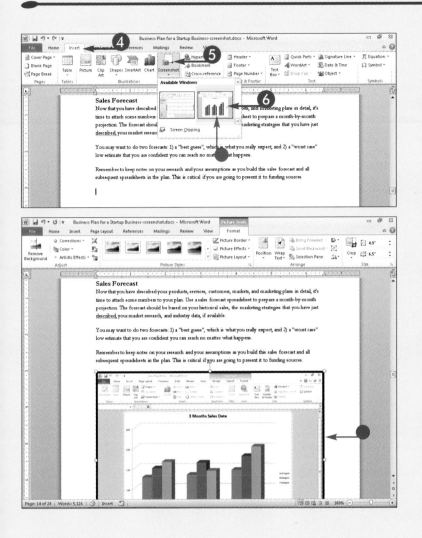

4 Click **Insert**.

5 Click **Screenshot**.

● The Screenshot Gallery shows open programs and available screenshots of those programs.

6 Click the screenshot you want to insert in your Word document.

● The screenshot appears selected in your Word document.

Click anywhere outside the screenshot to continue working.

Simplify It

Can I use the Screenshot feature to insert a screenshot of the current Word document into the same document?
No, but here is a workaround. Open the document in which you want to insert a screenshot and then open a second, blank document. From the blank document, shoot a screen of the first Word document. The screen appears in the blank document, already selected. Click **Copy** (🗎). Then switch to the Word document, click where the screenshot should appear, and click **Paste** (📋).

Can I use the Screenshot feature to take a picture of my desktop?
No, but you can take a picture of your desktop and insert it into a Word document. While viewing your desktop, press `Print scrn`. Then switch to Word and position the insertion point where you want the screenshot to appear. Press `Ctrl` + `V` to paste the image into your Word document.

Add a Clip Art Image

You can add clip art images to your document to help get your message across and add graphic interest to your document. Clip art images are typically graphic drawings rather than photographs. Word comes with a Clip Art gallery from which you can select a clip art image to insert in your document. Or you can search the Internet, where you will find thousands of clip art images available for download. Many are free but some charge a fee to use them.

Add a Clip Art Image

1 Click in your document where you want to place an image.

2 Click **Insert**.

3 Click **Clip Art**.

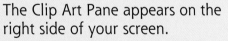

The Clip Art Pane appears on the right side of your screen.

4 Click here and type one or more words to describe the image you want to find.

● You can click here (☐ changes to ☑) to search online at Office.com for additional clip art.

Note: *This example does not search online.*

5 Click **Go**.

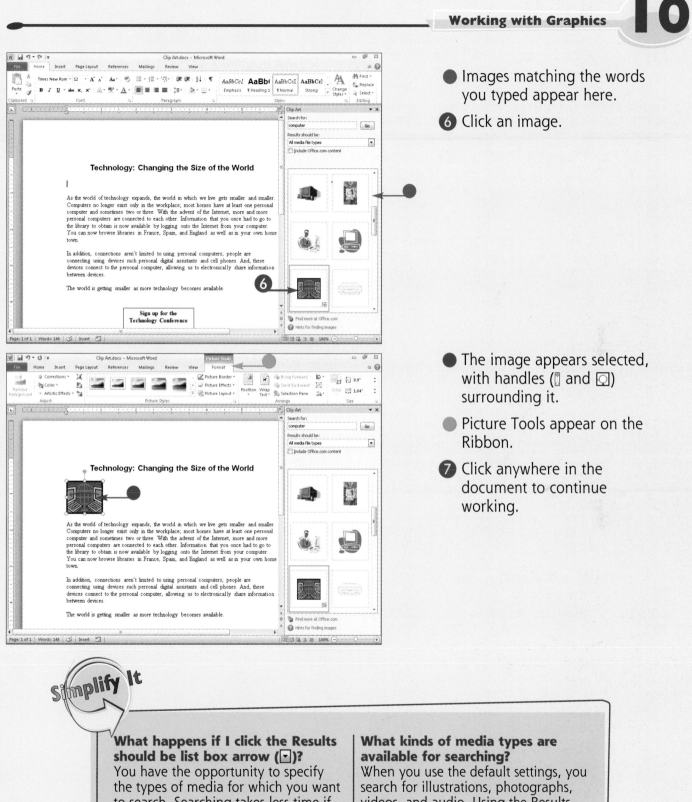

● Images matching the words you typed appear here.

⑥ Click an image.

● The image appears selected, with handles (▯ and ▢) surrounding it.

● Picture Tools appear on the Ribbon.

⑦ Click anywhere in the document to continue working.

Simplify It

What happens if I click the Results should be list box arrow (▾)?
You have the opportunity to specify the types of media for which you want to search. Searching takes less time if you limit the search, but the search may not display as many clip art images if you limit it.

What kinds of media types are available for searching?
When you use the default settings, you search for illustrations, photographs, videos, and audio. Using the Results should be list, you can limit the search to any one or a combination of those media types.

Add a Shape

To give your Word document pizzazz, you can add graphic shapes such as lines, arrows, stars, rectangles, triangles, flow chart symbols, callouts, and banners. Shapes are more like drawings than photographs. They are less complex than most clip art images, and, unlike WordArt, they do not contain or use text. However, you can use text boxes to place text inside a shape; see the section "Add a Text Box" for details.

Shapes are visible in Print Layout, Web Layout, and Reading Layout views.

Add a Shape

① Click the **Insert** tab.

② Click **Shapes**.

The Shapes Gallery appears.

③ Click a shape.

The mouse pointer (I) changes to ⊞.

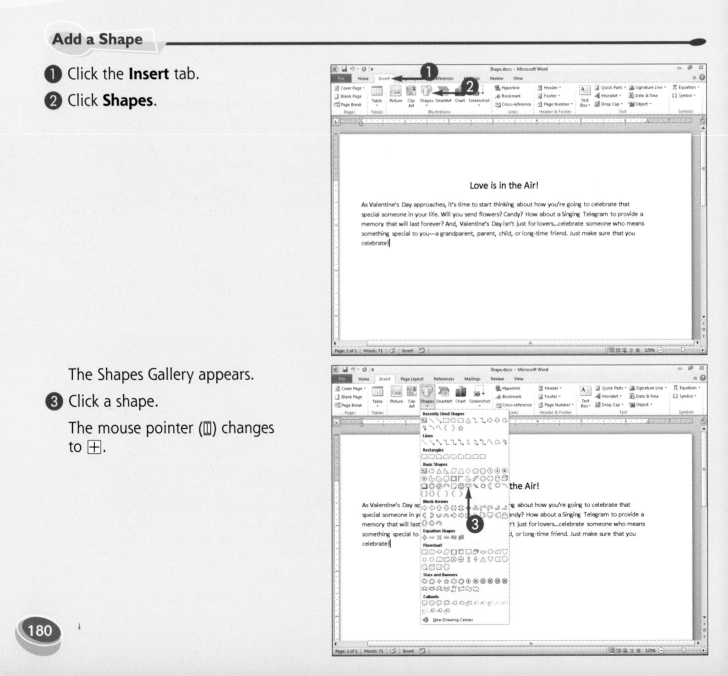

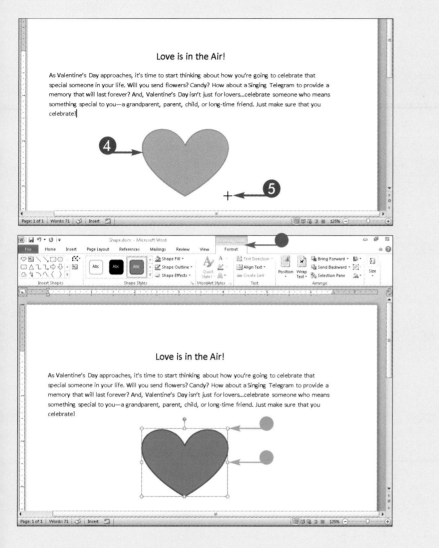

④ Position the mouse pointer at the upper-left corner of the place where you want the shape to appear.

⑤ Drag the mouse pointer (⊞) down and to the right until the shape is the size you want.

When you release the mouse button, the shape appears.

● The handles (▯ and ▢) that surround the shape indicate that the shape is selected.

● Drawing Tools appear on the Ribbon.

You can press ⟦Esc⟧ or click anywhere to continue working in your document.

Simplify It

Can I change the color of a shape?
Yes. Follow these steps:

① Click the shape to select it.

② On the Ribbon, in the Shape Styles group, click the **Shape Fill** button.

③ Click a color.

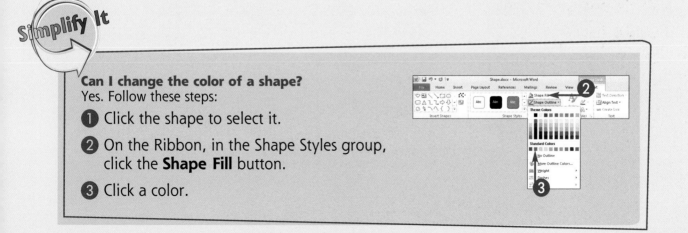

Add a Text Box

You can add a text box, which is another type of graphic, to your document to control the placement and appearance of the text. By default, most text boxes display a box outline around the text; hence the name *text box*. But you can eliminate the text box's outline if you

want. You can use text boxes in combination with shapes to incorporate text inside a shape, and, in this case, you might want to eliminate the text box's outline.

Text boxes are visible only in Print Layout, Web Layout, and Reading Layout views.

Add a Text Box

1 Click the **Insert** tab.

2 Click **Text Box**.

The Text Box Gallery appears.

3 Click a text box style.

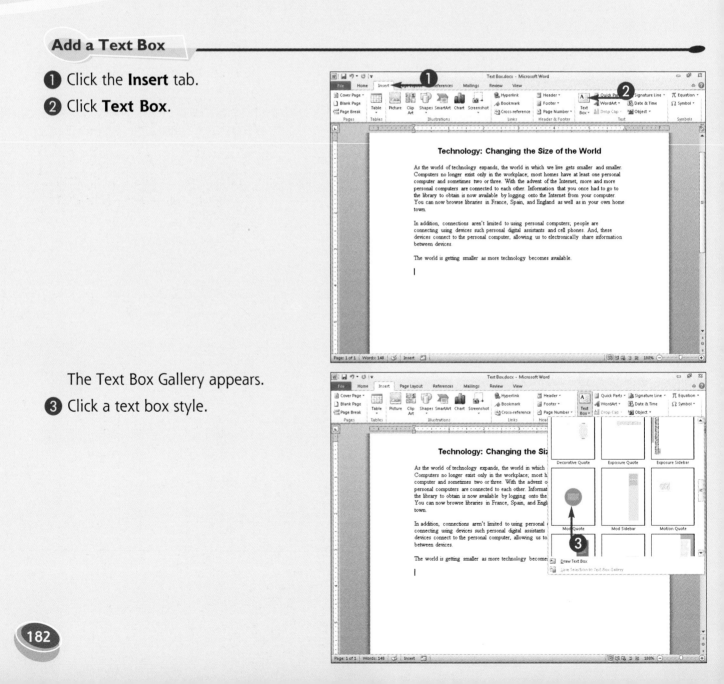

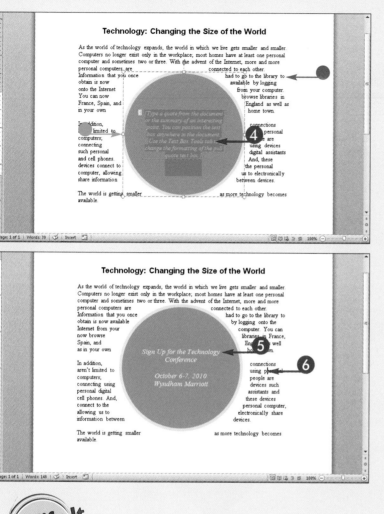

- Word places a text box in your document.

- Existing text flows around the box.

  Sample text appears inside a Pull Quote box, where you can type your text.

④ Position the mouse pointer inside the text box over the sample text and click.

  Word selects the sample text.

⑤ Type your text.

⑥ Click outside the text box.

  Your text appears in the box.

Note: *You can format the text using the techniques described in Chapter 5.*

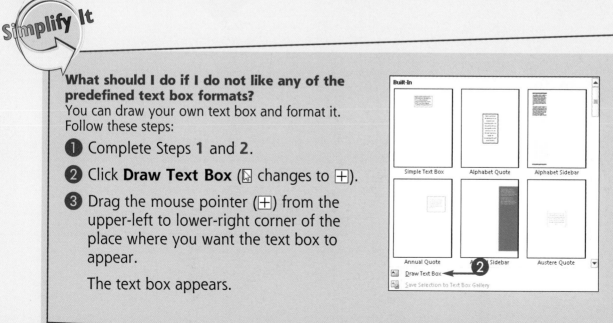

Simplify It

What should I do if I do not like any of the predefined text box formats?
You can draw your own text box and format it. Follow these steps:

① Complete Steps **1** and **2**.

② Click **Draw Text Box** (⬚ changes to ⊞).

③ Drag the mouse pointer (⊞) from the upper-left to lower-right corner of the place where you want the text box to appear.

The text box appears.

Move or Resize a Graphic

If you find that a graphic — a picture, Clip Art image, shape, text box, or WordArt graphic — is not positioned where you want it or if it is too large or too small, you can move or resize it. For example, if you insert a WordArt graphic without using existing text, Word automatically places the graphic at the upper-left edge of the page, but you can move it.

Similarly, suppose that you create a shape and then decide that it is bigger than you want it to be. You can easily resize it using the handles that surround any graphic when you select it.

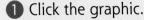

Move or Resize a Graphic

Move a Graphic

① Click the graphic.

● Handles (▯, ▢) surround the graphic.

② Position the mouse pointer over the WordArt image, picture, clip art image, or shape, or over the edge of the text box (▯ changes to ▧).

③ Drag the graphic to a new location.

● A lighter-shaded version of the graphic indicates the proposed position of the graphic.

④ Release the mouse button.

The graphic appears in the new location.

⑤ Click outside the graphic to cancel its selection.

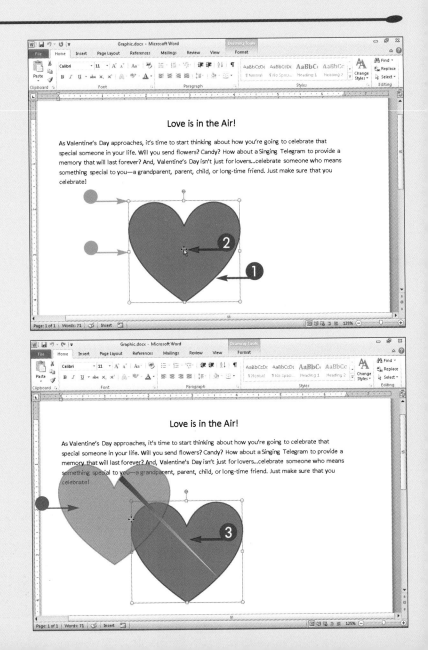

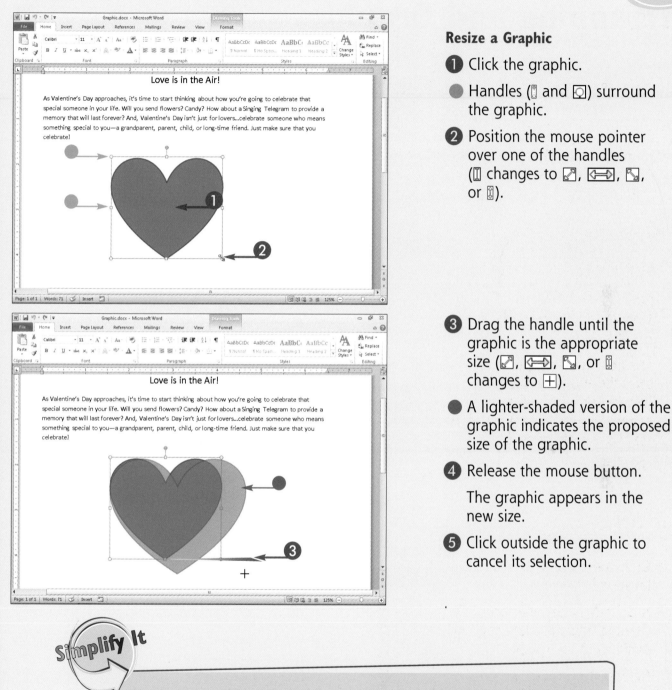

Resize a Graphic

1. Click the graphic.

● Handles (▯ and ⬭) surround the graphic.

2. Position the mouse pointer over one of the handles (▯ changes to ⬈, ⬌, ⬉, or ▯).

3. Drag the handle until the graphic is the appropriate size (⬈, ⬌, ⬉, or ▯ changes to ✛).

● A lighter-shaded version of the graphic indicates the proposed size of the graphic.

4. Release the mouse button.

The graphic appears in the new size.

5. Click outside the graphic to cancel its selection.

Simplify It

Is there an easy way I can make a graphic move only horizontally or vertically but not diagonally?
Yes. Press and hold the Shift key as you drag the graphic. Word allows you to move the graphic horizontally or vertically but not diagonally.

Does it matter which handle I use to resize a graphic?
If you click and drag any of the corner handles, you maintain the proportion of the graphic as you resize it. The square handles on the sides, top, or bottom of the graphic resize the width or the height only of the graphic.

Understanding Text Wrapping and Graphics

When you insert graphics into a Word document, you can control the way that text wraps around the graphic. By default, most graphics you insert have a relatively square boundary, even if the graphic is not a square, and most text-wrapping options relate to that relatively square boundary.

By editing a graphic's wrap points, you can change the square boundary to more closely match the graphic's shape and wrap text more closely around the shape. Word offers you seven different ways to wrap text in relation to a graphic image.

In Line with Text

With this, text does not wrap around the graphic. Word positions the graphic exactly where you placed it. The graphic moves to accommodate added or deleted text, but no text appears on the graphic's right or left.

Square

Wraps text in a square around your graphic regardless of its shape. You can control the amount of space between text and all your graphic's sides.

Through

With Through, if you edit a graphic's wrap points by dragging them to match the shape of the graphic, you can wrap text to follow the graphic's shape.

Top and Bottom

Wraps text around the graphic's top and bottom, but leaves the space on either side of a graphic blank.

Tight

Wraps text around the graphic's outside edge. The difference between this and Square is apparent with a nonsquare shape; with Tight, you can control the space between the text and the graphic's right and left sides. Word leaves no space between text and the graphic's top and bottom sides.

Behind Text

With this, the text runs over the graphic, as if the graphic were not there.

In Front of Text

With this, the graphic blocks the text underneath the graphic's location.

Wrap Text Around a Graphic

You can control the way that Word wraps text around a graphic image in your document. In the section "Understanding Text Wrapping and Graphics," you can read about the seven choices Word offers you when wrapping text around a graphic. Text wrapping becomes very important when you want to place graphics in a document where space is at a premium, such as a two-columned newsletter. You can use text wrapping to maximize the space allotted to text surrounding the graphic.

The information in this section shows text wrapping for a shape but applies to wrapping text for any kind of graphic.

Wrap Text Around a Graphic

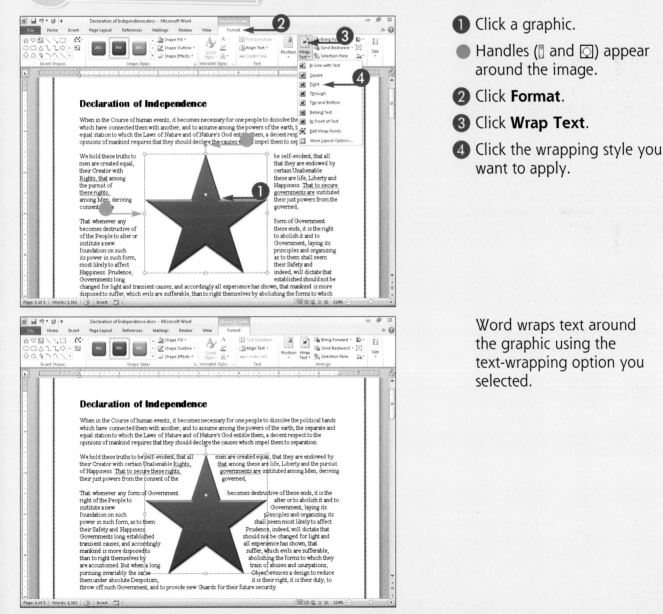

1 Click a graphic.

● Handles (and) appear around the image.

2 Click **Format**.

3 Click **Wrap Text**.

4 Click the wrapping style you want to apply.

Word wraps text around the graphic using the text-wrapping option you selected.

187

Work with Diagrams

Using SmartArt, you can add any of a variety of diagrams to your document to illustrate a concept. You can create organization charts, process diagrams, diagrams that represent cycles, and diagrams that present list information as well as other types of diagrams. These diagrams can illustrate your point concisely to the reader. For example, readers typically understand a diagram of a process better than a written description of it, and using both only increases the odds readers will clearly interpret your information.

The example in this section demonstrates adding an organizational chart.

Work with Diagrams

Add a Diagram

1 Click in your document where you want the diagram to appear.

2 Click the **Insert** tab.

3 Click **SmartArt**.

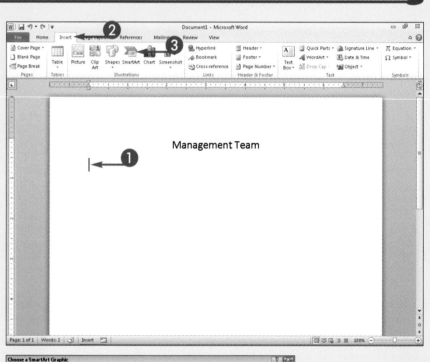

The Choose a SmartArt Graphic dialog box appears.

4 Click a diagram category.

5 Click the type of diagram you want to add.

● A description of the selected diagram appears here.

6 Click **OK**.

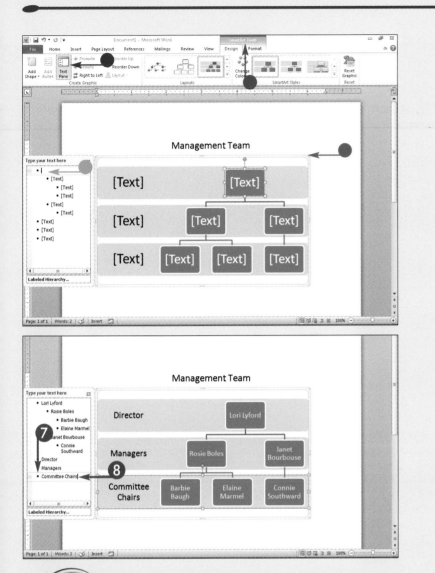

Word adds the diagram to your document.

● The graphic border surrounding the diagram indicates that the diagram is selected; the border will not print.

● SmartArt Tools appear on the Ribbon.

○ The Text pane appears here.

● If the Text pane does not appear, click **Text Pane**.

Each object within the diagram is called a *shape*.

Add Text to the Diagram

❼ Click next to a bullet in the Text pane.

❽ Type the text you want to add.

❾ Repeat Steps **1** to **2** for each shape in the diagram.

Note: *You do not need to use the Text pane; you can type directly in a shape.*

How can I add two lines of text to a shape?
After you type the first line of the text in the Text pane, press Shift + Enter. Then type the second line, and Word adjusts the font size of the text to fit the shape; for consistency, Word also adjusts the font size of all text in the diagram. Pressing Enter alone adds another shape to the diagram and adjusts the size of all shapes in the diagram.

Can I control the size and position of the diagram on the page?
Yes. Click the **Format** tab, click **Size**, and then click the spinner arrows (⬍) to change the height and width. Word sets the default position on the diagram inline with your text. You can use the Position Gallery to place the diagram in one of nine predetermined positions on the page. On the Format tab, click **Arrange** and then click **Position** to display the Position Gallery.

continued

Work with
Diagrams (continued)

To keep your diagrams current and interesting, you can add or delete shapes and apply styles to diagrams.

For example, the people who handle various jobs in most organizations change from time to time, and often as an organization grows, new responsibilities, handled by new people, arise.

You can easily keep diagrams up to date by adding or deleting diagram shapes as needed.

Word also gives you the option to apply styles to a diagram; these styles can make diagrams look extremely professional, as you see in this section.

Work with Diagrams (continued)

Add or Delete Shapes

1 Click the **Design** tab.

2 Click the shape above or beside which you want to add a shape.

● Handles (▯ and ▢) surround the shape.

3 Click the **list box** arrow (▼) beside Add Shape and select the option that describes where the shape should appear.

● The new shape appears.

You can add text to the new shape by following the steps in the subsection "Add Text to the Diagram" on the previous page.

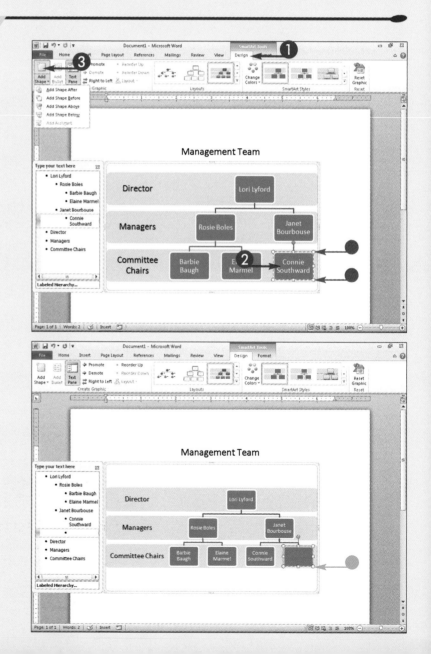

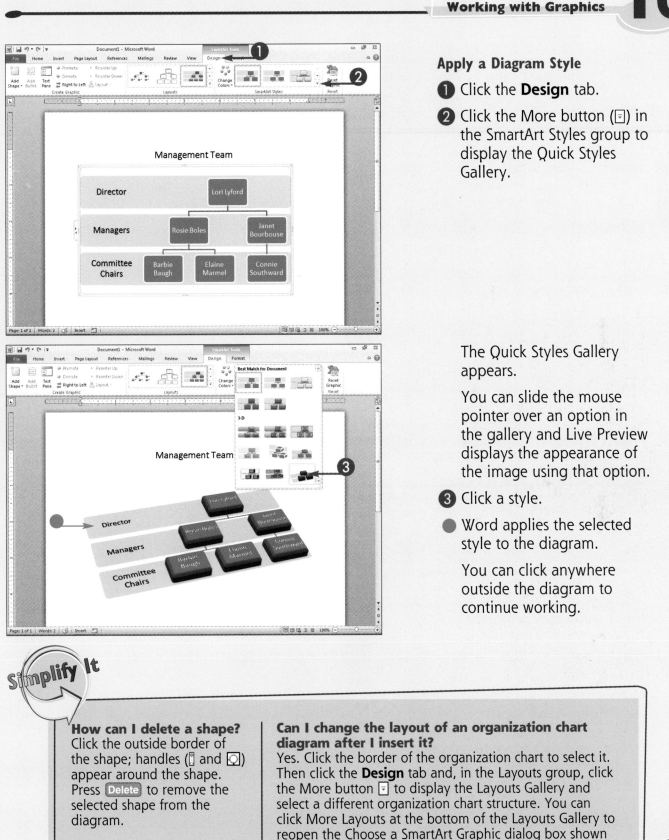

Apply a Diagram Style

① Click the **Design** tab.

② Click the More button (⊡) in the SmartArt Styles group to display the Quick Styles Gallery.

The Quick Styles Gallery appears.

You can slide the mouse pointer over an option in the gallery and Live Preview displays the appearance of the image using that option.

③ Click a style.

● Word applies the selected style to the diagram.

You can click anywhere outside the diagram to continue working.

Simplify It

How can I delete a shape?
Click the outside border of the shape; handles (□ and ○) appear around the shape. Press Delete to remove the selected shape from the diagram.

Can I change the layout of an organization chart diagram after I insert it?
Yes. Click the border of the organization chart to select it. Then click the **Design** tab and, in the Layouts group, click the More button ⊡ to display the Layouts Gallery and select a different organization chart structure. You can click More Layouts at the bottom of the Layouts Gallery to reopen the Choose a SmartArt Graphic dialog box shown earlier in this task.

191

Chapter 11

Customizing Word

Do you like the default Word settings? If not, you can easily customize portions of the Word program to make it perform more in line with the way you work.

For example, if you want to see characters that represent nonprinting characters, such as spaces or tabs, you can display formatting marks.

You can customize the information that appears on Word's status bar and, if screen real estate is important to you, you can display only the tabs on the Ribbon until you need the buttons.

But best of all, you can customize both the Quick Access Toolbar and the Ribbon.

Control the Display of Formatting Marks

For some people, it is very important to see nonprinting characters such as spaces between words or tabs, or paragraph marks. Word enables you to display all formatting marks — tabs, spaces, paragraph marks, hidden text, optional hyphens, and object anchors — directly from the Ribbon, but, if you prefer, you can limit the formatting marks that Word displays to view just the ones that interest you.

You can display all formatting marks using the Show/Hide button in the Paragraph group on the Home tab. This section shows you how to select formatting marks to display.

Control the Display of Formatting Marks

1 Click the **File** tab.

The Backstage view appears.

2 Click **Options**.

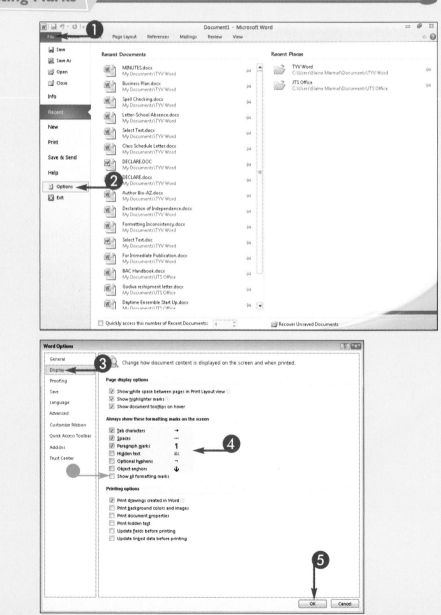

The Word Options dialog box appears.

3 Click **Display**.

● You can select the **Show all formatting marks** option (☐ changes to ☑) to display all formatting marks.

4 Select the check boxes of the formatting marks you want to display (☐ changes to ☑).

5 Click **OK**.

Word displays only the selected formatting marks in your document.

194

Customize the Status Bar

The status bar appears at the bottom of the Word screen and can display a variety of information that can help you while you work. For example, you can opt to display page numbers and the vertical position of the insertion point on the page. You also can display the line number. And when working in a document that you have broken into sections, you might also want to view section number information.

You also can use the status bar to switch between Insert mode or Overtype mode when inserting text. For details describing ways to insert text, see Chapter 3.

Customize the Status Bar

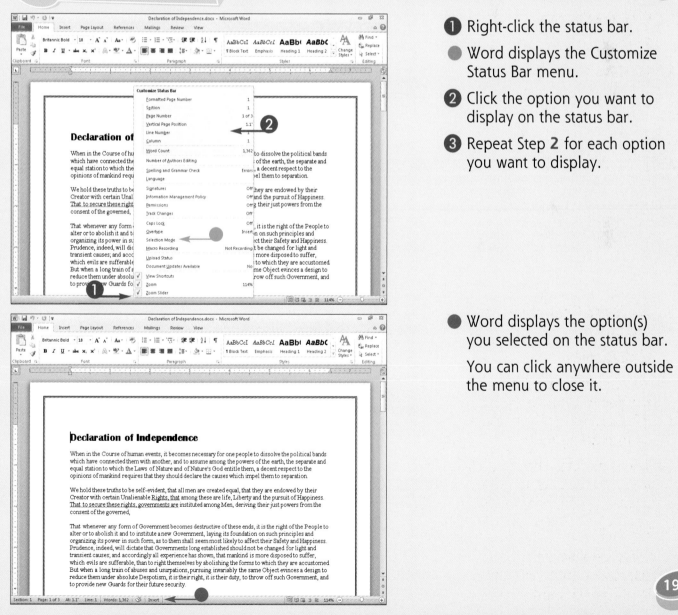

1 Right-click the status bar.

● Word displays the Customize Status Bar menu.

2 Click the option you want to display on the status bar.

3 Repeat Step 2 for each option you want to display.

● Word displays the option(s) you selected on the status bar.

You can click anywhere outside the menu to close it.

Hide or Display Ribbon Buttons

If screen real estate is important to you and you want to be able to see more of your document while you work, you can hide the buttons on the Ribbon and display only the Ribbon tabs. When you need the buttons on the Ribbon, you can easily redisplay them. Hiding the buttons on the Ribbon can make your screen appear less crowded.

When you hide the buttons on the Ribbon, you can easily redisplay them by simply clicking any tab. Once you are familiar with Word's Ribbon, you can click the tab that contains the button you want to use to save time.

Hide or Display Ribbon Buttons

- By default, Word displays the Ribbon.

1 Click the **Minimize the Ribbon** button (⌃).

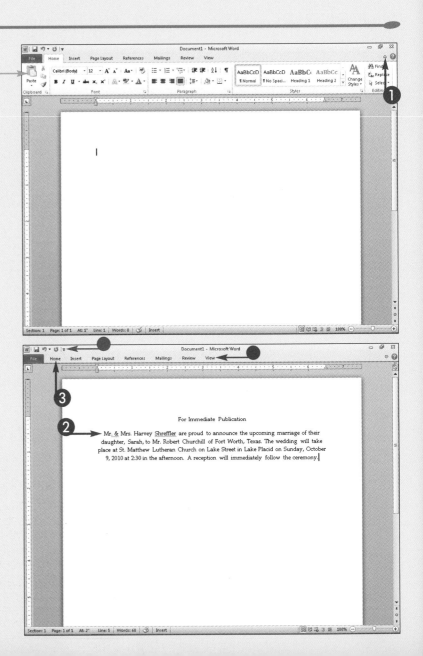

- Word hides the buttons on the Ribbon but continues to display the tabs.

- The Quick Access Toolbar continues to appear.

2 Type in your document as usual.

3 When you need a Ribbon button, click that Ribbon tab.

Note: *You can click any Ribbon tab, but you will save time if you click the tab containing the button you need.*

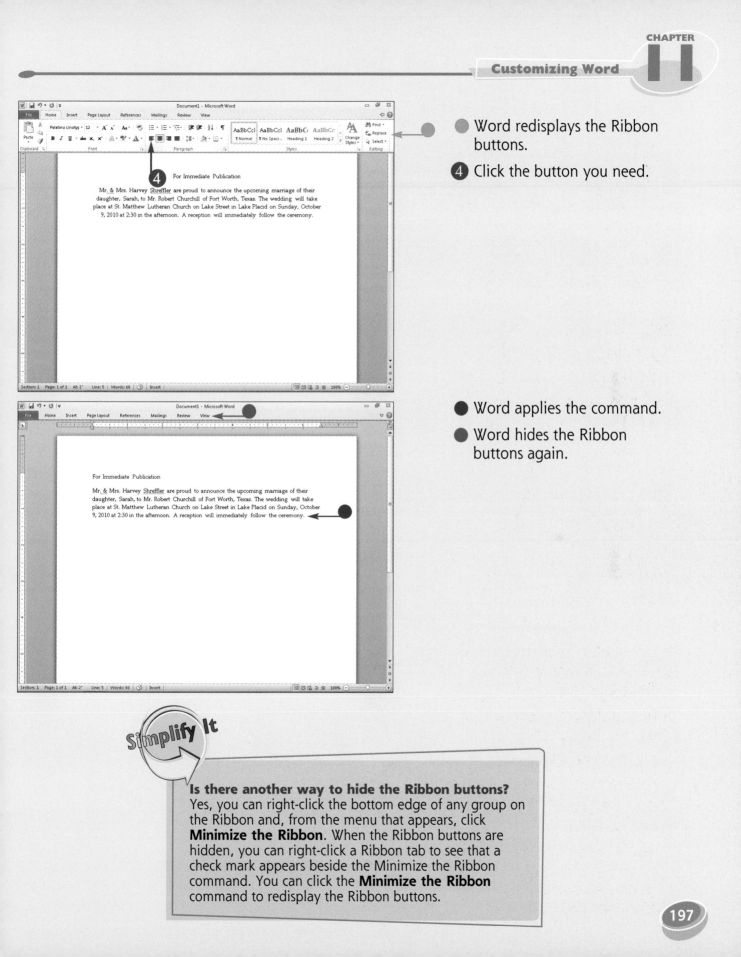

● Word redisplays the Ribbon buttons.

④ Click the button you need.

● Word applies the command.

● Word hides the Ribbon buttons again.

Simplify It

Is there another way to hide the Ribbon buttons?
Yes, you can right-click the bottom edge of any group on the Ribbon and, from the menu that appears, click **Minimize the Ribbon**. When the Ribbon buttons are hidden, you can right-click a Ribbon tab to see that a check mark appears beside the Minimize the Ribbon command. You can click the **Minimize the Ribbon** command to redisplay the Ribbon buttons.

Add a Predefined Group to a Ribbon Tab

Many people find that they use only a few of the tabs on the Ribbon regularly. And on those tabs, they use only a few groups of buttons. You can set up Word so that you can work more efficiently if you customize the Ribbon to place the groups of buttons that you use most often on a single tab.

For example, suppose that most of the buttons you need appear on the Home tab, but you often use the Page Setup group on the Page Layout tab to change document margins and set up columns. You can add the Page Setup group to the Home tab.

Add a Predefined Group to a Ribbon Tab

① Click the **File** tab.

The Backstage view appears.

② Click **Options**.

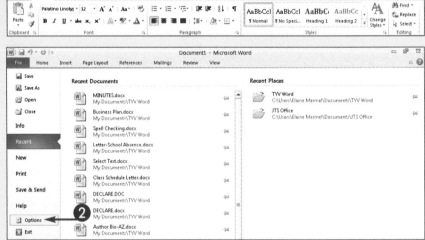

③ In the Word Options dialog box, click **Customize Ribbon**.

④ Click the list box arrow (▾) and select **Main Tabs**.

⑤ Click the plus sign (⊞) beside the tab containing the group you want to add (⊞ changes to ⊟).

⑥ Click the group you want to add.

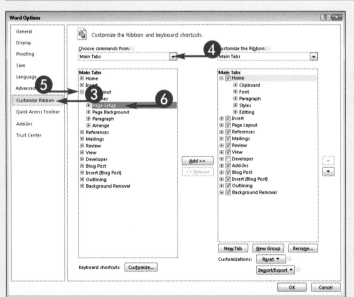

198

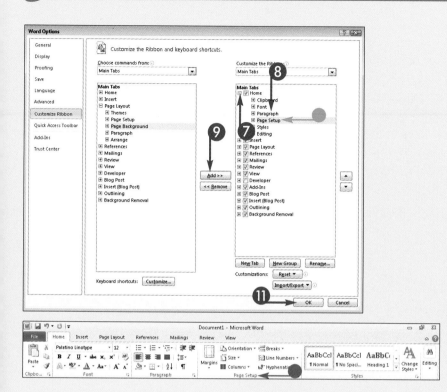

7 Click ⊞ beside the tab where you want to place the group you selected in Step **6** (⊞ changes to ⊟).

8 Click the group you want to appear on the Ribbon to the left of the new group.

9 Click **Add**.

● Word adds the group you selected in Step **6** below the group you selected in Step **8**.

10 Repeat Steps **5** to **9** as needed.

11 Click OK.

● Word adds the group you selected to the appropriate Ribbon tab.

Note: *Word might collapse other groups to fit the new group on the tab. In this example, Word collapsed the Quick Styles gallery.*

Simplify It

How do I add a single button — instead of a group — to one of the existing groups on the Ribbon?
You cannot add or delete a button to one of the default groups on the Ribbon. But, you can create your own group that contains only those buttons you want to use and then hide the default group Word displays. See the section "Create Your Own Ribbon Group" later in this chapter.

If I change my mind, how can I eliminate the changes I made to the Ribbon?
Complete Steps **1** to **3**. In the column on the right, select the Ribbon tab and group you added. Just above the OK button, click **Restore Defaults**, and from the menu that appears, click **Restore only selected Ribbon tab**. Then click OK.

Create Your Own Ribbon Group

You cannot add or remove buttons from predefined groups on a Ribbon tab, but you can create your own group and place the buttons you want in the group. Creating your own groups on the Ribbon can help you work more efficiently. For example, you can create a group on each Ribbon tab that contains the buttons on that tab you use most often. That way you do not need to search for those buttons; you know that the buttons you use most often on Ribbon tab will always be in the same position.

Create Your Own Ribbon Group

Make a Group

1 Click the **File** tab.

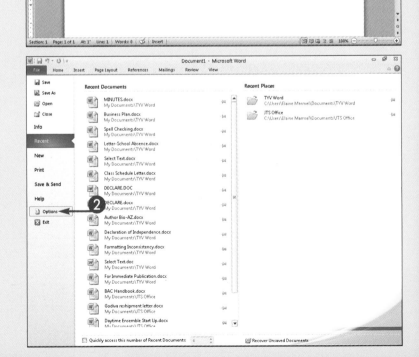

The Backstage view appears.

2 Click **Options**.

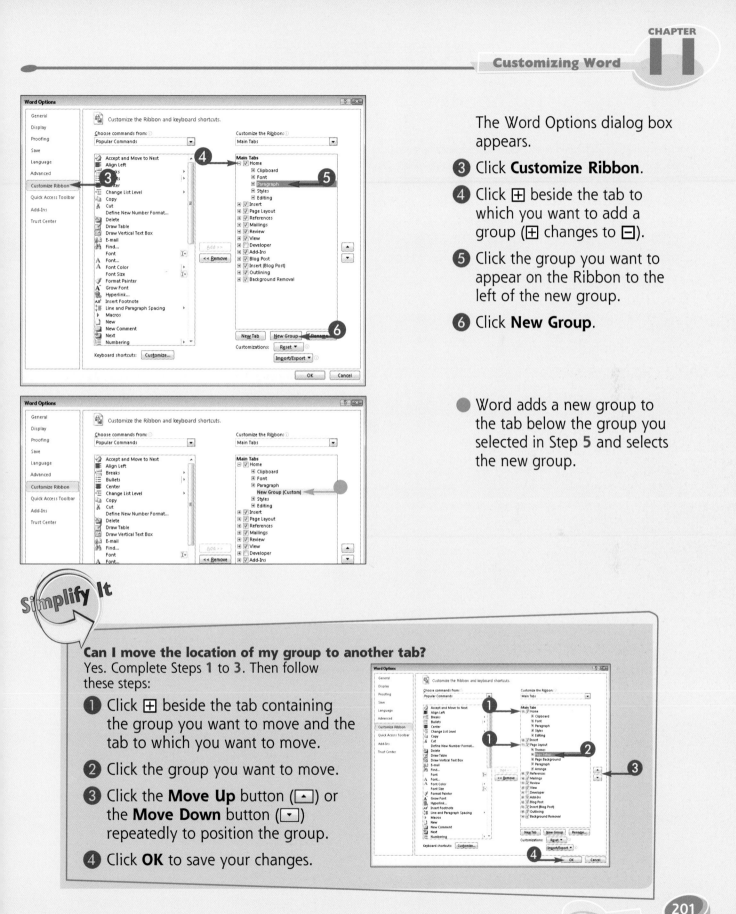

The Word Options dialog box appears.

③ Click **Customize Ribbon**.

④ Click ⊞ beside the tab to which you want to add a group (⊞ changes to ⊟).

⑤ Click the group you want to appear on the Ribbon to the left of the new group.

⑥ Click **New Group**.

● Word adds a new group to the tab below the group you selected in Step **5** and selects the new group.

Simplify It

Can I move the location of my group to another tab?
Yes. Complete Steps **1** to **3**. Then follow these steps:

① Click ⊞ beside the tab containing the group you want to move and the tab to which you want to move.

② Click the group you want to move.

③ Click the **Move Up** button (▲) or the **Move Down** button (▼) repeatedly to position the group.

④ Click **OK** to save your changes.

continued

Create Your Own Ribbon Group *(continued)*

When you add a group to a tab, you can assign a name to it that you find meaningful and then you can add whatever buttons you need to the group.

Regardless of the Ribbon tab on which you place your group, you can name the group anything you want, including a group name that already exists on another Ribbon tab. You also are not limited to adding buttons to your group that appear on the Ribbon tab where you place your group; you can add buttons to your group that appear in another group or even another tab.

Assign a Name to the Group

1. Click **Rename**.

   The Rename dialog box appears.

2. Type a name for your group.

3. Click **OK**.

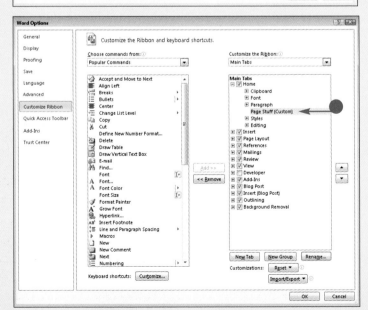

● Word assigns the name to your group.

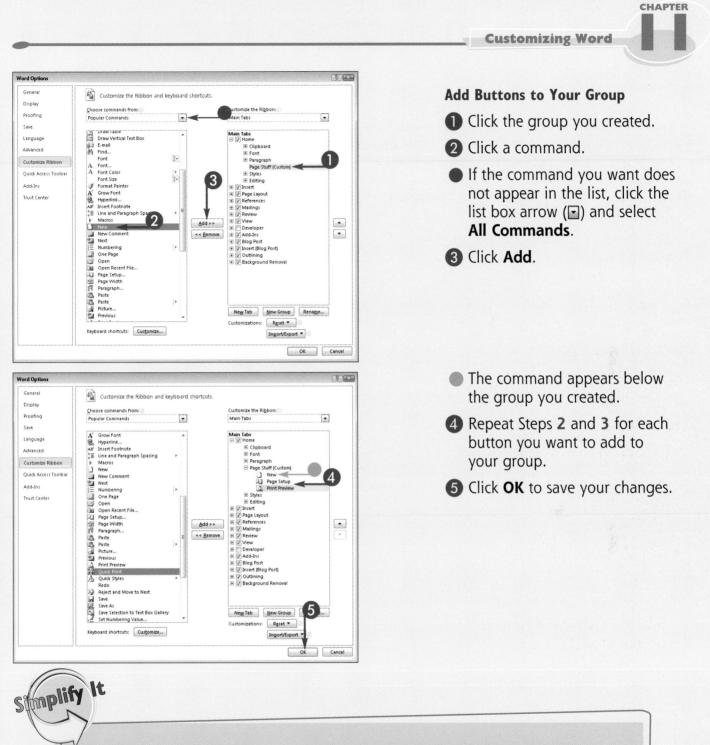

Add Buttons to Your Group

① Click the group you created.

② Click a command.

● If the command you want does not appear in the list, click the list box arrow (▾) and select **All Commands**.

③ Click **Add**.

● The command appears below the group you created.

④ Repeat Steps **2** and **3** for each button you want to add to your group.

⑤ Click **OK** to save your changes.

Are there any restrictions for the names I assign to groups I create?

No. In fact, you can use a name that appears on the Ribbon, and you can place that custom group on the Home tab, where the predefined group already exists, or on another tab.

How do I assign keyboard shortcuts to the buttons I add to my group?

Word assigns them for you, based on the keys already assigned to commands appearing on the tab where you placed your group. If you can place the same button on two different tabs, and if you do, Word assigns different keyboard shortcuts to that button on each tab. You cannot change the key Word assigns to buttons in your group

Create Your Own Ribbon Tab

Creating your own tab on the Ribbon can help you achieve maximum efficiency. If you create your own tab on the Ribbon, you can then add groups to that tab and store the buttons you use most frequently from all the tabs on the default Ribbon. If you place your new tab to the left of the Home tab, your tab will appear by default when you open Word. And you can leave the Ribbon positioned on your tab, saving you the time of locating the buttons you need on the various Ribbon tabs.

Create Your Own Ribbon Tab

Make a Tab

① Click the **File** tab.

The Backstage view appears.

② Click **Options**.

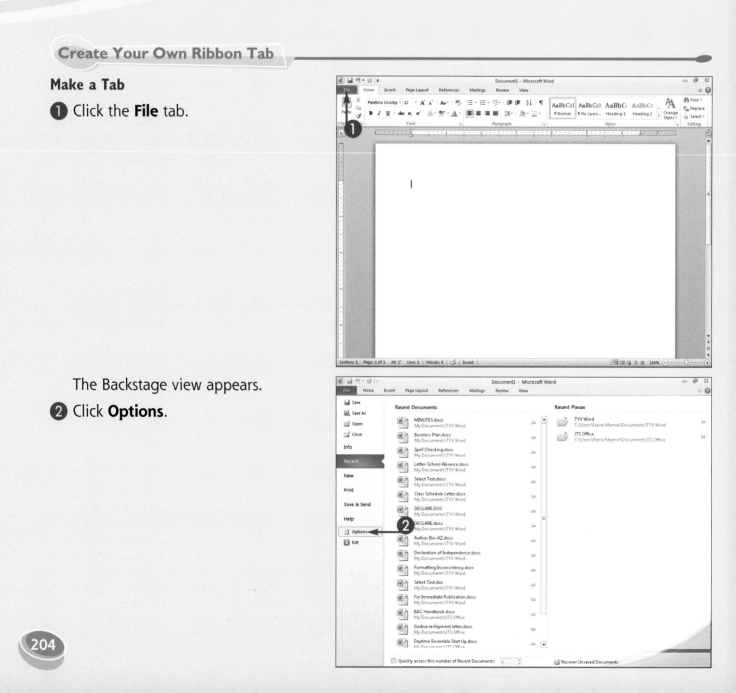

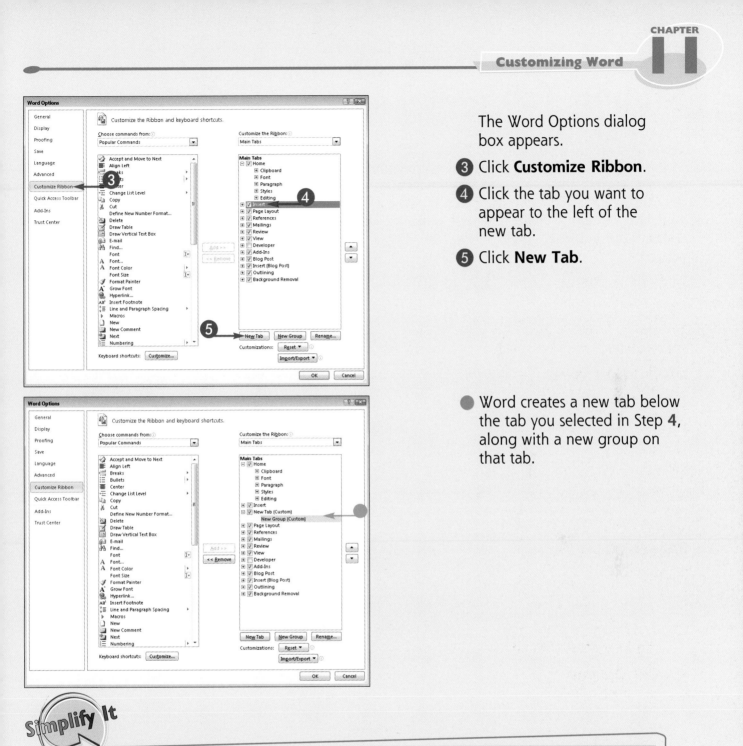

The Word Options dialog box appears.

3 Click **Customize Ribbon**.

4 Click the tab you want to appear to the left of the new tab.

5 Click **New Tab**.

● Word creates a new tab below the tab you selected in Step **4**, along with a new group on that tab.

Simplify It

Can I reposition a tab?
Yes. You reposition tabs the same way you reposition groups. Complete Steps **1** to **3** to open the Word Options dialog box to the Customize Ribbon pane. In the list on the right, click the tab and then click ▲ or ▼; these buttons appear on the right edge of the Word Options dialog box.

What is on the Developer tab and why does no check mark appear beside it?
The Developer tab contains tools used by those who write programs to make Word perform actions automatically. When no check mark appears beside a tab, Word does not display that tab on the Ribbon; in the case of the Developer tab, most users do not need the tools on that tab, so Word does not display it by default.

continued

Create Your Own Ribbon Tab (continued)

When you create a custom tab, Word automatically creates one group for you so that you can quickly and easily add buttons to the new tab. You can assign names that mean something to you to both your tab and the group Word automatically creates. You can add other groups to the tab; see the section "Create Your Own Ribbon Group" earlier in this chapter.

After you assign names to your Ribbon tab and groups on that tab, you can add buttons to your tab. Also remember that you are not limited to creating a single tab; you can create as many tabs as you want.

Assign Names

1. Click **New Group (Custom)**.

2. Click **Rename**.

   The Rename dialog box appears.

3. Type a name for your group.

4. Click **OK**.

5. Click **New Tab (Custom)**.

6. Repeat Steps **2** to **4**.

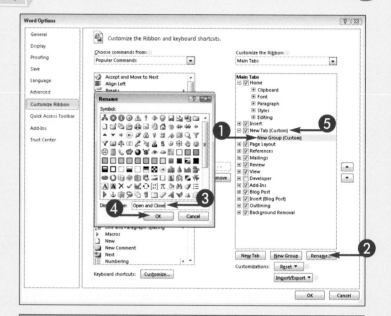

● Word assigns names to your tab and your group.

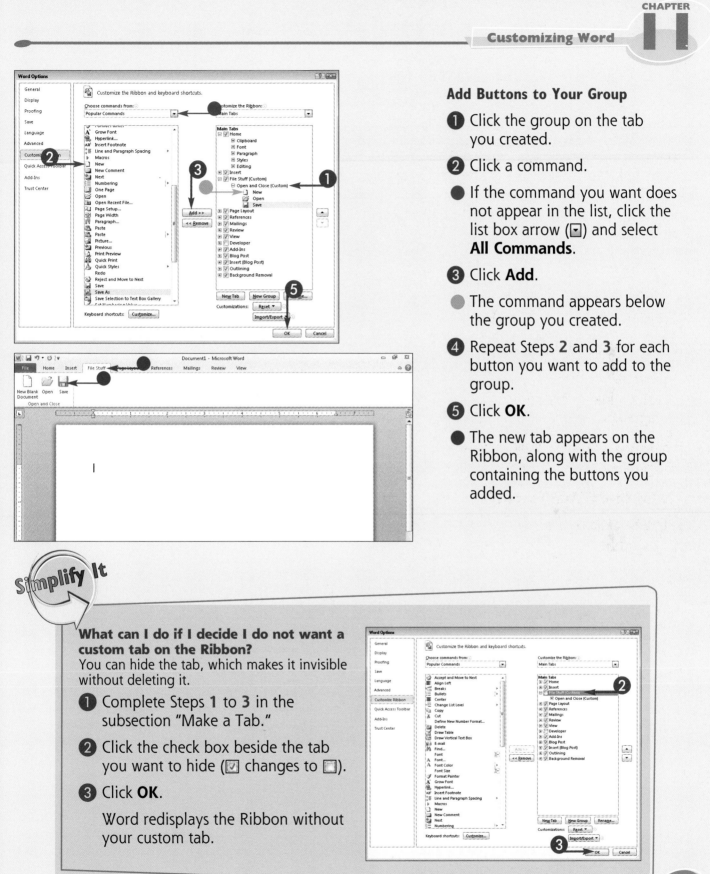

Add Buttons to Your Group

1. Click the group on the tab you created.

2. Click a command.

● If the command you want does not appear in the list, click the list box arrow (▾) and select **All Commands**.

3. Click **Add**.

● The command appears below the group you created.

4. Repeat Steps **2** and **3** for each button you want to add to the group.

5. Click **OK**.

● The new tab appears on the Ribbon, along with the group containing the buttons you added.

Simplify It

What can I do if I decide I do not want a custom tab on the Ribbon?
You can hide the tab, which makes it invisible without deleting it.

1. Complete Steps **1** to **3** in the subsection "Make a Tab."

2. Click the check box beside the tab you want to hide (☑ changes to ☐).

3. Click **OK**.

Word redisplays the Ribbon without your custom tab.

Work with the Quick Access Toolbar

You can customize the Quick Access Toolbar (QAT) in Word 2010 by changing both its location and its content.

You can position the QAT in its default location on the program title bar or, if you prefer, you can position the QAT below the Ribbon. Some people prefer to position the QAT below the

Ribbon because it places the buttons closer to the working area and makes the Word interface feel more like Word 97-2003 and earlier.

You can quickly add some buttons to the Ribbon from the QAT menu. Or you can add other commands to the QAT from the Word Options dialog box.

Work with the Quick Access Toolbar

Change Placement

① Click the **Customize Quick Access Toolbar** button (▾).

Word displays a menu of choices.

② Click **Show Below the Ribbon**.

● The Quick Access Toolbar (QAT) appears below the Ribbon instead of above it.

You can repeat these steps to move the QAT back above the Ribbon.

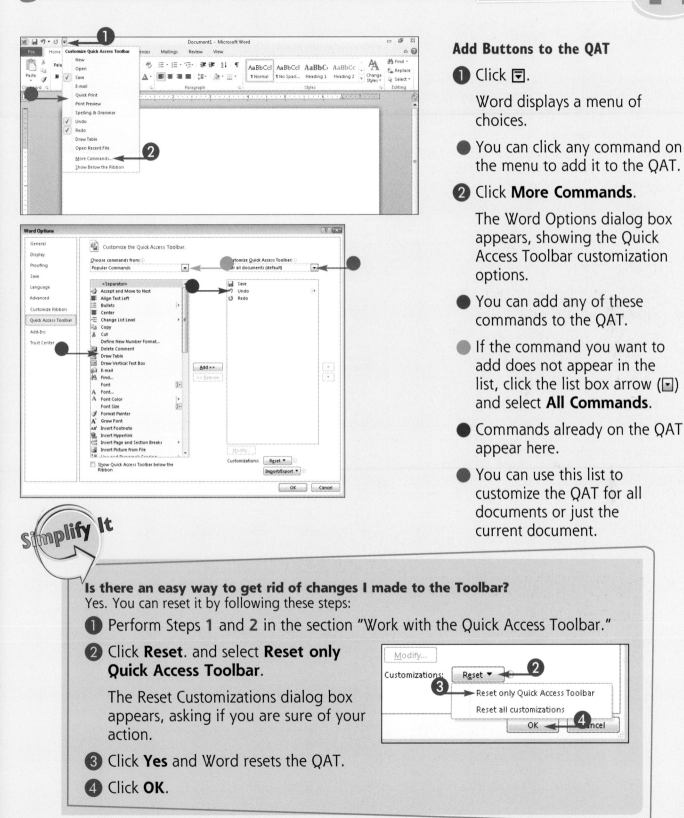

Add Buttons to the QAT

1 Click .

Word displays a menu of choices.

● You can click any command on the menu to add it to the QAT.

2 Click **More Commands**.

The Word Options dialog box appears, showing the Quick Access Toolbar customization options.

● You can add any of these commands to the QAT.

● If the command you want to add does not appear in the list, click the list box arrow (▼) and select **All Commands**.

● Commands already on the QAT appear here.

● You can use this list to customize the QAT for all documents or just the current document.

Simplify It

Is there an easy way to get rid of changes I made to the Toolbar?
Yes. You can reset it by following these steps:

1 Perform Steps **1** and **2** in the section "Work with the Quick Access Toolbar."

2 Click **Reset**. and select **Reset only Quick Access Toolbar**.

The Reset Customizations dialog box appears, asking if you are sure of your action.

3 Click **Yes** and Word resets the QAT.

4 Click **OK**.

continued

Work with the Quick Access Toolbar *(continued)*

You can add commands to the Quick Access Toolbar and reorganize the order in which commands appear on the QAT.

When adding buttons to the QAT, you select commands from a list. Word organizes the buttons into several lists that help you find the buttons you want; for example, you can display a list of popular commands or a list of commands not found on the default Ribbon. You also can display a list of commands on any Ribbon tab.

Once you add all the commands you want on the QAT, you can order them any way you want.

Work with the Quick Access Toolbar *(continued)*

③ Click the list box arrow (⬇) to display the various categories of commands.

You can select **All Commands** to view all commands in alphabetical order regardless of category.

④ Click a category of commands.

This example uses the Commands Not in the Ribbon category.

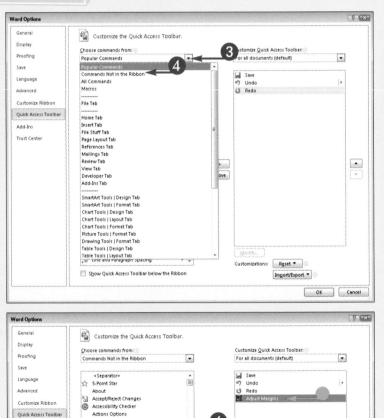

⑤ Click the command you want to add to the Toolbar.

⑥ Click **Add**.

● Word moves the command from the list on the left to the list on the right.

⑦ Repeat Steps **3** to **6** for each command you want to add to the Quick Access Toolbar.

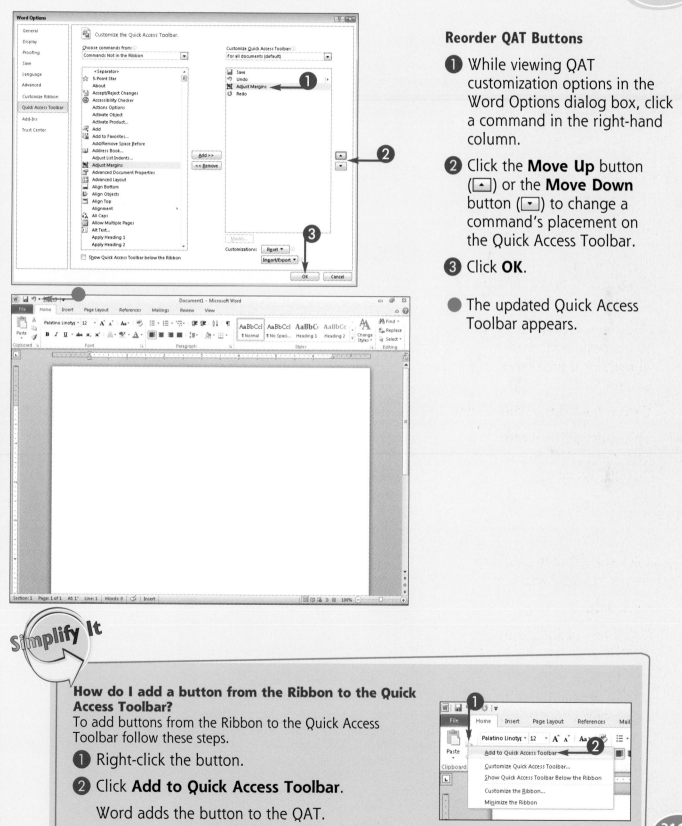

Reorder QAT Buttons

1 While viewing QAT customization options in the Word Options dialog box, click a command in the right-hand column.

2 Click the **Move Up** button (☐) or the **Move Down** button (☐) to change a command's placement on the Quick Access Toolbar.

3 Click **OK**.

● The updated Quick Access Toolbar appears.

Simplify It

How do I add a button from the Ribbon to the Quick Access Toolbar?

To add buttons from the Ribbon to the Quick Access Toolbar follow these steps.

1 Right-click the button.

2 Click **Add to Quick Access Toolbar**.

Word adds the button to the QAT.

Chapter 12

Mailing Documents

You can use Word to help you mail documents using both e-mail and *snail mail* — the commonly and affectionately used moniker for the United States Postal Service's standard delivery.

You can e-mail a document directly from Word in a variety of formats, including a Word document file (DOC) attachment or a PDF, among others.

When it comes to mass mailings, why do the work yourself? You can use Word's mass-mailing tools to create form letters, add envelopes to those form letters, or create mailing labels for the holiday cards you send to friends and family.

E-mail a Document

You can e-mail a Word document while you work in Word; you do not need to open your e-mail program and send the document from there. Word can attach the document to an e-mail message as a Word document file (DOC), a PDF file, or an XPS file. Word also can create an e-mail containing a link to a document stored in a shared location, and can send a document as an Internet Fax. This example shows you how to create an e-mail message with a Word document file attachment.

After you create the e-mail message and attachment, you must open your e-mail program and send the message.

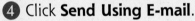

① Open the document you want to send by e-mail.

② Click the **File** tab.

The Backstage view appears.

③ Click **Save & Send**.

④ Click **Send Using E-mail**.

⑤ Click a method to send the document.

This example sends the document as an attachment.

An e-mail message window appears.

● The e-mail attachment appears here; in this example, the attachment is the Word document.

⑥ Click here to type the e-mail address of the recipient.

● You can also type the e-mail address of someone to whom you want to send a copy of the message.

Note: To send to multiple recipients, separate each e-mail address with a semicolon (;) and a space.

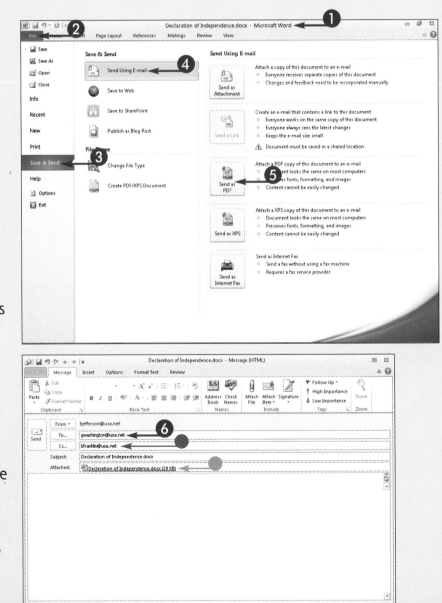

7 Click here to type a subject for the e-mail message.

Note: *Subjects are not required but including one is considerate. Word automatically supplies the document name for the subject; you can replace the document name with anything you want.*

● You can type a message here.

8 Click **Send**.

Word places the message in your e-mail program's Outbox and closes the e-mail message window.

Note: *You must open your e-mail program, and, if your e-mail program does not automatically send and receive periodically, send the message.*

Simplify It

What should I do if I change my mind about sending the e-mail message while viewing the e-mail message window?
Click ⊠ in the e-mail message window. A message appears, asking if you want to save the message. Click **No**.

What happens if I choose Send as PDF in Step 5?
Word creates a PDF version of the document and attaches the PDF version to the e-mail message instead of attaching the Word file. The recipient cannot edit the PDF file with Word; to edit the document, the recipient would need special software.

Create Letters to Mass Mail

Using a form letter and a mailing list, you can quickly and easily create a mass mailing that merges the addresses from the mailing list into the form letter.

Typically, the only information that changes in the form letter is the addressee information, but if you have other information that will change in the letter, include that information in the mailing list file. You can create the mailing list as you create the mass mailing, or you can use a mailing list that exists in another Word document, an Excel file, or your Outlook Contact List. This example uses an Excel file.

Create Letters to Mass Mail

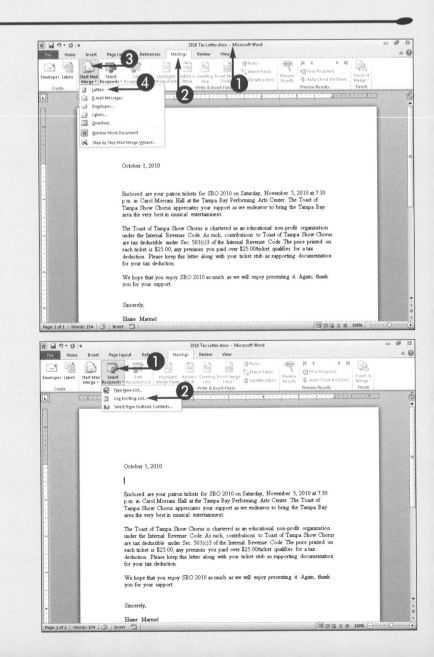

Set Up for a Mail Merge

1 Open the Word document that you want to use as the form letter.

Note: *The letter should not contain any information that will change from letter to letter, such as the inside address.*

2 Click the **Mailings** tab.

3 Click **Start Mail Merge**.

4 Click **Letters**.

Nothing visible happens on-screen, but Word sets up for a mail merge.

Identify Recipients

1 Click **Select Recipients**.

2 Click to identify the type of recipient list you plan to use.

This example uses an existing list in an Excel file.

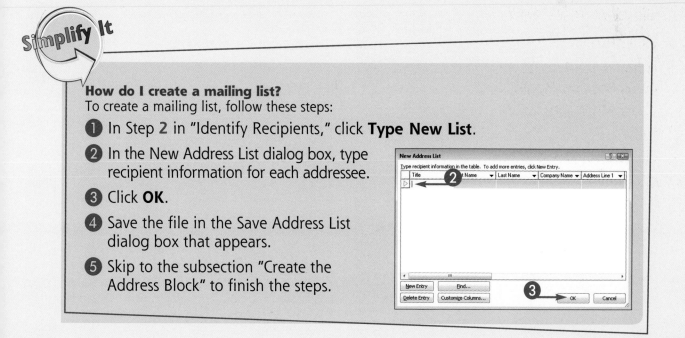

The Select Data Source dialog box appears.

③ Click here to navigate to the folder containing the mailing list file.

④ Click the file containing the mailing list.

⑤ Click **Open**.

Word links with Excel and the Select Table dialog box appears.

Note: If the Excel notebook contains multiple sheets, you can select a specific sheet in the Select Table dialog box.

⑥ If necessary, select a sheet.

⑦ Click **OK**.

Simplify It

How do I create a mailing list?
To create a mailing list, follow these steps:

① In Step **2** in "Identify Recipients," click **Type New List**.

② In the New Address List dialog box, type recipient information for each addressee.

③ Click **OK**.

④ Save the file in the Save Address List dialog box that appears.

⑤ Skip to the subsection "Create the Address Block" to finish the steps.

Create Letters to Mass Mail *(continued)*

You do not need to send your letter to all recipients stored in the mailing list file; you can select specific recipients from the mailing list to receive the form letter. You use *merge fields* to specify the place in your document where the recipient's address and greeting should appear. If your mailing list file contains more information than the recipient's address, you include merge fields in the letter for that additional information.

When you insert a merge field to specify the recipient's address, Word gives you the opportunity to specify the format to use for the recipient's name.

Create Letters to Mass Mail (continued)

⑧ Click **Edit Recipient List**.

The Mail Merge Recipients window appears.

● A check box (☑) appears beside each person's name, identifying the recipients of the form letter.

⑨ Click beside any addressee for whom you do not want to prepare a form letter (☑ changes to ☐).

⑩ Click **OK**.

Create the Address Block

① Click the location where you want the inside address to appear in the form letter.

② Click **Address Block**.

The Insert Address Block dialog box appears.

③ Click a format for each recipient's name.

● You can preview the format here.

④ Click **OK**.

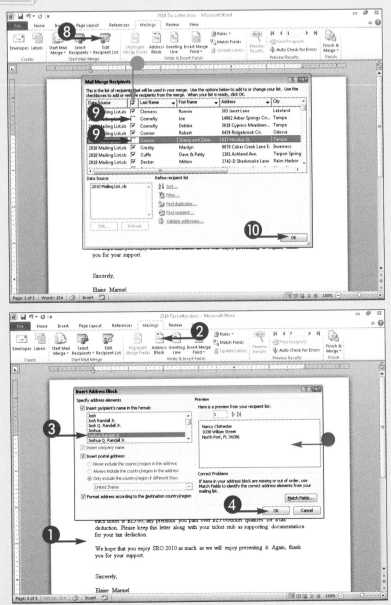

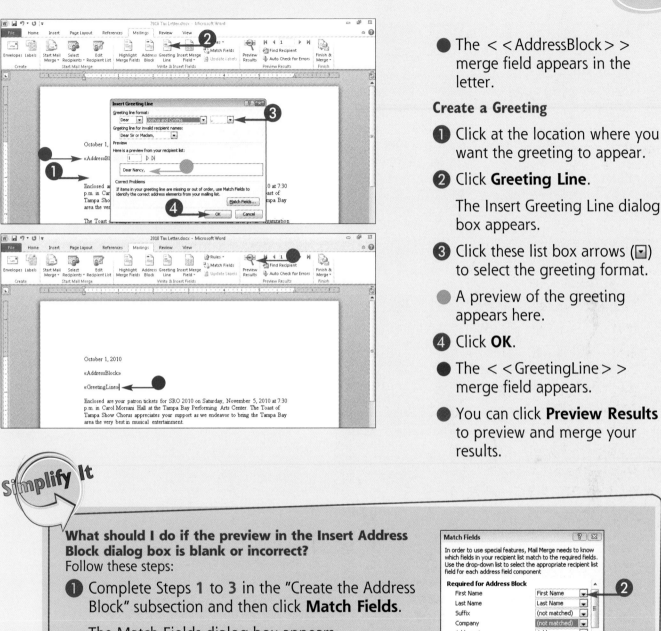

● The < <AddressBlock> > merge field appears in the letter.

Create a Greeting

1 Click at the location where you want the greeting to appear.

2 Click **Greeting Line**.

The Insert Greeting Line dialog box appears.

3 Click these list box arrows (▼) to select the greeting format.

● A preview of the greeting appears here.

4 Click **OK**.

● The < <GreetingLine> > merge field appears.

● You can click **Preview Results** to preview and merge your results.

Simplify It

What should I do if the preview in the Insert Address Block dialog box is blank or incorrect?
Follow these steps:

1 Complete Steps **1** to **3** in the "Create the Address Block" subsection and then click **Match Fields**.

The Match Fields dialog box appears.

2 Click the list box arrow (▼) and select the corresponding field name in your mailing list file.

3 Click **OK** and continue with Step **4** in "Create the Address Block."

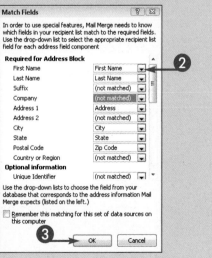

Create Letters to Mass Mail *(continued)*

After you finish adding merge fields, you can preview the letters and you again have the opportunity to select specific recipients for whom to create the letters. Most people typically create individual letters for each person in the mailing list file. Word places one letter per person in a separate Word document that you can review before printing.

If you prefer, you can merge the letters directly to your printer. In this case, Word does not create a separate document that you can review. And if your mailing list includes e-mail addresses, you can send the letters as e-mail messages.

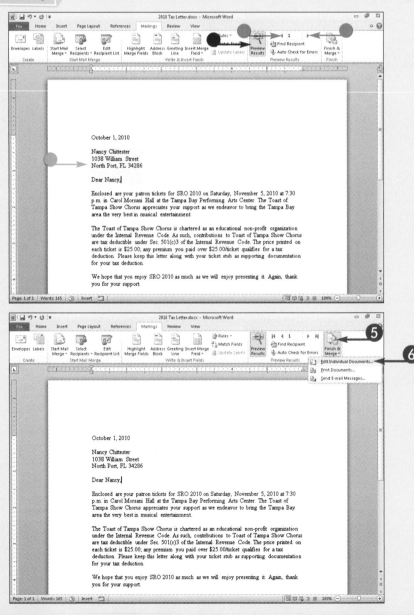

● Word displays a preview of the merged letter, using the unchanging content of the letter and information from the address file.

● You can click the **Next Record** button (◀) to preview the next letter and the **Previous Record** button (▶) to move back and preview the previous letter.

● You can click **Preview Results** to redisplay merge fields.

⑤ Click **Finish & Merge**.

⑥ Click **Edit Individual Documents**.

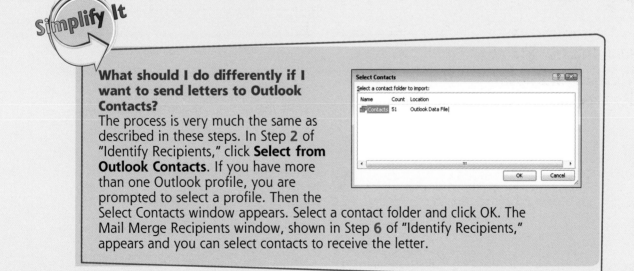

The Merge to New Document dialog box appears.

7 Select an option to identify the recipients of the letter (◉ changes to ◉).

8 Click **OK**.

● Word merges the form letter information with the mailing list information, placing the results in a new document named Letters1.

● The new document contains individual letters for each mailing list recipient.

9 Click the **Customize Quick Access Toolbar** button (▼).

10 Click **Quick Print**.

● You can click the **Save** button (🖫) on the QAT and assign a new name to save the merged letters.

Simplify It

What should I do differently if I want to send letters to Outlook Contacts?
The process is very much the same as described in these steps. In Step **2** of "Identify Recipients," click **Select from Outlook Contacts**. If you have more than one Outlook profile, you are prompted to select a profile. Then the Select Contacts window appears. Select a contact folder and click OK. The Mail Merge Recipients window, shown in Step **6** of "Identify Recipients," appears and you can select contacts to receive the letter.

Add Envelopes to Mass Mailing Letters

You can add addressed envelopes for letters you create using the Mail Merge feature in Word. You start by creating your letter using the information in the section "Create Letters to Mass Mail," earlier in this chapter, and then you add envelopes.

To use this technique, your printer must have two trays — one in which to hold the paper for the letter and the other in which to hold the envelopes.

If your printer does not have two paper trays, you can still create envelopes for your mass mailing; see the information in Simplify It at the end of this section.

Add Envelopes to Mass Mailing Letters

① Create letters for the envelopes.

Note: *See the section "Create Letters to Mass Mail" for more on creating letters.*

② On the Windows taskbar, click the form letter you used to create the merged letters.

● Word displays the letter you set up to create the mail merge.

Note: *This example shows merge fields; click **Preview Results** to switch between merge fields and final text.*

③ Click **Envelopes**.

The Envelopes and Labels dialog box appears.

④ Click **Add to Document**.

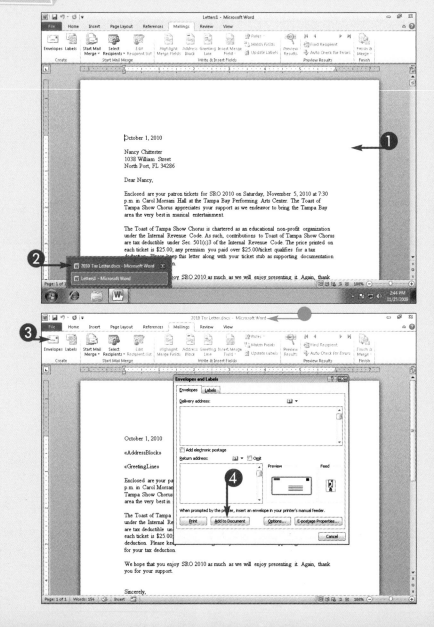

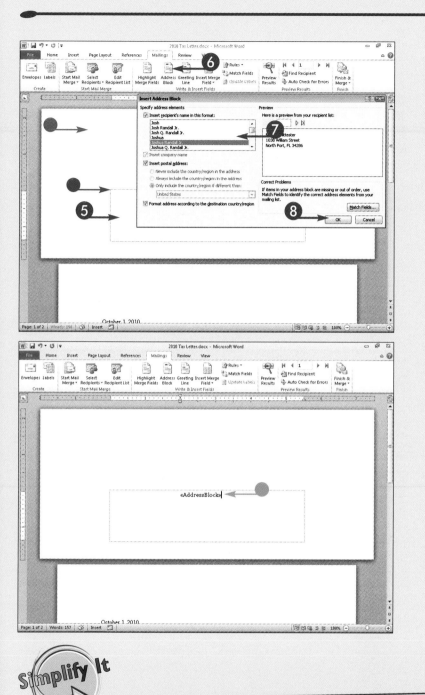

An envelope appears in your document.

● You can type a return address.

⑤ Click in the lower center of the envelope to locate the address box.

● Dotted lines surround the address box.

⑥ Click **Address Block**.

The Insert Address Block dialog box appears.

⑦ Click an address format.

⑧ Click **OK**.

● The < <AddressBlock> > merge field appears on the envelope.

Note: *Follow the steps under "Preview and Merge" in the preceding section "Create Letters to Mass Mail" to preview envelopes, merge address information on envelopes, and print envelopes along with your letters.*

Create Labels for a Mass Mailing

In addition to creating personalized form letters for a mass mailing, you can use Word's merge feature to create mailing labels for mass mailing recipients. Many people like to create mailing labels when they send holiday greeting cards.

The process of creating mailing labels mirrors the process of creating letters to mass mail in

many ways because you use a mailing list and insert merge fields. When you create labels, you take one action that you do not take when you create letters: you select a specific label format so that Word sets up the labels correctly.

Create Labels for a Mass Mailing

Select a Label Format

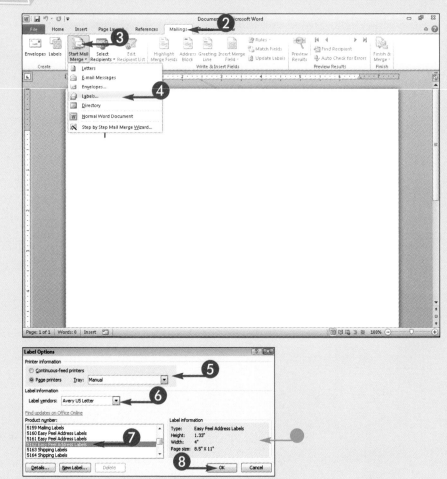

1 Start a new blank document.

   Note: See Chapter 2 for details starting a new document.

2 Click the **Mailings** tab.

3 Click **Start Mail Merge**.

4 Click **Labels**.

   The Label Options dialog box appears.

5 Select a printer option (◻ changes to ◉).

6 Click ▾ to select a label vendor.

7 Use the scroll arrows (▲ and ▼) to find and click the label's product number.

● Information about the label dimensions appears here.

8 Click **OK**.

   Word sets up the document for the labels you selected.

   Note: If gridlines identifying individual labels do not appear, click the **Layout** tab and then click **View Gridlines**.

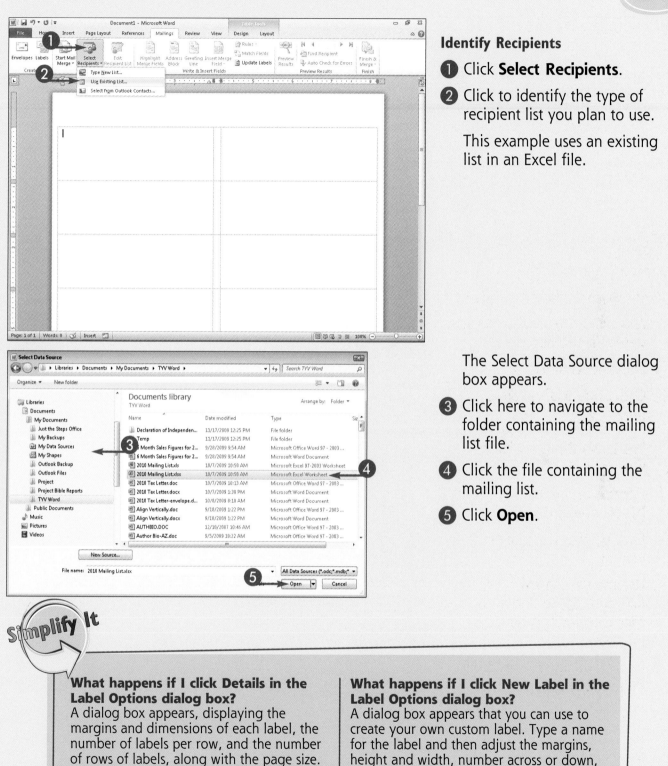

Identify Recipients

1 Click **Select Recipients**.

2 Click to identify the type of recipient list you plan to use.

This example uses an existing list in an Excel file.

The Select Data Source dialog box appears.

3 Click here to navigate to the folder containing the mailing list file.

4 Click the file containing the mailing list.

5 Click **Open**.

Simplify It

What happens if I click Details in the Label Options dialog box?
A dialog box appears, displaying the margins and dimensions of each label, the number of labels per row, and the number of rows of labels, along with the page size. Although you can change these dimensions, you risk having information print incorrectly.

What happens if I click New Label in the Label Options dialog box?
A dialog box appears that you can use to create your own custom label. Type a name for the label and then adjust the margins, height and width, number across or down, vertical or horizontal pitch, and page size as needed.

Create Labels for a Mass Mailing *(continued)*

Using the label options you specify, Word sets up a document of labels. To specify label options, you select the vendor whose labels you plan to use and then select the vendor's product number. You attach a mailing list containing recipient information to the Word document and then you add merge information. You can create your mailing list as you create labels, or you can use a mailing list stored in another Word document, addresses in an Excel file, or contacts stored in Outlook. This example uses addresses stored in an Excel file.

Create Labels for a Mass Mailing *(continued)*

Word links with Excel and the Select Table dialog box appears.

⑥ If necessary, select a sheet.

⑦ Click **OK**.

Word inserts a
< <NextRecord> >
field in each label
but the first one.

Add Merge Fields

① Click the first label to place the insertion point in it.

② Click **Address Block**.

The Insert Address Block dialog box appears.

③ Click a format for each recipient's name.

● You can preview the format here.

④ Click **OK**.

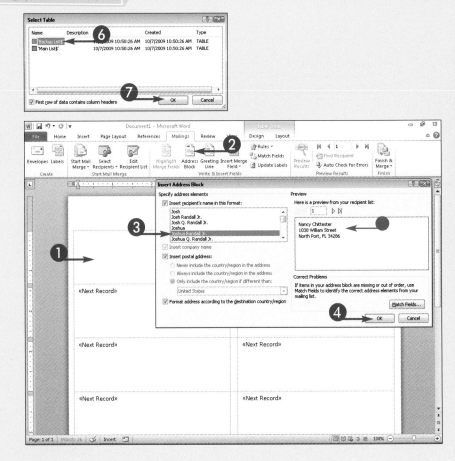

● Word adds the
< <AddressBlock> >
merge field to the first
label.

*Note: When you merge the
information, Word replaces the
merge field with information
from the mailing address file.*

❺ Click **Update Labels**.

● Word adds the
< <AddressBlock> >
merge field to every
label.

● You can click **Preview Results**
to preview and merge your
results.

Simplify It

Can I selectively create labels using an existing file?
Yes. Follow these steps:

❶ Click **Edit Recipient List**.

The Mail Merge Recipients dialog box appears.

❷ Click beside any addressee for whom you do
not want to create a mailing label (☑ changes
to ☐).

❸ Click **OK**.

continued

Create Labels for a
Mass Mailing *(continued)*

After you finish adding the Address Block merge field to your labels, you can preview the labels before you print them, and when you complete the merge, you have another opportunity to select specific recipients for whom to create labels.

You can opt to create a Word document of labels or you can merge directly to your printer.

If you merge to a document, you can review your labels for accuracy by previewing the document on-screen, printing it to plain paper, or both. If you merge to your printer, you print your labels onto label paper and have no opportunity to review the labels.

Create Labels for a Mass Mailing *(continued)*

Word displays a preview of your labels, replacing the merge field with information from the mailing list file.

● You can click ◀ to preview the next label and ▶ to move back and preview the previous label.

⑥ Click **Preview Results** to redisplay merge fields.

⑦ Click **Finish & Merge**.

⑧ Click **Edit Individual Documents**.

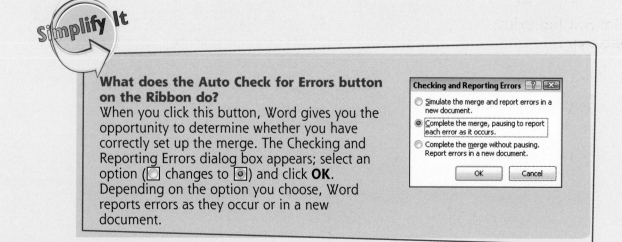

The Merge to New Document dialog box appears.

9 Select an option to identify the recipients of the letter (○ changes to ◉).

The **All** option creates a label for all entries on the mailing list; the **Current record** option creates only one label for the recipient you are previewing; and the **From** option creates labels for recipients you specify.

10 Click **OK**.

● Word creates the labels in a new Word document named Labels1.

The new document contains individual labels for each mailing list recipient.

11 Click 🔽.

12 Click **Quick Print**.

The labels print.

Simplify It

What does the Auto Check for Errors button on the Ribbon do?
When you click this button, Word gives you the opportunity to determine whether you have correctly set up the merge. The Checking and Reporting Errors dialog box appears; select an option (○ changes to ◉) and click **OK**. Depending on the option you choose, Word reports errors as they occur or in a new document.

Checking and Reporting Errors

○ Simulate the merge and report errors in a new document.

◉ Complete the merge, pausing to report each error as it occurs.

○ Complete the merge without pausing. Report errors in a new document.

OK   Cancel

Index

Index

Index

Index

Index

SmartArt Tools, 189
space marks, 112
spacing
    line spacing, 107, 108
    Tab key, 16, 17
    table cells, 159
special characters, searches, 73
Spelling & Grammar option, 78
Spelling and Grammar Checker, 78–79, 80–81
spelling corrections as you work, 79
Split Table button, 161
splitting tables, 161
Square text wrapping, 186
starting new documents, 32–33
status bar
    customizing, 195
    document information, 5
    insertion point location, 5
stock charts, 169
strikethrough text, track changes and, 86
Styles gallery
    paragraph formatting, 14
    Subtitle style, 14
substituting text, 72–73
Subtitle style, 14
suggestions on typing, 17
surface charts, 169
switch between documents, 34–35
Switch Windows option, 34
switching document views, 60
Symbol dialog box, 64–65
symbols, 64–65
synonyms in Thesaurus, 82–83

T

Tab key, 16, 17
Table button, 148
Table Options dialog box, 158
Table Style gallery, 164
Table Tools, 149
tables
    cell margins, 158
    cell text alignment, 163
    cells, 149
        combining, 160
        space between, 159
    column width, 151
    columns, adding/deleting, 154–155
    creating, 148–149
    deleting, 149
    formatting, 164–165
    formulas, 162
    Live Preview, 165

    mouse, 148
    moving, 156
    resizing, 157
    row height, 150
    rows, adding/deleting, 149, 152, 153
    splitting, 161
tabs
    Bar tab, 116
    Center tab, 116
    commands, 9
    Decimal tab, 116
    deleting, 117
    leader characters, 118
    Left tab, 116
    moving, 117
    Ribbon, 10
    Right tab, 116
    setting, 116–119
    using, 117
taskbar
    buttons, removing, 35
    switch between documents, 34–35
templates
    description, 33
    documents, 32
    Normal, 33
text
    alignment, 16, 106, 126
    blank lines, 16
    bold, 96
    bulleted lists, 110–111
    case, 97
    centering, 106
    color, 98
    copying, 52–53
    copying several selections, 56–57
    deleting, 44–45
    diagrams, 189
    emphasizing, 96, 98
    entering, 16
    entering automatically, 17
    footers, 133
    formatting, copying/removing, 100, 101
    frequently used, inserting, 76–77
    headers, 133
    hidden, 112
    highlighting, 99
    inserting, 42–43
    italic, 96
    moving, 52–53
    moving several selections, 56–57
    new lines, 16
    numbered lists, 110–111

238

Index